D1548014

Sima Joon,

Not so many people are as lucky as me to have a true friend like you.

And I am grateful for that everyday.

May you always dance to the nicest melody.

Love always,

Soheila

Dancing
to the Darkest Light

A remarkable true story of life, its challenges
and triumph over the ultimate heartbreak

*"He who has a 'why' to live for
can bear almost any 'how.'"*—Nietzsche

Soheila Adelipour

Dancing to the Darkest Light
A remarkable true story of life, its challenges
and triumph over the ultimate heartbreak

ISBN 978-1-7337126-1-3 (hardcover)
ISBN 978-1-7337126-2-0 (paperback)
ISBN 978-1-7337126-3-7 (eBook)

To my mother, my smart, capable and strong Momon.
And my children, Justin, Stephen, Cameron and Jordan.
Thank you for choosing me as your mom. I admire, respect and love you.
You are my "Why" to live for.

To my dear friends, family members and everyone that was there
and prayed for us during those tough times: You know who you
are and I LOVE you dearly. Your kindness, your support and
your compassion were our rock, our caisson and our safety net.
You are the reason we can still smile. Thank you for being there,
day in and day out. We are blessed to have you in our lives.

My "I" Story

My dear friends and readers:

I started writing my book in 2014, and it is now 2019. It was a difficult and heartbreaking road, but I had decided that I would travel that unfamiliar and challenging path to the end no matter what. I started writing and finally stopped at page 585. Looking at that thick manuscript, I realized how much has happened in my life and to my loved ones. Then came the unexpected difficult part...I had to make it shorter! I was told "a book more than 400 pages is difficult to sell."

I found "deleting" much more difficult than "writing." Every page held a story that deserved to be told and shared. But as always, I did what I had to do. As I wiped my tears, I erased 200 pages of my manuscript.

I wrote this book first, because I had promised my brother; and second, because I wanted to be an example for people who are going through difficult times and challenges. So much has happened in my life. "My Story" has become what many people would call a "horror story." I am well aware of that; however, that perception is what I am trying to change. It is true that my family has suffered great tragedies. That will always remain part of "my story," but it will not stay a "horror story." I prefer to see it as an "inspiring story."

Mr. Itzhak Perlman, the world-famous violinist, was giving a concert at Lincoln Center in New York. Mr. Perlman was stricken as a young child with polio; as a result, he wears braces on both legs and walks with crutches. The great musician enters the Hall, walking slowly towards his chair at the center of the stage, holding his violin case and crutches. He sits down, places the crutches to the side, opens the braces, takes out his violin, puts it under his chin, and nods to the conductor. The orchestra starts full force and he is deep into his music, playing with devotion and dedication. As he plays every note intensely and passionately, one of the strings on his violin suddenly snaps. The sound travels across the room like a gunshot. The room becomes silent. The musicians, the members of the audience, and the conductor stay frozen. Everyone is expecting Mr. Perlman to get up and limp his way off the stage or ask for another violin. But those were not his options.

Instead, he closed his eyes, took a deep breath and signaled the conductor to begin again. He started the Concerto with only three strings and reinvented and recreated his music as he was going forward. When the Concerto was finished, the audience was stunned and silent. Then came the applause. Everyone rose and gave a standing ovation, cheering and applauding for a man that had just re-defined his music. When he was asked why he continued on playing with only three strings, he replied, *"You know, sometimes it is the artist's task to find out how much music he can still make with what he has left."*

So, my dear and beloved friends, that is what I want to do and am trying to do now: "still make beautiful music with what I have left." The same tune, just played differently.

If, after everything that has happened, my book could inspire just a few people in this unpredictable, ever-changing and bewildering world to change their "challenging life stories" to "inspiring life stories" then my task would be complete.

Love, Light and Life,
Soheila Adelipour

Contents

Prologue

New York, July, 2013

A black hole; Dante's fifth ring of hell; a Roach Motel... you check in but you can't check out. For us, Mount Sinai hospital—especially the MICU floor, medical intensive care unit, for people with little chance of survival—had become a grim, depressing, and hopeless place, every inch of it permeated by disappointment, heartbreak, fear, and profound sadness.

We had struggled for so long to be positive and strong; to keep each other smiling and laughing; to move on and embrace each day with an all-too-transparent masquerade of normalcy. Eventually our expectations of a return to some version of our previously ordinary lives dwindled, even as we defied the black cloud that hovered and threatened. Our outlook had turned gloomy. Our resolve was weakening, and we were anticipating the very worst.

Our family had always been staunchly anti-drug. Taking a pill for a headache or a capsule for indigestion was a big deal, an act we carefully considered, distrusted, and resisted. And yet, there we were, all of us hungrily pursuing, divvying up, and then gulping down Vitamin X. Xanax was the essential quick-fix. Vitamin X was now part of the new normal: a comforting friend; a source of confidence; a new safety net; our new Hamptons getaway; our new yoga. Without that magic pill, sleep had become impossible. Even my elderly mother was on Vitamin

X. We were a close-knit unit; all for X, and X for all. And so, we shared our pills. We had become our own professional drug dealers. This was our new normal.

"Hey, how many do you have left? Can you spare a few?"

Anxiously: "No, I only have enough for three more days!"

"Okay, no problem. Let me have a few. I promise I'll give them back as soon as I can fill my new prescription."

Nervously: "I don't know. What if I run out and go dry?"

We all knew enough to have a couple handy for when our mother started to sob. We'd push one in her mouth and beg her to swallow. She'd cry and shake her head, resisting its comfort. "I want to die, I want to die. I cannot bear the thought of me still here and him gone."

It was crushing to see her like that.

Twenty minutes after giving in and swallowing, she'd be sitting on a chair in the waiting room—the visitor's lounge that had become our makeshift living room/kitchen/dining room and my bedroom—like a zombie.

"Now, how many do you have left?" We immediately started checking inventory. "Momon should be good for another five hours. The vitamin is working again," we whispered to each other.

None of us smoked or drank; recreational drugs were not even in our vocabulary. The idea of prescription drugs left us feeling uneasy. Years before, after foot surgery, my doctor had prescribed a considerable supply of Vicodin for pain—more than enough to see me through a future nose job or facelift. After a single dose, I stopped, preferring to endure the pain rather than suffer the miserable side effects of those dreaded pills.

This was an altogether different type of suffering, though. This was not post-surgery swelling, throbbing, and cramping. This was not a migraine. This was an emotional ordeal—cruel, unrelenting, and interminable. But worse still, it was familiar. We were once tormented during the revolution in Iran in 1979 when we left behind everything we knew and headed towards what would become our first new normal. The freedom we lost, the home that was confiscated, the identity we left behind—eventually replaced by the freedom of democracy, a new home, and eventually naturalization papers and a new hyphenated identity.

Then... Stephen. Losing my precious twenty-two-year-old prince catapulted me into a devastating *new* new normal. I had to learn to stop waiting for him to walk through the front door and listening for the sound of his car coming up the driveway. I had to remind myself every second of every day that I owed it to my other precious sons to keep pushing through without letting anyone see that a huge part of my heart had been lost on the day I hugged him good-bye for the last time. And just like the first time around, this new new normal also led me to a new town, a new home and a search for a new life.

And then... Zohreh. After a very long battle with a brain tumor, my sister Zohreh died an untimely death a few years after Stephen. But this brand-new new normal, was no ordinary normal. By the time of my sister's death I had fallen back and forth through the looking glass so many times that nothing would ever be normal again.

On the day we buried Zohreh, my brother, Fariborz stayed at home, telling everyone he was recovering from a walking pneumonia. The truth was that he had already been diagnosed with leukemia and started a first round of chemo. His immune system had been compromised, and a simple handshake could have proven fatal. Other than his wife, I was the only one entrusted with this secret. But less than two months after the burial of our sister, my brother's secret was out. His condition deteriorated so quickly that he had to be hospitalized in MICU. We could no longer keep it from my mom. His life was hanging by a thread.

In this brand-new new normal, Xanax came reliably to our rescue each and every night. The very notion of growing dependent on a drug freaked us all out, but there seemed no other way. Ironically, the tables had turned. My kids, nieces and nephews worried about my siblings and me. They hid our precious stash, giving us quotas and doling out dosages. They threatened us, recoiling as they watched us fighting over the last pill. They were concerned and afraid. It seemed the natural order of our family, along with everything else, had simply turned upside down.

But in the stifling environment of the MICU region of the hospital, ever-present anxiety, constant minute-to-minute worry, and cloying stress consumed us. We needed to be strong and present for our only brother, Fariborz, and my terrorized mother. At any cost. Even if doing so meant creating a bunch of pill-popping addicts out of us all.

Life in Ahwaz: The Bloody Girl In the Carpet

"We are all born ignorant, but one must work hard to remain stupid." —Benjamin Franklin

Iran, 1955

Late one night my young newlywed parents were awakened by an unexpected pounding on their front door. "Open up, Mrs. Doctor," an angry voice ordered as strong fists pounded. "We have a patient for you."

"Who is that?" my father asked frantically.

"I have no idea," my mother replied, while quickly putting her clothes on.

"Open the door, I said," demanded the man outside.

"Should we call the police?" my father suggested, nervously looking out the window.

My mother tried to remain calm behind the locked door. "It's the middle of the night," she called out. "Please come to my office in the morning."

"No! We can't wait till tomorrow. Open the door now or I will break it down. Your patient is here with us," the man yelled. "We won't wait."

Nearly frozen with fear, my father struggled to undo the locks and slowly began to open the door. With violent force, he was slammed against the wall as three visitors pushed their way inside. Two men dressed in

5

tribal clothing, accompanied by a woman covered head to toe in a black chador, were carrying a rolled-up Persian rug. It was soaked through and dripping, leaving a bloody trail behind them on the shiny wooden floor. The intruders dropped the rug onto the floor in the middle of the living room and kicked it open with blood-stained shoes. As the rug unrolled, my parents took a step back in shock and horror. A young teenage girl, semi-conscious, her clothes and hair saturated with blood, lay moaning and crying from pain in front of their eyes.

The older man moved forward and stood over the girl. He grabbed her long, knotted wet hair in his large, threatening-looking left hand and held her head up roughly, while using his right hand to hold his machete to her neck.

"As Allah is my witness, I will kill this piece of filth."

Until the day they got married, my parents lived in Shiraz, a beautiful city in southern Iran, which is famous for its wine and happy-go-lucky people (probably as a result of the wine). Not particularly ambitious, Shirazees are said to be all about music, food, flowers and, of course, the wine of their region.

The Jewish community in Shiraz was tight and cohesive; they married their own kind and stayed together. My mother was a beautiful, educated and independent twenty-year-old; my father a handsome, tall and broad-shouldered twenty-four-year-old young man who had just started his own business in import/export. They met through a Jewish youth organization and fell in love, which in those days was neither a normal nor conventional route towards marriage. Seven decades ago, most Iranian marriages were arranged when the future couple were both still young children. Girls were expected to marry as teenagers, move into the homes of their new husbands and obey their in-laws unquestioningly.

This was the tradition and the rule, but my mom was an exception. Compared to most Jews in Shiraz, she and her family led charmed lives.

They didn't reside in the Jewish Quarter; they had a beautiful house on a major street, surrounded by verdant orange and lemon trees and a pond filled with brightly-colored red and gold fish. My grandfather was an educated man. He never felt compelled to marry his first daughter off simply to follow custom. My mother wanted to continue with her education, and her father approved. After high school (very few females received a diploma in those days) she applied to medical school, determined to become a midwife, which required three years of study.

My grandmother had married when she was only thirteen, and had my mom a year later. By the time my mother became a midwife, my grandmother was pregnant with her seventh child. When she went into labor, my mom helped to deliver her brother, a nine-pound baby. A year later, my mom gave birth to her own first child, Nahid, my oldest sister. For a while mother and daughter were reproducing simultaneously. By the time my grandmother welcomed her eighth and final child, she was thirty-seven, an age where many modern women are just getting started with motherhood.

Shortly after their marriage, my parents moved to Ahwaz, a southern city close to the Persian Gulf. Living could be difficult there. Summers were brutal, extremely hot and humid. Temperatures rose as high as 120 degrees Fahrenheit. My parents chose the area because of its booming export and import business. My mother started working as a midwife (at the time, there were no gynecologists available) in the local clinic, and my father began trading goods. Little by little, they got to know other Jewish families who had settled there in hopes of making better incomes. Despite the extreme summer heat and my mom's horrible nausea with her pregnancies, life was good.

My parents joined the private social clubs, became permanent fixtures at every party, and traveled often. After giving birth to three girls in 8 years—Nahid, Zohreh and me—they were quietly longing for a boy. My mother continued working even with three young children; she had a prestigious job, one in which she excelled. She was loved and respected by her patients, who showered her with gifts, whatever they could afford. They brought her fruit baskets, fresh dates, beautiful fabrics, and even chickens and goats. Many of those gifts came from the people who lived in tribes outside of Ahwaz. Each tribe had its own chief who ruled and controlled the people. They were mostly Arabs who'd moved there years before. They relied upon my mother's services; the idea of taking their wives and daughters to a male doctor, even for a minor examination, was unthinkable. It was members of one of these tribes who made an unexpected appearance at our home late one night.

"Oh no! What are you doing?" My mother instinctively reached out her arm, putting one hand on the man's wrist holding the machete to his daughter's throat. With her other hand, she grabbed hold of the brutalized girl's wrist to check her pulse. "What has been done to this poor child?"

"Poor child? She is a whore, a slut. I'm ashamed to be her father. It was her wedding tonight—to him," he shouted, pointing to the other man. "She was not a virgin; there was no blood on her wedding night. I am going to kill her. Before I finish her off, I want you to examine her and tell me if she has dishonored us or if she was born like this. My wife said that it could be an act of God. You better tell us the truth. If she has lost her virginity I will cut her throat from ear to ear to protect the honor of the family."

The woman, trembling in the corner, started sobbing under her veil and cried, "My daughter is pure. She is innocent. She is clean. Have mercy for her, she has done nothing wrong."

"Shut up, woman, or I will kill you too! It's your fault. You gave birth to this filth. Not another word from you," her husband yelled, holding his machete over his wife's head as if daring her to make another sound. His eyes were burning with rage, his nostrils flaring. He looked like an injured panther ready to attack and kill.

My mother jumped forward and planted herself between the husband and wife. "Please, let's take a breath here. You are not my first family with this problem. I have one every week. Let me examine your child first, then you can honor kill both: your wife and your daughter. But your wife happens to be right. I have seen many cases of virgin girls that were born this way. A lot of them are pure and have done nothing wrong. I can tell you within only a few minutes after a simple exam. I will do that, but I need you to promise that if the result is negative, you will do your killing somewhere else. Not here. Not in my house."

My father, utterly stunned, stared at my mother with his mouth open, as if to say, "Kill her somewhere else? Have you gone mad?"

Ignoring my father's shocked look, my mother asked the men to drag the carpet to the other room. "Please take her to my bedroom, and leave her there," she said, pointing the way. "I can't examine her in front of you two. I need privacy."

The men, seeming to completely believe that this medical professional would tell them the truth, held the corners of the blood-soaked carpet and pulled it to the bedroom. My mother followed them, trying very carefully not to step in the thick lines of blood left behind. She asked the men to wait outside and locked the door behind her. She then joined her patient, giving the girl some water to sip on and then washing her face. She struggled to focus and not shake as she tenderly explored the young bride's battered body. The examination revealed the girl was not a virgin—and Allah had nothing to do with it.

"What have you done, child? You know the rules. Your father will kill you for this," my mother said. The girl started crying and reached with her bloody hands for my mother's feet, which she repeatedly kissed. "Please do something. I beg of you. It was not my fault. My uncle is the guilty one. He threatened me if I didn't do as he said, he would kill me. Every time I went to get water, he was there waiting for me. I was so afraid. Please Mrs. Doctor, help me. Please." The girl was trembling.

"Poor girl, how old are you?"

"I will be fifteen next month," the young victim answered.

My mom took her hands. "Okay, now listen to me. Stay right here and don't make a sound," my mother instructed. Leaving the girl, she walked back to the living room.

"Allow me to kill her, to slice her filthy body into small pieces, to throw them in the desert. Let the wild beasts feast on her impure, disgusting, and repulsive body," the father yelled, while waving his machete.

"Calm down, please," my mother urged. "Your daughter is pure. She has done nothing wrong. She is as Allah created her. The same way that he has made people with bigger noses or bigger eyes. They're all Allah's creations, and so therefore, perfect. Her virginity is intact."

The woman in the black veil dropped to the floor and cried out, "Allah is great, Allah knows best. I told you my daughter is clean." The father, whose face had temporarily softened, turned towards his daughter's husband, directing his still-simmering anger at him. "Did you hear that? Our family's honor is intact. She is a virgin. Maybe we should blame it on your shortcomings! Our name is good and our dignity unharmed." For the first time since they had entered the house, he kept his machete pointing downward as he spoke.

My mother interrupted, "Now you must tend to your innocent daughter. She needs to be taken care of." She looked at the girl's husband and continued, "You are not allowed to touch her until she is 100% healthy. She has lost a lot of blood. She needs to be fed and pampered. And left alone to rest and recover." She took a deep breath and said, "And if you want healthy babies, send someone else to fetch water for the family from now on. Preferably a man!"

The father looked down at the floor, and quietly said, "Yes." He took out a roll of cash and held it in front of my mother in his two huge hands. "Mrs. Doctor, please take this. We apologize for the trouble. Take as much as you want. You deserve all of it and more."

"I will take just my regular fee, plus the cleaning charges. You have made a mess in my house." She took a portion of the money, and then directed the family towards the door. "Take your daughter and nurse her. She needs to get strong again. Please make sure her husband doesn't touch her for another two months."

"Yes, Mrs. Doctor. You have my word."

The family left. As soon as the doors were closed behind them and the coast was clear, my parents exhaled. Then it was my father's turn to blow a fuse. "You can honor kill both, but promise me you won't kill them here! Have you lost your mind?"

"Calm down and let me explain," my mother insisted. "I had to make sure they would trust me; that they'd believe I was on their side; that I understood their shame. Otherwise he would have suspected my made-up story."

"You lied?" my father was even more shocked, if possible.

"What did you expect? That I'd let that monster cut her throat? Of course, I lied. Now everyone is relieved and alive."

My mother was proud of her stories from her working years. She was written up in the newspaper when she delivered healthy triplets in a tent, and again when the head of a local tribe threatened to burn their hospital down. Hassan was a tall, strong man, with an impressive beard and a huge turban. He came to my mother's office with his pregnant wife, who was having labor pains, and a massive entourage. Hundreds of Hassan's men on horses held their swords in the air and stood guard.

"She has been in labor for more than twenty-four hours and nothing has happened yet." He approached my mom aggressively and in an intimidating tone said, "If anything happens to my wife, I will burn down your hospital. I have my people surrounding this place. No one is allowed to leave until my child and my wife come home healthy. You will do your best or else. I love my wife and I can't go on living without her."

The wife was a pretty, small-framed young girl. My mother knew it would be very difficult for her to give birth just by looking at her hips. To make matters worse, the baby was bridged. The staff and my mom tried to turn the baby around by putting pressure on the mother's stomach from different angles. The poor girl kept screaming from the combination of the physical force, my mom's weight on her, and the labor pains. Her husband, meanwhile, paced back and forth outside of her room, yelling out every once in a while, "Fatima, I am here. I will protect you. I will not let anything happen to you."

My mom knew she could not wait any longer, and a C-section was performed on her young patient. If any kind of infection set in, the girl would die for sure. My mother asked for penicillin, which was being widely used across Europe, but in that small hospital in Ahwaz, availability was extremely limited. They just had to keep their fingers crossed and hope the patient would pull through.

My mother stayed in the hospital next to the girl's bed for the next two days, cleaning and disinfecting her stitches. The husband's anger had dissipated with the arrival of a bouncy and healthy boy; he was proud and happy. He had an heir. The wife was a different story. She was weak, with a high fever, and her breathing was difficult. My mother's team did their best, but the girl did not survive. The doctors and my mother huddled in her room, deciding how to break the news to her husband.

"Even the police will be outnumbered by Hassan's men."

"But he will be beside himself when we tell him that his wife is dead," one of the doctors said, nervously looking out the window at the men still massed outside on horseback.

My mom got off the chair, headed towards the nursery, and said, "I will take care of it."

She walked out, holding the baby in her arms. She handed the newborn to the father and said, "Hold your son, your pride and joy. He will rule your tribe one day. He is strong and robust, just like you. Your wife asked me to tell you to take care of him. To make him a powerful and big man like his father. This was her last request, before she left us." My mother took a deep breath.

"Now, if you want to burn the hospital down, I can't stop you, but you will end up in jail and never get a chance to see your beautiful son grow." She paused, letting her words sink in, then added, "Take your son home and do as Fatima wished. She will be watching you from heaven."

Tears rolled down the man's face. Holding his infant child, he held his chin up proudly and showed off his male offspring to everyone. Looking at my mother, he nodded, and left the hospital.

My mom collapsed onto a chair, legs giving out from an equal mixture of mental and physical exhaustion. When she told us that story years later, I wondered how it would have ended if the wife had given birth to a girl.

Life in Tehran

"Family is like the branches on a tree, we all grow in different directions, yet our roots remain as one." —Unknown

Tehran, 1960s

I was three years old when my parents, having earned enough money to start a new life in the capital city, moved our family to Tehran. Life was simple, mostly happy, what we thought of as "normal," with nothing more to trouble us than the ordinary day-to-day problems of a busy, ever-growing family.

Tehran in the '70s was calm, safe, and largely uneventful. The evening news was dominated by coverage of the Vietnam War, with its gruesome pictures and footage. That, and the Munich massacre of eleven Israeli athletes during the 1972 Summer Olympics, left a permanent tattoo upon my memory. While the rest of the world still seemed to think of Iranians as backward commuters on camels and donkeys, our lives were pleasant, modern and peaceful.

We respected our parents, never touched drugs or alcohol, and did as we were told. The main religion was Islam, and depending on the neighborhood, almost every religion was accepted or tolerated. Our friends were Jewish as well as Arminian, Christian, Bahai, Zoroastrian and Muslim. No one cared about our beliefs; if they did, they kept their thoughts to themselves.

The fashions were the latest from Europe: skirts were very short, heels were high, and bikinis tiny. The "camels" that were our preferred mode of transportation were either Chevrolets, Cadillacs, BMWs, Mercedes-Benzes, Fiats, or Peykans, a model manufactured in Iran with great pride that was unfortunately neither functional nor safe. Rolls-Royces and Bentleys belonged to the royal family and were forbidden to the general public.

The Shah and his family were respected and feared. Everyone spoke about them with the utmost politeness and caution. One could never be sure who was listening. Making anti-Shah comments or criticizing the government was the kiss of death. Members of SAVAK (the Shah's secret service) were everywhere, listening carefully to everything.

Jews in Iran were exempt from that fear. The Shah and the royal family knew very well that we appreciated the freedom and the safe haven we were living in. Every city still had its Jewish Quarter, with poor living conditions and constant verbal attacks from Muslims, who considered Jews impure and filthy, but that was their belief system and had nothing to do with the official government stance. The Jews tried hard to succeed in business and little by little they started leaving those horrible conditions. The ones that made it in the business world lived charmed lives and enjoyed the fruits of their hard work.

Nightclubs and cabarets were destination playgrounds for anyone who could afford them. They were all given Western names: Cafe Lido, Chattanooga Restaurant, Cabaret Baccarat, suggesting a hint of that opulent land far, far, away, where everything was bigger, more beautiful, and far more interesting. The shows were wannabe Vegas revues, with singers dressed in the latest fashions. Money was a non-issue for people who had it, and the good life was available for them to enjoy.

We spent most of our hot summer days in Khadem Abad, a region verdant with lush fruit trees and flowers on the outskirts of Tehran. The drives to our vacation home there were always filled with laughter and enthusiasm. We settled in excitedly after arriving, eagerly looking forward to swimming, playing volleyball, and climbing trees in the great outdoors. Our mother prepared and packed up lunch early each morning, and then we'd spend the whole day outdoors by the public pool. Of course, there were also the diving lessons my father oversaw. A tough and strict taskmaster, he ran the show. When I tried to complain, he wasn't swayed.

"My back hurts," I appealed. "Look, it's all red from landing on the water the wrong way."

"Go put on a T-shirt. That will lessen the impact," he ordered. "And make it quick."

"Babajoon, please. My skin is on fire. Can I stop now?"

"If you want to learn how to flip from a diving board, this is the time and place to do it. You can't give up now. Go put on your shirt. Now. Run!" His tone was firmer. I walked down the diving board ladder, water dripping from my skin-and-bone body, back stinging, and began searching for something protective to wear. There was no point in arguing. There never was.

My younger siblings Nazee, Fariborz, and I played, swam, talked to friends, climbed trees, picked fresh fruit, and threw Frisbees under the sun all day long. But our father made sure we were always learning and improving our skills, whether it be swimming, diving, volleyball, or even holding our breath under the water for long periods of time. To do otherwise would have been a waste of a good day for him.

Our father was well-read, self-taught, very informed—but also serious, opinionated, authoritarian, and, at times, a dictator. If he thought that I was a good athlete and an opportunity arose for me to learn to flip off a diving board, I had to practice flipping like a dolphin until I did so to perfection. Each of us kids knew what was expected from us: to do our "best" and do so "extraordinarily," because merely "good" was simply not "good enough." His children's grades had to be perfect. If not, he'd be in the principal's office the next day, report card in hand, talking to the teachers.

No one ever dared to say "No" to my father. He was feared and respected like the rest of the Persian men of that era. Where he differed was that at a time when girls were supposed to marry early and get on with their new lives with their husbands and children, my father insisted that his girls should have higher education and master as many diverse skills as possible.

Poor Nahid was always in trouble. She was the first child and endured tremendous pressure; much was expected of her and she tried. But she was just never terribly interested in studying or schoolwork. She was a dreamer and an artist at heart. She simply had no use for Calculus or Algebra. When the teacher was giving a lecture, Nahid was busy drawing faces or flowers in her notebook. Her marks were deemed unsatisfactory by my father. He clearly did not understand her artistic temperament.

He eventually shifted his attention away from Nahid, focusing all his efforts on his second daughter. Zohreh was a better student, but a rebel. My father hoped she would become the doctor or engineer of the family, but she, too, had other plans and dreams. Zohreh was only interested in the concepts of design and space. She decorated her room to perfection and allowed no one in without her permission. She was stubborn and fearless. While the rest of us kids followed our father's orders to the letter, she'd do the opposite. When we were all frightened, she would laugh. When we were all home studying, she'd be out with her friends.

She knew what she wanted to do and which college she wanted to attend. My father was under the impression that Zohreh had applied to certain universities as he had instructed. When it was time for acceptance letters to arrive and he discovered she'd only applied to the School of Interior Design, he was beside himself, a volcano on the verge of eruption.

"How dare you disobey me? Didn't I ask you to apply to medical school?"

"I don't want to be an engineer or a doctor. I want to be an interior designer," she argued.

"There is no prestige in that field. I told you where to apply and what to study."

"Well, I don't care. I want to do what I enjoy," she yelled back, running to her bedroom and locking the door behind her.

The rest of us, meanwhile, hid in the corner, doing our level best to avoid the conflict and our father's fury.

"This is not the end of it. You will not go to that stupid college."

True to form, Zohreh did, in fact, pursue her further education at "that stupid college," where she was one of the best students in her class.

She was a nonconformist, against the institution of marriage. When a suitor called to ask her out, she typically answered with, "I am not interested in getting married and likely never will be. If I feel like having children, I'll adopt. There are tons of children out there who need homes." To which my mother would look at her daughter, her mouth open in seeming shock, her hands on her face in obvious disbelief. "Why are you saying these things to people? They will start talking. Think of your reputation, your family's reputation."

Forty years ago, in Iran, Zohreh's ideas were radical; too much for anyone's ears. But she had a strong sense of herself and wasn't concerned with approval or pleasing others. Shrugging her shoulders, she'd say, "Why should I get married and let a man decide for me what to do or not to do, when I can make my own money and decisions?" In response, my mom shook her head, and, looking distressed, simply walked away.

Then there was me. Third in line, never a star student, but I worked and tried hard, even if I had to cheat in school a bit here and there to get a better grade. I wanted to avoid any unnecessary conflicts. I knew what was expected of me, and a solid academic performance was essential, topping the list of requirements. When I had free time, I was a mainstay at my mother's side, helping with the housework or supermarket shopping. But, I was also the clown of the family and loved making everyone laugh. Full of energy, I was always busy doing something or getting involved in a project.

Nazee was the family's star student, with her perfect grades. She was the answer to my father's prayers, even though with three daughters already, he'd been wishing for a son. Born with long, black eyelashes, huge black eyes, and a head full of thick hair, my sister was a beautiful baby. As a child, she was quiet and gentle, in stark contrast to my loud and hyper personality. She was three-and-a-half years younger than I, but we shared everything: a room, friends, ideas, and secrets. We went everywhere together and were each other's closest companion.

Two years later Fariborz arrived to complete our family; he was the love of all our lives. He was the most adorable little boy, with dark eyes and a deep cleft on his cute curled-up chin. He was a good and sweet child, with a big heart. He studied at Andeesheh, a coveted Catholic school for boys offering the highest level of education available in Tehran. It was, naturally, the academic institution of choice for my father's one son.

The fact that he was the only boy surrounded by sisters gave my father great motivation to ensure he didn't grow up to be a spoiled brat. My mother inhaled and exhaled to each of Fariborz's breaths. He was the apple of her eye; she couldn't get enough of him. He was a smart and hardworking boy, and I absolutely loved being and playing with him and Nazee. I was the "go-to" babysitter of the family, which was never a problem for me because I adored babies and children. While Nahid and Zohreh went to parties and restaurants with our parents, I happily stayed behind with my younger siblings, entertaining them.

Our Changing Lives In Iran

"In three words I can sum up everything I've learned about life: 'It goes on.'" —Robert Frost

Tehran, 1970s

Nahid was working as an executive secretary at a hotel in Tehran in the early seventies when she met her future husband. Ike was in his 30s, recently divorced and fell hard for my sister. She was only 19 years old. My mother was against the match from day one, but Ike knew well how to capture a young girl's heart. In short order, they married, started a family and made plans to leave Iran. They moved to New York in 1974 with their two daughters, Liza and Linda, still in diapers. My mom was profoundly upset. America was too far away; it felt like another world. She held her young granddaughters in her arms and said mournfully, "I will miss you. When will I ever see you again?"

Our daily visits and talks were replaced with long-distance phone calls and lengthy letters, until the summer of 1977, when Nahid returned to Tehran with her daughters for a visit. We were truly happy to be together again. That same year, Zohreh had graduated with degrees as an architect and interior designer, and had applied to Pratt Institute in Brooklyn for her master's. Her decision to continue her education in New York was against our father's wishes. But my sister couldn't wait to get out of Iran and start life on her own, something she had long planned and fought for. In the end, as she always had, Zohreh did what she wanted to do.

On the day of her departure, Zohreh walked out of her room, dressed up in a beautiful blue and white floral outfit, her hair and makeup perfect, luggage in hand.

"Shall we leave now? I don't want to miss my flight."

"But we have plenty of time," my mom replied, sadness in her voice.

"Please! What if there's traffic or the lines are too long? Let's go."

We all piled into the car to take her to the airport. She was joyful; we were not. She was restless to leave; we were holding onto every minute, wishing we could slow the clock. After dropping her off, saying our lengthy goodbyes, and sharing long, tight hugs, we drove directly to Khadem Abad to spend the day by the pool.

We were swimming and playing in the water with Liza and Linda, while my mother sat under the shade of a tree, alone. She was worried about Zohreh. We sat down for lunch, insisting that she have something.

"I am not hungry."

"But, Momon, you have to eat. You can't stress over Zohreh and have such anxiety. She's on the plane now, as happy as she can be, and you are here in this beautiful place with the rest of your family, torturing yourself."

"I have been told Brooklyn is not safe."

"Only some parts of Brooklyn aren't safe," Nahid replied. "She will be fine. She's a capable girl."

While we were trying to cheer up our mom, I looked up and noticed a tall and skinny girl in a blue and white floral outfit approaching us.

"Nazee, doesn't that look like Zohreh?" I asked.

My sister looked up and exclaimed, "Oh my God, it is Zohreh. What is she doing here?"

"Momon, look! Zohreh is here," Nahid said excitedly. My mother stared in disbelief, and started running towards my sister with the rest of us. We formed a circle around Zohreh and began firing questions at her:

"What happened?"

"Was there a problem with your flight?"

"Is everything okay?"

As if she'd been waiting for the producer to yell out "Action!" Zohreh, who had remained composed until that second, started to cry. "I checked my luggage, went to the gate, and then sat there, waiting to board. I was way too early for the flight, so I put my jacket under my head, leaned on the wall, and fell asleep. I only woke up because a baby was screaming and crying. I walked over to the agent and asked her for an update on my flight." Zohreh blew her nose into a tissue and continued. "The agent looked at my boarding pass, pointed at a plane in the sky and said, 'Miss, do you see that airplane? That was your flight. We have been calling your name but you didn't show up, so the plane left without you!' Momon, can you believe this? I was asleep the whole time and didn't hear a thing. Only twenty feet away from the gate and I missed my flight."

Her sobs grew more intense and our laughter became stronger as she recounted the story. It was too funny and all-too-typical of Zohreh. Sleep was her favorite thing. She slept soundly all night and would sleep all through the day if given the opportunity. Which made my dad crazy. "This house is not a lazy home!" he would yell.

But she loved her rest. No one dared to wake her up and nothing could. She never let go of that habit. And now, she had missed her magic carpet ride, her "Beam me up Scotty," her chance to escape to a whole new world.

"Why are you laughing? Don't you see how upset I am?" she asked. She was distressed, but we were on the grass, rolling with laughter.

"Is anyone hungry?" my mom asked, turning her face to conceal her big smile.

"Did they say when you can travel again?" my father asked with an angry face, obviously trying very hard to keep his cool.

"In two days," Zohreh answered. "They were sold out for tomorrow's flight. I just hope my luggage will be safe there."

"Come on, let's go eat," my mother said.

We returned to the pool and resumed playing. We were happy to be together again—four sisters, my brother, my parents, and my beautiful nieces.

It would take a major revolution, lives destroyed and lost, turmoil in the Middle East, an incapable American president, and the collapse of an empire before we'd be reunited again.

"Throw the tear gas," the commander yelled. "Throw the goddamned tear gas."

The chaos had begun. The Shah's army started throwing tear gas at the students who were protesting and chanting, "Marg Bar Shah" (*Death to Shah*) at the school of engineering at Pahlavi University. In the mass pandemonium, everyone was either trying to find cover or flee the dreadful scene. I stood there stunned and confused, watching bodies appearing and disappearing within the heavy smoke.

It was October of 1978, and life outside of the universities in Iran was almost normal. Life inside of the universities was another story altogether. It was utter madness. I was on campus just to check my grade on my latest exam and then meet friends for lunch at a local restaurant. A routine visit under normal circumstances. But nothing about those college days was either routine or normal.

Walking in as I always did, through the massive gates, I moved across the courtyard and climbed the two steps to enter the school building. It was a beautiful day, but unusually quiet with few students around. Passing through the long hallway towards my classroom, I checked the list posted inside of the glass showcase, looked for my name, followed the dotted lines until I saw my grade, gave myself a satisfied smile, and turned around and walked back out, proud and happy.

I was alone. The hallway was deserted and eerily quiet. The only noise I could hear was the echo of my heels tap-tap-tapping on the floors. But I didn't give that much of a thought. I was content with my grade and happily lost in my own world.

I pushed the heavy doors open and started to exit the building. Upon my first step out, I heard someone yelling, "Soheila, don't! Go back inside."

It was too late. I was already in the courtyard. I looked to my left, where the voice was coming from, and saw a friend hunched down behind a chair. He looked at me and pointed at the iron fences. There, I witnessed what I'd only ever seen in the movies: our whole school was surrounded by armed soldiers. They were down on one knee, holding their guns pointed directly at the courtyard, and looked ready to fire.

I stopped myself from taking another step forward and looked around me. There were revolutionary students all over the courtyard. They were throwing stones at the soldiers and chanting, "Down with the Shah. Down with the Shah." They were an angry mob, with messy beards, unkempt hair, and soiled-looking clothing. They seemed not to care that the guns were pointing straight at them. As if they were ready to do whatever was needed, no matter the consequences.

"Throw the tear gas," the commander ordered again.

The canisters came flying over by the dozens. The chanting grew stronger for a few seconds, and was then replaced by heavy coughing and choking sounds. The soldiers stormed the courtyard and started running after the revolutionaries, grabbing them and beating them up with their batons. The students were running in different directions, holding their hands or pieces of clothing in front of their mouths. The gate was blocked by the soldiers; no one was able to escape. We were trapped.

I was still standing frozen in front of the building, too frightened to take a step or make a move. Ten minutes before, it had been a quiet, beautiful, and clear sunny day. Too quiet, in fact. Now bedlam and madness had replaced the tranquility, and the sun was barely visible through the smoke. A guy tumbled and fell right in front of me. I took one step back. The soldiers got to him quickly. One grabbed him by his hair and another started kicking him.

"You bastard, you. You son of a bitch. You go against the Shah? I will kill you right here and deliver your worthless body to your mother."

The protestor was in obvious pain. There was blood all over his face and shirt. "Stop. Please. *Ghalat kardam, Goh Khordam* (I made a mistake), stop. I beg you, stop."

It was a nightmare, a war scene, total chaos, the beginning of the revolution. I took a step back and leaned on the wall trembling in my high heels, a pencil skirt, and a button-down shirt. Damn lunch attire! I stood there in shock, watching both sides of the fight without making a move.

Suddenly, someone grabbed my hand and pulled me with a strong force. It felt like I had woken from a coma. I turned around and started running in the direction the hand was taking me. Someone was dragging me, while yelling, "Run, Soheila." I managed to do so without falling. He made his way inside the building and I followed behind him. When I landed in the lobby, I looked to see who it was through eyes that were stinging and burning. Tears were rolling down my face; breathing was difficult, my throat was burning, and I could not stop coughing. He was the same friend who had warned me not to leave the engineering building earlier. He was one of the older students, a senior I had gotten to know in the few months since enrolling at Pahlavi University. He screamed again and again, "Run, Soheila. We have to go up to get away from the gas."

I was not exactly dressed to join the marathon, and not being able to see or catch my breath didn't help, but I did as I was told and kept running. He was holding onto my hand as tightly as he possibly could as he headed towards the stairs and started climbing them, one floor after another. I was concentrating on keeping my balance in those damn shoes, and miraculously stayed right with him.

We ran up to the fourth floor, the highest, and opened the door to one of the rooms. We entered a classroom, crawled to a corner and collapsed to the floor. Standing up straight next to a window was far too dangerous with the possibility of a stray bullet.

My friend started crawling around the room, searching for a piece of paper, finding only a brown shopping bag in the wastebasket. He took out his lighter, set a piece of the paper on fire, held it in front of me, and said, "Take couple of deep breaths." I looked at the fire in front of me, still coughing, and didn't dare move.

"Go ahead. Take a few breaths. It neutralizes the tear gas," he said reassuringly. I held my face on top of the fire and started inhaling the smoke. It worked like magic. I stopped coughing and the burning in my eyes started to ease. When he was sure that I was able to breathe, he took the paper and held it under his own nose and took deep breaths.

Once I'd caught my breath, I looked around the room and realized we were not alone. There were strangely-shaped creatures covered in brown fabric on the floor. Mullahs, the Muslim clergies, were hiding with their heads under the seats, asses sticking up in the air. All I could see were rows of wide brown butts pointing up. They looked like neatly packed and organized piles of manure!

While they had instructed the young students to fight and put their own lives in great jeopardy, these men were hiding. They had taken cover and were shivering like cowards on the fourth floor, away from all the danger.

"What are you doing here?" my friend whispered to me. "Didn't you know no one was supposed to come to engineering school today?"

"No," I said, "of course not. No one told me anything. I came here to check my grade. What is going on?"

"There was a meeting here for Khomeini's people. The Muslim fanatics gathered around a big group of the students for an underground meeting. It was leaked to the secret police somehow. The Shah's men got here in time to arrest them. Now the leaders of the meeting are hiding here and innocent students are getting arrested in the courtyard."

"So, why are you here?" I asked.

"I wanted to witness it and collect some information. I thought no one would question me if I walked around dressed like this."

I could almost see his point. He was clean-shaven, well-groomed, and very well-dressed head to toe in European clothing. However, in that chaos, I didn't think anybody would bother to check the designer label on the back of his shirt before pummeling and arresting him.

We sat in the classroom for a couple of hours, every once in a while checking out the window to see if it was safe to leave the building. The clergies were not moving; they were clearly too scared to leave that room. There was no need to check their labels. Those dirty long brown and black outfits, their lice-infested turbans, their unruly, curly beards, their worn-out plastic slippers, their cracked and filthy feet—all spoke for themselves.

Zohreh's Sad Living Room

"You've got to take the good with the bad, smile with the sad, love what you've got, and remember what you had." —Christine J. Collins

New York City, April, 2015

"Kids, you had to see *Mahalleh* in Shiraz, or the other Jewish Quarters in different cities in Iran." My mom sighed deeply before continuing. "They were filthy, over-crowded, and rundown. The streets were narrow, muddy, and dirty. Most people were tired and poor, and so many were hungry. I never lived there, though," she said, with an air of pride. "We lived in a big house with lemon trees on a great street in Shiraz. But I did join my father a few times when he was taking food for people in need. It was sad."

Our entire family was sitting in Zohreh's living room. Folding chairs were arranged in rows behind us for the people who came every day to pay their respects; on each was placed the customary Kippah (brimless skullcap) and a holy book. The mirror was covered by a cloth, as is customary in Jewish tradition to acknowledge the somber mood of the family of the deceased. Next to it hung a large picture of Zohreh, looking beautiful and smiling.

As she reminisced, Momon was leaning on the couch, holding and comforting Roya in her arms, caressing her granddaughter's long hair and wiping each tear as it rolled down her face. Roya's eyes were glued to her mom's picture on the wall. Arya, her twin brother, was sitting on the floor leaning on her chair. The rest of the grandchildren were circulating around her, some seated Indian-style on the Persian carpet, a few leaning against the wall, the others seated on the chairs. They knew what to do—the mission was to keep their grandmother distracted for as long as possible.

We were trying to keep her thoughts moving and busy with any subject but Zohreh's death. My mother had been crying most of day, but was finally calm now, thanks to Xanax. She was deeply into her stories, which she told in her heavy Persian accent. It was clear she was trying to use the best of her English vocabulary in front of the kids. She loved to talk about her childhood and life in general for the Jewish people in Iran.

"Was the Jewish Quarter in an enclosed area like the ghettoes in Europe?" one of the kids asked.

"Oh no, the Jews in Iran were never locked in a gated area or told not to leave on Sundays or rainy days, even though they were considered impure by the Muslims. They concentrated themselves in one place because together they could protect each other against the Muslims who were trying to make their lives miserable. They created their own market, butcher, and bakery, simply because at the time if a Jew wanted to buy something from a Muslim merchant or from a store, they had to put their money down on the floor or the counter so their skin wouldn't touch the shopkeeper's, even accidentally. If a Jew's hand touched the produce, it would be considered contaminated and filthy; it would be unsellable, and then thrown in the garbage. Then, the Jews were put in the same category as stray dogs in Islam—dirty and disgusting."

"Yes guys, your grandmother is right." I turned around and faced the kids. "I had a very good friend in high school, who was always hanging out at our house. Once, when I stopped over at her place, she seemed uncomfortable. She told me I was not allowed to enter her house. I asked why not, and she explained that her mom didn't like to have Jews in their home. We were considered the *untouchables* of Iran. To be honest, that was my only brush with anti-Semitism. I never had a bad experience with any other friends. In fact, most of my friend were Muslims. I didn't attend a Jewish school."

"The Jews before the 1950s were treated very badly in Iran," my mom said, looking around at the kids. "When your grandfather was a teenager in Shiraz, he was assaulted numerous times. He was a champion in track and an all-around excellent athlete. But every time he won, the boys followed him, ganged up against him, and beat him up in a back alley. One time, they hung him up on a hook on the stable wall for donkeys. He was missing for 24 hours!"

"Funny, isn't it?" Camy said with a smirk. "The Jews were not supposed to be touched, but it was okay to beat the crap out of them with their fists!"

"At the time of Reza Shah, things started to change," my mother explained. "Shah's father was against the Mullahs and wanted to westernize the country. He was friendly with the Jews, and saw no threat in them. But how we were treated depended on the neighborhood we lived in as well. In areas like downtown and around the old bazaar, they still called us 'Bad Jew' or 'Dirty Jew' in schools or on the streets."

"Grandma is right. In the sixties and seventies, many Jews in Iran were successful and financially set, and involved in a lot of different businesses. They were living the good life. They owned beautiful homes, factories, jewelry stores, real estate, and much more," Nazee added.

"But when Khomeini came, we all thought he was another Hitler. Most of the Jews left everything behind and fled the country. However, he turned out to cause more death for the Muslims than he ever did for any other religious group."

"What does Fariborz always say? 'We have to thank Khomeini for forcing us to leave Iran and migrate to this great country,'" Nahid said. "Our brother is one proud American."

"When I had my own practice in Ahwaz, in the south, I was never bothered by the Muslims. They respected me as a physician, and they brought me gifts to thank me," my mom added.

"But Momon, weren't you sad to leave Iran?" Arya asked.

"I really believed we would go back. No one thought that the situation could stay like that. Life in Iran was ideal for us. I always said if the regime had stayed the same, the Iranian Jews would have been among the luckiest people in the world. We had nice homes, in beautiful neighborhoods. We had our group of friends, Jewish and Muslim. We traveled all over the world. We owned a variety of businesses. We wore the latest fashions from Europe and listened to the Beatles, Frank Sinatra, and Nat King Cole. It was a comfortable life. We didn't have issues with drugs, alcohol, or guns."

"And then came the revolution..." Liza prompted.

"Yes, and then came the revolution. The constant gunshots, the 'Allah Akbars' screamed from rooftops, the killings, the total chaos." My mother repositioned herself on the couch and said, "This part of the story, Soheila would know better. She lived through the whole revolution. The rest of us left at the very beginning." She looked at me and yawned. "Why don't you tell them what happened? I'm tired. I think I will go to bed now."

We all looked at each other, desperation in our eyes. I tried to think of something, quickly, to keep her up and involved. "It is much too early for you to go to bed. Please, sit with us some more."

"I feel a bit dizzy," she said. "Almost like that time I tried marijuana." The kids all stared at their grandmother, obviously shocked, and then turned to look at each other and started laughing.

"Momon, you tried drugs?" Mitchie, Nazee's son, asked.

"Yes, I did. What's the matter? Your grandma was young once!" She held her chin up and said, "I tried it with Grandpa, right here in New York, about forty years ago. A friend of ours offered us a puff. I took a couple. Oh my God, my head became so big. I was laughing non-stop. I wanted to go to the window and fly out, but I couldn't move." She looked around at her grandchildren and said, "Ha! You think your grandma is so old-fashioned that she would never touch a joint?"

The kids couldn't stop laughing.

"What else did you try?" Linda asked.

"Opium!" she answered, with a mischievous smile.

"Whaaaat?"

"No you didn't!"

"Justin, did you hear that?"

"Camy, I'm not deaf, I heard that."

"Is Momon hallucinating?" Matthew, Nazee's son, sat straight up. "She couldn't have done opium!"

"I did, I did, I did. In Iran, it wasn't considered a horrible thing. No one who I knew was an actual drug addict. But when close friends got together, they arranged for it. They sat around and took a couple of puffs each and had fun and told jokes. But you should also know that years ago, opium was used as a drug that took care of a lot of illnesses. Now, here in United States, they are trying to legalize the use of marijuana for medical reasons. You see, Iran was way ahead of the West." She started chuckling.

"I had no idea I had such a cool grandma. High five, Grandma," Mahtab, Nazee's daughter, said with a huge smile.

Momon high-fived Mahtab with one hand as she wiped the tears from laughter with the corner of her skirt. She said, "Your grandma used to be cool, just like you."

"Yes she was, and still is."

I exhaled. The "Mission Impossible" had been accomplished. Momon had forgotten about Zohreh for at least a couple of hours, thanks to the power of love from her family. Nahid, Nazee, and I looked at each other; we didn't need to speak as our eyes told the story without words. Of course, this was not even a Band-Aid on the pain and agony she had gone through during Zohreh's suffering—not to mention the pain and agony to come when she would learn about her only son's illness.

Mercifully, she had no idea that during that exact week of Zohreh's death, Fariborz was at home, under quarantine. She did not know that he was recuperating from pneumonia, a result of aggressive chemotherapy to treat his leukemia. She did not know that this was another part of a difficult test, a long series of unfortunate events, and another round in our back-and-forth wrestling match with God. We kept that secret to ourselves for now.

Shiraz, 1978

THE LIBRARY AT PAHLAVI University in Shiraz was massive. It was a modern, state-of-the-art and impressive structure for the 1970s. It was built on top of a hill and could be seen and admired from most parts of town. Pahlavi University, named after the Shah's family, was considered a prestigious and competitive university. Most of its students came from out of town, therefore when it came time to study, they had the choice of either their dorm or the library. The dorms were always busy and noisy, so the library was a place of refuge for them. It was a place to hang out, a place to mingle, a place to meet everyone, a place for an occasional nap—as well as a place to study. I was proud and happy to be accepted to Pahlavi University in 1978.

I was there with one of my best friends, Shahriar. We were both in school of engineering. Shahriar, Vahid and I were the Three Musketeers. We were always together. We walked to our classes together, we ate together, and we studied together. We were like siblings. They were my mother's second cousins from different sides.

We walked out of our classes and decided to grab something to eat. The environment around the university was tense. Young students went missing and disappeared almost daily. Those days everyone was deathly afraid of the Shah's secret service. They were everywhere and kept everyone under a watchful eye. They arrested anyone on the slightest suspicion of being a member of Khomeini's religious and fanatic group. Vahid and Shahriar stayed with me to protect me. Not from the SAVAK—the secret service people knew we were Jewish and had nothing to do with Khomeini and the uprising—but from the fanatics.

They wanted girls to dress extremely modestly, and for their hair to be covered. I hadn't signed up for the new fashion trend or their preferred hair accessory. Nor was I ready to give up my European clothes because a mob of heavy-bearded, hairy, angry, power-hungry, ignorant men demanded that I do so.

"If it makes them feel uncomfortable, tell them not to look at me!" I used to tell my friends.

I still walked around as I always had: in jeans, T-shirts, skirts short and long; tight pants, full make-up and long, blown-out hair. The Khomeini devotees looked at me with disgust, but at the time I ignored those hostile looks. No one believed these radical ideas would ever catch fire and spread. The word was that "America and the CIA were supporting the Shah and nothing would go wrong. Carter was on top of everything." How little we knew.

Pictures of Khomeini were posted all over the university, and his devotees were hardcore, committed, and uncompromising. They were not afraid of anything. They thought that they were serving Allah, and if that meant ending up in custody with SAVAK and in their torture chambers, losing their lives while following their religious leader, so be it. It was a small price to pay for such a big purpose. They would be paid back handsomely when they reached the gates of heaven. There would be 72 virgins waiting for them on the other side.

The atmosphere around the university had changed dramatically in recent months, but we assured ourselves that it was only temporary. "President Carter and the CIA are on top of it all. It will be taken care of."

After we were done eating, Vahid left, and Shahriar and I decided to go to the library and study. The library was unusually crowded. It took us a couple of minutes to find empty seats next to each other. We took our textbooks out and got busy with our studies.

The mood and the feeling at the library on that day were atypical. Normally there was laughter in one corner or a heated conversation in the other, but on that day, the huge room was extremely quiet. I kept looking up and around me. The library was filled with students seated in the rows of grey tables and metal chairs. Everything looked normal, but I felt uneasy.

"Shahriar," I said, "why is it so quiet here?"

He paused and said, "I don't know."

"Listen," I said, "you do not hear anyone talking, and look, the library is full."

He looked up at the room and said, "It is crowded for sure. Almost every seat is taken. But you are right, it is too quiet."

And then it started, voices erupting in complete harmony: "SHHHHAAAAAAAAAAH! *Marg-Bar Shah!* (Down with the Shah!) *Marg-bar Shah!*" Everyone got up from their chairs at once and yelled, "*Allah Akbar* (God is great), *Marg-Bar Shah.*"

We had unwittingly entered the eye of the storm.

The radical insurgents stood either on their chairs or tables, holding their fists up, chanting and screaming "*Marg-Bar Shah*" non-stop in anger and disgust. Things quickly spiraled out of control. They picked up their metal chairs and smashed the glass windows with them. They lifted the large tables and turned them over, pushed the bookshelves over on top of people, took out the books and threw them all over the place, climbed the counters, stood tall, held their arms in the air and chanted "*Allah Akbar, Allah Akbar.*"

Shahriar and I were stunned. We didn't know which way to go or how to get out of that chaos. The calm, quiet, and organized library had become a complete war zone in just a few seconds. We were in a state of utter upheaval and confusion. I grabbed my purse and crawled under a large table with Shahriar. It was a good enough idea, but for a short while only. Almost every table was turned over and ours would be soon. We looked at the exit of the library, at the end of the hall—it was blocked by the radicals. We were stuck.

All of a sudden we heard a huge shattering sound. We looked towards the noise and saw two men throwing the massive metal tables into the huge glass walls next to us. Pieces of broken glass were flying all over the library. We went deeper under the table to avoid the sharp objects. We could see people's legs running in different directions in the utter chaos. It was complete havoc. The militants had managed to destroy our beautiful library in just a few short minutes.

Khomeini's mob, we would later come to realize, had a special talent for destruction—in particular, destroying anything beautiful that they could not have. Beautiful buildings, beautiful homes, beautiful lives, beautiful culture, beautiful city and our beautiful country. If they could destroy such a massive and beautiful structure with no opposition or repercussions, they could do the same to anything that came in front of them.

Shahriar took my hand and said, "Time to go."

I slung the strap of my purse over my shoulder and started running towards the big opening through the broken glass wall. Books, backpacks, tables and chairs were flying over our heads as we ran for our lives. We were not the only ones who had thought of that escape plan. The rest of the innocent students also made a beeline for the new "Emergency exit!"

Shahriar and I got to the opening, jumped through, landed on the grass and kept on running. As we were getting away, we could still hear the noise from a distance, the chanting and the screaming was non-stop, *"Allah Akbar. Marg-Barg Shah. Marg-Barg Shah."* We did not look back. There was no need. Things would never be the same.

The Shah Leaves

"It is unusual," said Christina, "for a revolution to call for fewer rights for people, not more." —Cassandra Claire, Lord of Shadows

Tehran, 1979

From the beginning of the revolution, the government and the non-religious people were waiting for President Jimmy Carter to step forward and take action. The discussions were always about the American President and the CIA: "The CIA will never let Khomeini's people take over. They need an ally in the Middle East."

"Don't worry, someone will do something. Between powerful forces like England and America, nothing will happen to this regime."

"Where is Carter? What is he thinking? Is he thinking at all? He should go back to his peanut farm! What foreign policy? He has none!"

"The revolution is anti-America, anti-Israel, anti-Western world, anti-everything. Every president before has been supporting the Shah! Why is Carter so weak?"

These were days of uncertainty and fear. The situation in Iran was extremely dangerous. Almost every night we got together at one of the neighbor's homes and discussed the revolution and the news. No one dared travel far; between the military curfew, the volatile circumstances, and the unsafe roads, there were no guarantees for anyone's safe return. At the end of each heated conversation, they all reached the same conclusion, "The

United States would never let these people take over. Carter will protect the Shah. It's the right thing to do. It's good politics," and walked home.

My father and I had gotten used to living with each other. We were the only two family members left in Iran. My mom, Nazee, and Fariborz had left in October with only one suitcase each. I would have been with them in New York had I been living with my family in Tehran and not at Pahlavi University in Shiraz when they had applied for their visas. I was still unable to get a passport and a visa, so my father stayed behind with me.

We had nothing to do but read, watch the news or go to visit neighboring friends. At one of the gatherings, while we were listening to the evening news on one of the major TV stations, the serious and professional anchorman suddenly got up in the middle of his report and yelled out, "Help! Please! Help! The revolutionaries are taking over the TV station! Please help. People, help me!" The gunshots were loud and clear in the background.

He scrambled under his desk for cover right in front of the camera. Our apartment building was not too far away from the TV station. We ran to the balcony and heard the constant noise of machine guns—the same sound that was coming from the TV set. The anchorman was still holding onto his microphone, pleading and begging for help from under his desk. Ten minutes into the chaos, people started going to the rooftops and chanting, "*Allah Akbar*" in support of the revolutionaries attacking the TV station.

The chanting became more and more powerful by the minute with guns and machine guns going off at every corner. We went inside to take cover for fear of a stray bullet and sat in front of the TV in shock. The camera was left on an angle; there were sounds of fighting in the background. The anchorman kept begging for mercy. They grabbed him from under his desk by the collar of his jacket, dragged him across the floor and pulled him away. The TV went blank.

Once they took over the national TV station, they could say or do as they wished and get their message out to the whole country. They were angry, hateful, fearless, and determined—a powerful combination. They were loyal and committed to Khomeini. They wanted Shah out, and they got him out.

On January 16, 1979, Mohammad Reza Pahlavi, the Shah of Iran, left his country for good. We were all glued to our TV sets. No one wanted to witness it alone. Twenty of us gathered at the neighbors' apartment and watched his departure in horror. The Shah was crying and so were all his deputies. We knew that the moment he left, the country would descend deeper into even greater chaos.

The Shah's entourage was following him to his plane. His wife, Empress Shahbanoo Farah Pahlavi, in her winter coat and a fur hat, watched him with concerned eyes. Her husband, the emperor, Reza Shah Pahlavi, The Shahanshah, "The king of kings," the absolute power in Iran, was crying as he approached the steps. One of the generals ran to him, kissed his hand and kneeled to kiss his shoes. The Shah held his arm and tried to pick him up from the ground. Both their faces were filled with sorrow.

The Shah boarded his plane with his wife and took off for the Bahamas, the only place he was allowed to fly to. We sat there in silence and watched his departure. We were mourning the end of life as we knew it. The women sobbed and the men had teary eyes. It was the end of an era.

We were living on a street close to the main avenue in Tehran called Pahlavi (a name that was changed soon after!). Our attention shifted from the TV set to the noise from the streets. People were cheering and cars were blowing their horns nonstop. My father and I left our friends and walked towards Pahlavi Avenue. What an unforgettable scene that was! People were dancing on top of their cars, holding the Iranian flag with a hole in the middle. The lion and the sun in the center of the flag representing the Pahlavi regime had been cut out.

The celebrants glued Iranian currency to the windshields of their cars, again with the picture of Shah missing. They chanted, *"Marg bar Shah! Marg bar America!"* ("Down with the Shah! Down with America!") They cut American flags into small pieces, burned them and danced around the flames. The streets were packed. People came from everywhere to celebrate their victory. They had won. They had accomplished the seemingly impossible. They had gotten rid of the Shah.

My father looked at me, "Carter should be happy! The stupid guy doesn't know what kind of damage he has caused the world. This is only the beginning. He will never be able to fix this mess. No one can." He looked at the crowd cheering, dancing, laughing, and rejoicing. "And these people don't know what kind of damage they have caused themselves and the future generations. This country will go back 100 years. They will be sorry very soon."

A few feet away from us, I noticed a well-dressed man holding a young boy in his arms. He was smiling a big smile and his son was waving a small Iranian flag. The sun and the lion were missing on that flag as well, but the gentleman was obviously not an Islamic extremist. He was wearing a pair of perfectly ironed blue jeans, a crisp white shirt, a sports jacket and beautiful Italian shoes. He was proud to witness the victory. He wanted his young son to be part of this memorable day as well. He wanted to share the feeling of bliss and happiness with his pride and joy. He wanted the change, and he'd gotten the change. The young boy was smiling and waving the flag while his father was whispering in his ears.

I stared at the two of them. (To this day I wonder what became of that little boy. He would be in his early forties by now.) Did his father, with his expensive European clothes and perfect slicked-back hair, foresee the killings? The Iraq war? What about the inflation? Or the unemployment? Or the Arabic language replacing English? Or the injustice, especially towards women? Was he still smiling that big smile ten years later?

My father and I stood on the sidewalk and watched as our beautiful country was handed over to a bunch of close-minded and backward clergies. No one had ever had any respect for Mullahs before. People made jokes about them. People made fun of them. People looked down on them. In the popular series *Shahreh Ghesseh* (The City of Stories), the main character was a fox in a clergy outfit and turban. He was playing the role of a Mullah, and he was ridiculed throughout the program. But now they ruled the country.

"This is no longer a fit place to live," my father said, shaking his head. "We need to get out of this country as soon as I find a way to get you a passport and a visa."

The mob was getting bigger by the minute. The noise was deafening. But we didn't move. It was like a bad accident; we couldn't stop watching.

A guy yelled from one of the cars, "Sister, why aren't you celebrating? Say '*Marg bar Shah!*' Say it!"

"Let's go home," my father said grimly. "It might get out of control."

The next day, life in the now-lawless country started with executions. The new regime didn't waste any time. There were pictures of Shah's officials, ministers, generals, politicians, and close friends, dead, on the front page of the major newspapers. The sight of lifeless bodies, mangled faces, and bloody clothes complete with bullet holes became everyday news.

There was no longer any rule of law. Khomeini followers could go and arrest anyone and make a criminal file against them. Minoo was one of my closest friends in college. She was raised in a military household. She was a sweet, beautiful girl with stunning eyes. Iranian women are famous for their eyes, but hers were unique. They almost didn't look real. They were different shades of blue and green, framed by thick dark eyelashes. Minoo's dad held a high-ranking position in the army. He was among the first to be executed.

"We could hear my dad talking to them from the next room," she told me, sobbing. "'What have I done wrong?' he asked, 'Why do you want to kill me?'

"The firing squad yelled, 'Shut up! Not another word. We told you to shut up!' They counted from ten down to one and the gunshots started. My mom screamed and fainted. A few minutes later they dragged my father's blood-soaked dead body out and said in disgust, 'If you want him back, you have to go and pay for the bullets that we wasted on him first and then come back for this worthless piece of garbage.'

"I stared at the lifeless body. They didn't kill him at once, bullet holes were in his legs, his stomach, his chest, and face. They made sure he suffered. My dad was innocent!" she cried. "He never did anything wrong. They killed him so there were no enemies left." She was out of breath from crying. Her beautiful eyes were red and filled with sorrow. "They call themselves Muslims? I'm Muslim too! I would never kill anyone. They call each other brothers? Brothers killing brothers!"

Every day, citizens were hanged or executed by firing squads. What Khomeni's supporters had long criticized SAVAK for being, they had themselves become, and much worse.

Our lives continued in fear. We read books, watched the news and visited our neighbors. Electricity was no longer a given. Every neighborhood had its own quota, which was surprising since the power company had been working fine at the time of the Shah. We never had a black-out then. My father and I read for as long as there was light available. After that we either went to bed or to friends' nearby. The curfew was still on, so going far meant taking a big chance.

Oil and gas were also not so readily available as they had been before and my father became the "Oil Nazi." He was in charge of the hours that he thought heat was absolutely necessary. He turned it off for the building every night. When the tenants complained, he said, "Guys, put on an extra blanket. No one knows when the next delivery of oil will be. Better to be safe than sorry." True to his word, we were the only building with heat during cold winter days when everyone else was waiting for oil delivery.

I borrowed books from everyone; what I had plenty of was time. I was going through them at record speed. It reminded me of the episode I'd seen on the Twilight Zone, where the guy wanted nothing but time to read... until one day the whole world was destroyed by a nuclear bomb and he was the only survivor.

"And the best thing, the very best thing of all," he said, "is, there's time now. There is all the time I need and all the time I want. Time, time, time. There's time enough at last," he said, while walking to the library. The minute he tried to pick up a book, his glasses fell off. He slowly raised the shattered glasses and touched them with his fingers. They were destroyed. Without them he was blind as a bat. He sat on the staircase of the library and said, "That's not fair. That's not fair at all. There was time now. There was all the time I needed..."

I had all the time I needed, and I could see, too. I read *The Wandering Jew, War and Peace, Les Miserables* and *The Odyssey*. There were no computers, no internet, no interesting TV or radio shows, no social life. All I could do to make time go by faster was to read. And that's what I did. I lay down on my bed and read. If we lost power, I would continue reading with the help of a flashlight or a candle for hours.

Every night around sundown, the *"Allah Akbar"* chanting started on the rooftops, and the sound of machine guns followed. No neighborhood was immune to the nightly terror. We had no choice but to adapt to the situation. As soon as they started chanting, I called out to my dad in the next room, "Here we go again, the gunshots are going to start soon."

"Don't get close to the windows," he'd reply.

Most Persian Jews stayed in Iran at the beginning of the horrible times. They were still hopeful that Shah would return, and the United States would take care of the revolution. "But that's what the Jews thought in Germany during Hitler's rise," my father argued. "They thought they were so powerful that nobody could touch them. Look how wrong they were. They killed them all."

"But Jews have been living in Iran for more than two thousand years, we have roots here."

"German Jews also thought they were more German than Jews! They burned us alive in Spain, gassed us in concentration camps, killed us in the Middle East. Now it's Iran's turn. History keeps on repeating itself in different parts of this world for Jewish people." My father sighed in frustration. "This is not a place for us anymore. You better leave before it's too late." The common belief was that they were going to persecute the Jews as soon as they got rid of the Baha'is.

Baha'i, to some, was a peaceful "religion" and to others "a school of thought," but to the Muslims it was sacrilegious because they tried to convert as many people to their beliefs as possible. For extremist Muslims, this was not to be tolerated. The punishment for converting was death. Almost immediately they started burning their homes down and arresting them randomly. The Jews believed the Baha'is were one step ahead of us in terms of elimination; we ranked second.

On February 1st, 1979, Ayatollah Ruhollah Khomeini landed in Iran on a specially-chartered Air France Boeing 747 jet, after 15 years of exile in Turkey and Iraq. The Ayatollah had been born into a religious Islamic family. He was a Shiite, the branch of Islam practiced and followed by most Iranians. He memorized the Qur'an at an early age and lived in the holy city of Qom, devoting himself to the formal study of Shia Islam.

In 1963 when the Shah launched the "White Revolution," a program that called for the reduction of religious states, equal rights for women, and other modern reforms, Khomeini, by then known by the high Shiite title of "Ayatollah," condemned the Shah's program openly. He called for the overthrow of the Shah and the establishment of an Islamic state. He was imprisoned, which led to riots, and the Ayatollah Khomeini was expelled from Iran in 1964.

And now he was back, compliments of Air France, surrounded by clergies in their long brown layered robes and turbans, along with the Air France pilot and co-pilot standing next to him on top of the staircase of the airplane.

"What are these people doing? What are they planning behind closed doors? Why was he given permission to enter France? What was the President of France thinking? Why wasn't he compelled to remain in an Islamic country instead?" Everyone I knew was asking the same questions.

He emerged from the airplane and stood on top of the staircase looking solemn, unsmiling, expressionless, while people were jumping up and down with joy and happiness. It was as though God himself had landed on board that Boeing 747.

Millions of people came to Meydan Shahriyar, Iran's major monument, and celebrated, expressions of triumph and happiness tattooed on their faces as they shouted, "Long live Khomeini, Long live Khomeini." They were pushing and shoving their way forward just to get a glimpse of their leader. He waved at them from his car with a serious face. Khomeini had arrived to rule Iran. He condemned the way Shah's regime was "Westernizing" a Muslim country. He was against the United States and Israel and every country in-between.

Living a fearful life started in Islamic Republic. The Mullahs took over the country. The nightclubs, famous restaurants, public resorts, co-ed schools, co-ed swimming pools—co-ed anything—closed for good. People began trying to sell whatever they were able to turn into cash and leave the country—either legally, by plane, if allowed, or illegally, escaping across one of the borders on foot. The goal of many was to leave Iran and reach the safety of the rest of the world.

Life for my father and me remained pretty much the same. I still refused to cover my hair and go under the traditional chador. I was young and stupid. When the Muslim extremists stopped me a couple of times in the street and asked me to change the way I dressed and wore my hair, my father practically had a heart attack.

"I have to find a way for you to leave this country as soon as possible. I wish you had left with your mother." But I couldn't leave. I didn't have a passport or a visa... until the day my father met Rabbi Herschel at the local synagogue.

Rome

"A man who believes in freedom will do anything under the sun to acquire, or preserve, his freedom." —Malcolm X

March, 1979

I landed in Rome on March 14th, 1979. It was a beautiful day in a magnificent city, and it took only minutes for me to fall in love with this incredible new place. I couldn't have been happier. Life for me at that moment had become exactly the way I'd envisioned it: perfect. I was finally out of that miserable country, where everyday living had become unbearable, and I'd arrived in this vibrant and romantic place.

I jumped into a cab with my three heavy suitcases and showed the driver the address I'd been given back in Tehran. I remember thinking, *So this is how it feels to have wings and fly.* I felt free: free of fear, free of limitations, free of uncertainty. It was a glorious liberation, and it had only just begun.

We pulled up in front of an old massive stone building with statues of scary-looking creatures on the edges. I was hardly a world traveler, so for me everything was fascinating and interesting. My present had suddenly become exciting, and my future full of promises and possibilities. *And, I am not even in America yet*, I thought.

I entered the building, unsure of where I was going. Luckily, I saw Rabbi Herschel from our synagogue. "Hello Rabbi," I yelled out enthusiastically. "I'm finally here."

"*Shalom, Ciao* Soheila! Glad you made it. We were all worried about you."

"So, where should I go? Where is everybody? What is this place?" I asked eagerly, my happiness difficult to contain.

He laughed and said, "Why don't you follow me?" He started walking as he spoke. "Your friends are out sightseeing. This place is an orphanage, but we use this part of it to house you guys," he explained, pointing to his right.

"Should I leave my luggage here?" I asked.

He looked at my massive suitcases. "No. Let's bring them in. I'll give you a hand. By the way, how is your father?"

"Great. He will join my family in New York, soon."

We placed the bags in the hallway and walked towards the office. Rabbi Herschel's family had been among the few who had moved to Milan in search of a better life in the sixties. He'd been raised in Italy, and spoke Persian, English, and Italian fluently.

We entered a room with three desks, an elderly woman seated behind each. The personnel in the office greeted me, took my passport, and gave me a key and a room number in exchange.

"Follow me, Soheila." We entered a small room with beige walls and curtains, two chests of drawers, and two simple beds. I would not have been happier entering Buckingham Palace. It was not much, but it was mine and it was safe. I looked out the window and took in the scene: old cobblestone streets, tiny Italian cars, a fruit vender, and a bunch of kids playing on the sidewalk. No signs of any revolutionaries or "*Allah Akbar*" chanting on the rooftops. This was heaven. I thanked the rabbi and raced back towards the front door.

"Where are you running off to?" he called out.

"I want to walk around and see everything," I answered, while rushing down the staircase. "I just need to get my bags."

"Wait. I will help you." Together we brought my luggage to my new room and stowed it safely in a corner. I was on my way out when I heard him yell, "Please make sure you have the name and address of this place."

"Oh, I do. How do you think I got here? I just need to know how far away we are from the Coliseum."

"Not far... definitely within walking distance. Ask anyone, '*dov'e il Colosseo?*'"

"*OK, Ciao!*"

They say that in order to appreciate light, you have to experience darkness. Well, I was appreciating and inhaling every spark, every gleam, and every ray. I walked around the beautiful city of Rome with a bounce in my step and a smile on my face. I bought an ice-cream, savoring every lick and every bite. I watched and talked to those beautiful Italians. It was a magical day.

When I got close to the coliseum, I stood transfixed, staring at it from across the street. I had seen that image on postcards many times, but to be standing in front of the historic structure was a dream come true. It was for sure colossal. The line to get in was long and seemed never-ending. I decided against the wait, thinking that I'd rather keep walking and see more of the amazing city. Rome was joyful, Rome was vibrant, Rome was intoxicating, Rome was everything Tehran no longer was. Rome had me at hello.

Heading back, I showed the address of the orphanage to people in the streets, asking, as instructed, "*Dove?*" Some of those warm and welcoming Italians walked a couple of blocks with me, just to make sure I was heading in the right direction. *I love these people*, I thought, *they're so kind and friendly. Not angry and bitter.* When I finally arrived back at the orphanage, I saw my friends, Shahriar and Vahid, standing in the doorway, waiting for my return. I ran into their arms.

"Guys! We're in Rome," I gushed.

We hugged each other tightly. "I was worried about you," Shahriar said. "Tomorrow we'll all go sight-seeing together," he added.

"Tell us what happened at the airport and how you finally got your passport," Vahid said. "We felt so bad that you were the only one left behind."

"You should have seen my father at the airport, when your flight took off," I said, laughing. "He was arguing with the Pan Am people as if it was their fault that my passport was the only one missing. Poor souls. He'll be joining my mom and the rest of the family in New York, soon."

"You're here now, that's what's important," Shahriar said.

"True, and if everything goes well with our visas, I will be back with them next week." I filled them in about my almost Exodus-like experience back in Tehran's airport as we met up with the rest of the Iranian Jewish students in the dining room. Everyone was happy to see me, and I was equally delighted to see them.

The next morning we got up early, had breakfast, and hit the town. Vahid and Shahriar had a map to the city and were ready to go. We walked all over—to the Trevi fountain, Piazza Navona with the Bernini masterpieces, the Pantheon with its colossal dome, the ancient ruins. We found a gelato store at every corner and I sampled every flavor until I seriously felt green. "Guys, I've officially overdosed on ice cream!" I said, laughing. Even nausea couldn't threaten my contentment.

We decided to leave the Vatican for the next day and returned to the orphanage. We were sitting in the dining room having dinner when Rabbi Herschel announced, "Everyone, please pay attention. Tomorrow evening, we will all go to the American Consulate for your visas. Please make sure you are here and that you are not tired, because you will probably be out very late."

We began cheering and clapping. Rome was beautiful, but America was the promised land. The next morning, the three of us headed out to visit the Vatican. We walked by a *mercado aperto*, open market, with lots of stands selling leather goods and Italian handicrafts. Shahriar stopped and said, "Guys, let's split up for ten minutes and then meet back up in front of this gate."

We agreed and went our separate ways. Shopping was not part of my itinerary. My parents had paid a lot of money for each dollar in the black market in Iran, and the last thing I wanted to do was to spend those valuable bills, so I just walked around for a bit and then caught up with my friends as planned.

That evening there was a special energy in the dining room. Everyone's face was radiant and beaming with hope and happiness. The staff walked in, each one holding a box. They called our names one by one and handed us our passports. "Please find your way out in a line and wait by the entrance."

Around 10 pm, buses started to pull up in front of the building in succession. We boarded quietly and took our seats. We were all anxious and excited, but no one said a word. *It is time for celebration*, I thought. *What's with the somber mood? Who died?* I got up and yelled out, "Hey, let's have a bus party!" We started singing and dancing—mostly me dancing, them singing—until we got to the American Consulate.

We all fell silent at once as the bus pulled into the driveway of a stunning and imposing building with rows and rows of windows. The entrance was surrounded by large columns and massive gates. It was an impressive structure, free-standing in the middle of a green lawn and palm trees. Our bus made a turn towards the back of the building and stopped. We got off and were directed to a side entrance where we were told to wait.

After about fifteen minutes, an American officer cranked the door open and stood in front of us. He was clean-shaven, well-dressed, and extremely polite. He instructed us to stand in a straight line by the wall. We did as we were told. Quietly, we formed a line and walked one at a time towards the direction he pointed.

We entered a room and saw three immigration officers seated at their desks ready to receive us. It must have been around eleven o'clock in the evening, and yet they were still on duty, for us and only for us. *They probably know more than we do*; I thought, *they realize it is dangerous for Jews to stay in Iran*. We walked towards the immigration officers as we were called to step forward. No one spoke a word. They took our passports, glanced at our faces, and bam! We had our freedom—our permission, our wings—to enter the land of opportunity, no questions asked. What was almost impossible for me to do in Iran was accomplished in the middle of the night in half an hour in Rome. France had arranged for Khomeini to arrive, and Italy arranged for Jews to leave.

We thanked the officers heartily, got back on the bus, and sang and danced all the way back to the orphanage. We had each other, our visas, and the rest of our lives to look forward to in the greatest country on the planet. Even though we had left ninety percent of our assets and belongings behind when we left Iran, we were given back our lives, our futures and our freedom that very evening.

We spent the rest of our Roman holiday exploring the majestic city. By the fifth day, I knew more than a few sentences in Italian, which I used wherever I went. We were having fun, but we were also anxious to get to America.

On March 21st, on our flight from Rome to New York, Shahriar took a small box out of his pocket and held it in front of me.

"Happy Birthday, Soheila."

I was truly touched that he'd remembered my birthday. To give me a gift was beyond generous. We all knew that we were supposed to hold on tight to every dollar. For him to have gone and bought this for my birthday was an act of love and kindness, and it meant the world to me.

"Oh my God, thank you." I ripped the wrapping paper open and saw the most beautiful leather wallet with the word "Rome" embossed on the front.

"It's beautiful," I said, "but when did you buy this? We were constantly together in Rome."

"Remember the *mercado aperto?* I had only ten minutes. I hope you like it."

"I love it. But you shouldn't have. You probably paid too much."

He laughed out loud. "You're right—I probably did. The bastard wouldn't come down with his price. But it's worth it if you like it."

"Of course I do. Thank you so much!"

I still have that embossed wallet, safe in my drawer next to the artwork of my children and the locks of hair from their first haircut. If only life could always feel as promising and reassuring as it did on that wonderful and amazing day.

It was a cold but sunny day in New York. JFK airport was huge and chaotic. But we were more excited than tired as we stormed out of the airplane. Rabbi Herschel was more anxious than excited as he instructed us on what to do and where to go. "Please, stay together. Wait for me when you arrive at Immigration. We have to stay in a group."

Going through the passport office was a breeze. We all stood on the same line and walked forward one by one, got stamped, and walked towards the baggage claim. Buses were lined up for us in the parking lot. However, getting the luggage on the bus and organizing every tired body took a couple of hours.

After numerous head and luggage counts we finally all got onboard and headed towards... We had no idea where!

"Shahriar, do we know where we are going?" I asked.

"No idea, I was told we were coming to New York, after that, no clue," he answered.

"Well, my mom, my sisters, and Fariborz are here, so I guess I will be joining them soon."

"And I have relatives in Philadelphia. I will probably go there," he said.

"For now, we are going where the bus takes us!"

The bus ride took a long time. We went through various highways and streets until we finally stopped in a residential neighborhood.

"Leave your bags on the bus for now and come in the house right in the front," our dear Rabbi yelled out, "Follow me, everyone."

"Where are we?" I asked.

"You are in Crown Heights in Brooklyn," Herschel answered, "home to the religious Jewish community, the Lubavitchers."

We stepped off the bus and saw men wearing black top hats, long black coats and a massive beard. *What is this new universal fashion trend? We left one group of heavily-bearded men and traveled 5000 miles to live among another group of heavily-bearded men?* I thought.

Hasidic Jews were not part of the Jewish Persian culture. The big hats, the long coats, the up-to-the-knee white socks and the oversized beard were mostly for the Eastern European Jews, known as the Ashkenazis. We had never seen anyone in our community dressed in that fashion. Our

Rabbis had a beard, but it was a normal beard. They wore only a Kippah and a dark suit. But everything was different here.

Women helping in the office either had their head covered with a scarf or wore a wig (that was also something new to us). They wore big loose skirts—never pants—and oversized jackets or tops. Some of those wigs were elaborate and sexy, which was very confusing to us. The women had to cover their hair for modesty and avoid looking sexy, but instead some wore a more beautiful fake version of their own hair. What was accomplished with that? What was the point? Where was the "modesty?"

We stood in groups inside of a huge house that had been turned into small offices. A couple of small-framed, look-alike Rabbis in white shirts and black pants were fussing over paperwork while talking extremely fast. My English was good, but their American accent and special way of talking made it difficult for me to understand what they were saying.

"Who are these people?" I asked Rabbi Herschel.

"Three brothers out of seven, they are called Rabbi Hecht. No need for first names, they are known by their last name only. They are in charge here."

One of the trio asked me for my passport and the cash that I had with me. Each one of us had been allowed to leave the country with $3,000 in cash legally. I had no way of hiding any money from them; the amount had been marked on the last page of my passport at the airport in Iran. I handed him my passport and all my cash. In return he gave me a receipt and walked away.

I found Shahriar and Vahid, "Guys, they took my money and passport."

"Why did you give it to them?" Shahriar asked.

"I was caught off-guard. I couldn't think," I said.

"Well," Shahriar said, "I will not hand over my money to anyone. Vahid, if they ask, we have already given them everything. Play dumb."

They walked away and stood apart from the people on line. Everyone was done. One of the guys in the office approached them and asked for their passports. "We were first on line. They have everything," Shahriar said. The Rabbi shrugged his shoulders and left.

"You are definitely going to hell for lying to a Rabbi," I said, laughing.

"Maybe, but I prefer that option over this one!" Vahid laughed.

Next stop was at a different desk with another Rabbi Hecht, this one in charge of housing. The religious families in Crown Heights had offered their homes to the new immigrants. They knew most of us had no place to go and nowhere to stay. Depending on the size of their homes, they offered help. My second cousin Dina was with my group. She was only 15 years old. She was homesick. She didn't speak much English and was following me like a shadow.

"Dina, stay with me so we can share a room," I said.

"Thank you, Soheila, I don't know any of these people."

"Rabbi, I have to stay with Dina. Please do not separate us."

"OK. I will arrange it. Stand aside, don't follow the line. I know which house I want you to stay at. It is a beautiful house and they are among the very few that own a TV set. They are more open-minded than the rest of the Lubavitchers. They are lovely people. I want you there."

I was surprised by the act of kindness and the special interest. But I did not question it—the extra attention was helpful. Dina and I waited until everyone was assigned a home. It was our turn. Herschel signaled us to step forward. "I want Soheila and Dina in Mr. Gordon's home. I have talked to him already, and he knows about these girls. Please assign them there," he told one of the "Magnificent Seven."

"You have already handed in your passports and your money?" Rabbi Hecht asked us.

"Yes," we replied in unison.

He scribbled some notes and said, "Go and find your bags. The Gordons live close by."

We started walking. The streets were framed by rows of trees that seemed just about to wake up from the winter cold. It was a charming neighborhood. What amazed me was the diversity, Jewish people with their conservative black outfits and the black people in their colorful ones.

These people came from different worlds. They shared the same neighborhood in peace, but their cultures were altogether different. The only thing they shared besides the same ZIP code was probably the English language, and not even quite that. We heard the Hasidics speaking a certain dialect that was very unfamiliar to our ears. (Yiddish is a language mainly spoken by the Ashkenazi Jews. It originated in the 9th century with an extensive Germanic-based vocabulary.) That way of speaking didn't exist in Iran. No Jew spoke Yiddish where I grew up. The people in this neighborhood were not only black and white, they were day and night, they were oil and water. They did not mix, but they lived in peace, side by side.

However, as diverse as the people were, the houses and the neighborhood looked harmonious. They were attached to each other by common walls and almost looked the same. They all had a small garden in the front behind the fence, a small iron gate, and a stoop that led to the entrance. It was a lovely neighborhood. We stopped in front of one that was better maintained than the rest.

Why are we in Brooklyn? Why are we in an extremely religious area? I thought I left extreme anything behind in Iran. I want to move forward, not back. This is not what I have seen in the movies or read about in books or magazines! Why am I here? I wondered.

Herschel knocked on the door and a sweet lady in her mid-30s with her hair in a colorful scarf opened the door. She greeted us with a big smile as we walked in. Dina followed us without saying a word.

"Welcome to my home," Mrs. Gordon said. "Please, come in."

The furnishings were modest and simple. The staircase to the second floor was directly in front of the entrance. The combined living-dining room was to our right as we walked in. It was a cozy home.

"Mrs. Gordon," Herschel said, "this is Soheila and Dina. They arrived a couple of hours ago. I told them that I would make sure they stayed with the nicest family."

"My name is Freda, make yourself comfortable. Do you want to see your room?"

She pointed down at the staircase directly behind the one that was going up. We followed her to a basement. There were two beds, nice carpeting, a small table, two small windows on top of each bed and a full bathroom.

"I think I need to buy you a chest of drawers, the closet is very small for both of you," she said while opening the closet door. It *was* small, and it was nice of her to think of it.

"We will manage. It is kind of you to take us in," I said. "We should bring our bags downstairs."

I walked up and Herschel followed me. "Soheila, do you need anything?" he asked.

"No thank you, I am fine," I whispered. "I appreciate your help. Just tell me why do I have to stay here? My family lives in Scarsdale, I can just go to them."

"I will tell you later. I think I will head back to the office. They need help," he said. He thanked Freda and left.

We both got busy taking the necessities out of our luggage. An hour later we heard a strong, loud voice from the top of the staircase. "Where are they? Downstairs? Girls, can I come down?"

"Yes, of course," I said.

The footsteps on the staircase were heavy, and so was he. A tall guy with a round stomach, red beard, curly hair, thick glasses, a black hat and a black business suit appeared on the steps. He was sweating as he descended.

"Hi girls, I am Chapsy. I hope you like your room. Please make yourself comfortable. Do you need anything?" he asked.

"We are fine, Mr. Gordon. Thank you for opening your home to us," I said. "My name is Soheila, and this is my cousin, Dina."

"Nice to meet you. Are you happy here?" he asked.

"They need a chest of drawers, Chapsy. The closet is too small," Freda yelled from the top of the staircase.

"I will take care of it. Don't worry," he said, "We will have dinner at eight." And he went back upstairs. (The very next day, after work, Chapsy came downstairs carrying a chest of drawers on his back. He was sweating and out of breath but that didn't stop him. He did as he promised.) They were good people with kind hearts. They took us in, two complete strangers, and fussed over us as if we were their long-lost relatives.

We were in the kitchen at 8 exactly. Freda had made spaghetti for dinner and she, Chapsy and their three kids were already seated at the table. Their oldest daughter, Rachel (pronounced Rakhel), was about nine years old, Shaya was four, and the baby girl, Devara Leah, was around a year old. The little one was in her high chair trying to pick up small pieces of pasta and put them in her mouth. The kids wanted their spaghetti with ketchup only. That was not a problem, Freda handed them the bottle and they soaked their pasta in it. Chapsy started telling the kids about us and why we were there during dinner, and the "whys" started with Shaya:

"Why aren't their parents here?"

"Why they don't have their own home?"

"Why doesn't she speak English?"

Life was simple and delightfully uncomplicated in that household. There was a certain respect, understanding, and acceptance. Each person had his or her designated role and duties: Chapsy was the breadwinner. Freda was the homemaker. The rest was handed over to God. There were no other expectations, no demands and no arguments. Life had been figured out for them. They followed their dos and don'ts. Freda sent Shaya and Rachel to school every morning and stayed home and took care of the little one. She cleaned the house, cooked, watched her favorite soap opera while drinking her coffee. By the time the older kids were back home from school, she was ready to greet and feed them.

A couple of days later, at the breakfast table, we heard the doorbell. Freda called out, "Soheila, your friends want to see you."

I ran to the door and saw Shahriar and Vahid standing there with their suitcases. "Hi guys, where are you going?"

"We are taking off. We can't just stay and wait until they find out that we haven't handed in our passports and money. We are free to go. We heard everyone is supposed to stay here and study Hebrew and become religious, I didn't come to this country hoping and dreaming I would make it big as a Rabbi one day," Shahriar said.

"But I can't leave without my passport. I have to go and talk to them," I said.

"Sorry Soheila, but we have to go before it's too late. My uncle lives in Philadelphia, we are taking the next train there. I called him last night and he told me how to get to him," Vahid said.

"I will miss you guys," I said. "But let me give you the phone number here so at least you can keep in touch with me."

I ran in and asked Freda for their number, wrote it on two pieces of paper and brought the slips to them.

"Don't forget to call me," I said and kissed them goodbye.

"Sorry, but we have to leave now before someone from the office notices us. Our luggage is a dead giveaway," Shahriar said.

And they were gone. I was heartbroken. They were my buddies. *Not a problem,* I told myself, *I will go and ask for my documents and my money today and join my family too.*

After breakfast, Dina and I went to talk to Rabbi Hecht. The three brothers were busy moving around and talking fast as usual. It was ADD and ADHD at its peak.

I walked forward to one of the Hechts. "Excuse me, Rabbi, can I have my passport and my money back, please?"

"Why do you want them back?" he asked in a surprised manner.

"My family lives in Scarsdale, not too far from here. They are waiting for me."

"You can't go anywhere. You have a student visa with the Jewish school here and it is against the immigration laws if you move out. You will leave us no choice but to report you."

I had no idea about the student visa. I was shocked. Were they holding me there against my will?

"But no one told me that was the plan. Rabbi Herschel just told us that we will come to America. I thought I can join my family when I get here," I said.

"Well, you can't. We will hold on to your passport and money here for your safety. You have to start learning the Jewish laws and Hebrew language as of next week," he said in a firm voice.

How smart of Shahriar and Vahid to leave, and how stupid of me to be so naïve, I thought. *Extreme religions have so much in common.* "Do *as we tell you or else."* I left the office and went back home with Dina. I called my mom and told her about the situation we were in.

"Bottom line, Momon, I can't leave now, they are holding me hostage," I said.

"Are you allowed to come here and visit?" my mom asked.

"I guess!" I answered. "Even prisoners have visitation rights."

Optimistic as always, I quickly accepted and adapted to the situation. *This is only temporary. I'm here, I might as well make the best of it,* I told myself.

I studied Hebrew in the Jewish school and spent the rest of the day with my friends or at home. The Lubavitchers expected everyone to dress modestly and conservatively, but I had never in my life bought anything that could be described as either. It simply wasn't my style. I could do modest, but conservative? Hardly! I dressed in my jeans, T-shirts, pencil skirts, tight dresses and high heels. They looked at me as if I had just landed from another planet but didn't say a word. The Gordons didn't try to change me either. I wasn't dressed in a vulgar way, but it was not "rabbi's wife"-style either.

How funny is this world? I thought. *This is the same mentality as the Muslims in Iran but different packaging! Do they have any idea how similar they are? Do they know how much they have in common? And they have hated each other since the beginning of time!*

Then came the fun part... the Hasidic men started noticing me and called the Gordons to ask me out.

The idea was ridiculous to me. Date a Rabbi? Shave my long hair? Not show my legs? Give up my skinny jeans? Then again, out of respect to the family I was staying with, I dated any man who invited me out. Dinners were interesting, depending how you approached it. My dates were not allowed to touch me or even shake my hand. We went out and talked and I always found an excuse to make some kind of skin contact "accidentally" to make them uncomfortable. I tapped them on the back while talking or touched their hands as I spoke. Some of them would pull away as if they had touched a loose wire. Others didn't seem to mind. (Later on, if I complained about the kids, my husband would tell me without hesitation, "Oh, come on, you would have been taking care of twelve kids if you had married one of those Rabbis!")

One of the most interesting dates was with the son of the pharmacy owner on the street corner. He was religious but not Hasidic. He was usually in khaki pants and white shirt and wore the traditional Kippah. He was much more relaxed and cool than the rest of them.

He called me after the first date and asked, "You want to go out again?"

"Yes, why not?" I said.

"Great, where do you want to go?"

"Let me think," I said, "Can we go to Six Flags, Great Adventure this weekend? I've never, ever been on a roller coaster ride before."

"Yes, but not on Shabbat, I don't drive on Saturdays. How about Sunday?"

"Perfect, do you mind if I come with my sister?"

"Not at all, I'll pick you up at 9:30."

I hung up the phone and called Zohreh right away. "Zohreh, you want to go to Great Adventure with me? I'm going with a date."

"Yes, I'm dying to go, it would be fun," she said.

"Be here Sunday morning at 9."

Crown Heights was not a long way from where she was. Zohreh was studying for her Master's degree at Pratt Institute in Brooklyn. She was exactly where she wanted to be, doing exactly what she wanted to do. My dad had gotten used to the idea of her living alone in New York, even though his plans for her were completely different than her plans for her.

Sunday morning arrived and Zohreh was at the front door bright and early—in a T-shirt and a skirt!

"Zohreh, why are you wearing a skirt? We are going to an amusement park!" I said.

"It's a big skirt, it is not uncomfortable. See, it is a full skirt," she said while turning around on her heels.

"Well, I wouldn't!" I said.

My date arrived soon after. We got into his car and left for a great adventure. Zohreh and I were extremely happy and excited. I'd seen pictures of mega-amusement parks in America and read stories about them, but had never been to one.

We got there and went straight to the scariest one. The three of us were thrilled and nervous. The ride started with a loud crank and went vertically up slowly until it reached the top. At the peak, after pausing for a few seconds, our car free fell, face down on a huge curve. At the end of the curve it went up again, slowly coming to a full stop on the opposite side at the highest point for a few seconds and went straight down, full speed, but backwards towards the starting point. We were facing the sky, our backs towards the ground, legs dangling in the air.

Everyone was screaming at the top of their lungs. I looked over at Zohreh on the return ride and saw her "full" skirt covering her face and her naked legs dangling in the air. My date's eyes were popping out of their sockets watching the scene. I yelled, "Zohreh, your skirt!" But she was screaming and too scared to notice her rated-R mishap. I grabbed her skirt while free-falling down and tried to cover her legs. I held on to the skirt while shaking and screaming until we came to a full stop. I think my date was disappointed by my action. It was a funny scene for us and a memorable roller coaster ride for my religious friend. He would never be able to erase that sight from his memory. I am sure he had a new-found appreciation for the modest full skirts worn by the religious girls.

I stayed in Crown Heights for three months.

Leaving Crown Heights

"Toto, I've a feeling we're not in Kansas anymore." —Dorothy, Wizard of Oz

June, 1979

I *have been in Crown Heights long enough. I need to get out*, I thought. I knew there was no way I was going to marry a religious Hasidic Jew and reproduce like rabbits! Nor was I about to shave or cover my head or put my short skirts and jeans away in a retirement home! As nice as the Gordons were, that lifestyle was not for me. I had to leave and get on with my own new life. I was in "the land of opportunity" and there was none here, unless you were seriously looking for the opportunity of becoming a Rabbi's wife!

Every time I went to The Brothers Karamazov and asked for my passport, the answer was the same, a very well-rehearsed argument, spoken with complete authority. "How many times must we tell you, if you leave, we will report you to the immigration office and they will send you back to Iran," one of the brothers would tell me again in an angry tone.

It was frustrating. I didn't want to study Hebrew and Judaism all day and nothing else. I wanted to continue with my college education. I wanted to find a job, I wanted to see America, I wanted to be with my family, I wanted to start my new chapter. I wanted my freedom back.

My father was now living in Scarsdale with my mom, Nazee and Fariborz. He had stayed behind after I left in the hope of selling some properties in exchange for dollars in the black market. But word had gotten out, and since he was the only one left behind, the authorities started to ask questions. He began panicking. One day he was called to come to Komeeteh (the Islamic Police station). They held him for a couple of hours and asked him all sorts of questions, including "Where is your wife?" and "Where is your family?" He answered every question in the most politically expedient way possible, trying to keep his calm—something that didn't come naturally to my father.

The next day, he went directly to a travel agency. He asked for the first available flight out to anywhere, bought the ticket, locked the apartment door with everything inside and left. (I often wished he had at least brought our family pictures with him; it was the only thing from our old life that I truly miss.) He left Iran for good and never looked back, finally reuniting with my mother in Scarsdale.

I decided to call my parents and tell them about my hostage situation, knowing it would infuriate my father. Given his short temper, this news would quickly cause him to explode. Sure enough, he got extremely angry and yelled over the phone, "They have no right to keep your passport. I will take care of it myself. I will be there soon."

A couple of hours later he was in Crown Heights, standing in the doorway of the house, fuming. "Let's go. Take me to the main office," he said. "I want to meet the guy that is holding your passport."

We walked the few blocks without saying a word. I didn't dare speak. I knew the anger was building up inside him as we were getting closer to the office. He was a bomb ready to explode, a volcano ready to erupt. By the time we got to the front door, he was ready to kill.

"Which one is holding your passport?" he asked.

I pointed to one of the seven brothers behind the desk, secretly feeling sorry for the guy.

My father walked forward and said in a firm and loud voice, "I am here to pick up my daughter's passport and money. The name is Soheila Nobandegani. Please make it quick, I do not have much time."

My father was a tall and broad-shouldered handsome man with an intimidating personality. He had an impressive presence and was quickly noticed when he entered a room. If he wanted to create fear in people he knew exactly how to do it. His icy sharp stare was enough to send chills down anyone's spine, then up and around to warn every cell in the body: "Be fearful."

The lion that morning suddenly became a lamb in my father's presence. "She...sh.. she can't leave. Her, her vi-vi-visa is with the school here."

"Her visa is with me, here. I'm her father and that's why she will leave today."

He slammed his fist on the desk, sending cups, pens, reading glasses, and every other object flying all over the place. He bent over, looked straight into the Rabbi's terrified eyes and shouted, "And if you do not give me her passport right now, I will make sure you regret it. I will call every parent and together we will hire a lawyer to take care of this matter once and for all. You cannot hold anyone's passport."

He held his hand out and asked in a firm voice, "Now. Passport, please."

Grumpy-turned-Dopey looked at my father and then around the room for help, but no one came forward to offer assistance. He opened his mouth to say something but nothing came out, not even a squeak. He looked down at my father's tight fist still on his desk, the spilled coffee and the mess that it had created, got up from his chair, walked towards the file cabinets, and opened a drawer.

He walked back taking slow, small steps, carrying a brown envelope. When he reached his desk, he looked at my father again and held out his hand. My father took the envelope away from him, opened it up, checked my passport, counted the money, looked at the deflated, defeated and destroyed Rabbi and said, "Shalom, Rabbi."

And we left. It had only taken five minutes and I was free to go. We walked back in silence again. When my father popped a fuse, no one dared to talk.

I moved into the small apartment in Scarsdale, a town north of Manhattan, with my family that very evening.

Scarsdale

"You never know how strong you are... until being strong is the only choice you have." —Cayla Mills

Scarsdale, October, 1979

Nazee walked into the living room with a bruised face, sobbing. My mother rushed to her, "What's wrong? What happened to you?"

We were living in a small rented apartment in Scarsdale. It was a quiet suburb, very all-American, about forty minutes by train from the heart of Manhattan, and five minutes away from Nahid.

Nazee and Fariborz were attending the local public school, which was proving to be a challenge. They had come from an all-Iranian curriculum to an all-American one. My sister and brother had to study hard and work even harder to catch up with everyone else. They were looked at as "foreigners" and "outsiders." Nobody came forward to initiate a friendship or strike up a conversation. Fariborz was a 14-year-old-boy going through puberty, with dark eyes, black hair and a thick uni-brow. In a mostly blond environment, he stuck out like a sore thumb. Not only did the students make fun of him, the teachers were cruel to him too.

Things got even worse during the hostage crisis. On November 4, 1979, revolutionaries took over the U.S. Embassy in Tehran and took 66 American diplomats and citizens captive. Every news channel, radio station, and newspaper was reporting the smallest piece of information, twenty-four hours a day. The pictures of the bewildered hostages blind-folded among thousands of angry Khomeini followers broke everyone's hearts. My father spent most of his day watching the news and cursing under his tongue. "Damn Carter, it's all his fault."

During the hostage crisis life was difficult for Iranians in the U.S. People saw us as barbarians, as terrorists, as savages. They looked down on us and loved to hate us. Those days, ninety-nine percent of the Americans we met didn't even know where Iran was. There was no CNN, no internet and no social media. People were not exposed to different cultures.

My brother and sister were victims of the times. They were ridiculed and bullied in school every day, but that day it wasn't just emotional hurt. Nazee was black and blue. "I don't know how to go on in this school," she sobbed, "I was walking in the hallway to go to my next class. I felt a strong impact on the back of my legs. I fell on my face; my books went flying in the air. I looked back, and I saw one of the boys from my grade was standing behind me, laughing. He had run towards me while I was not looking and kicked me behind my knees. The circle of the students kept getting bigger and bigger. No one helped me. They all stood there and laughed at me. I picked up my books and walked to my class."

My mom's eyes were filled with sorrow. We knew what she was think-ing; she had said it many times: "Damn revolution, I left my beautiful home and my wonderful friends behind to come and live in this small apartment, where we are nobody and nothing to these people." She took Nazee to the bathroom, washed her face, and tried to calm her down.

The bullying of my brother and sister did not stop there. Their class-mates posted hate notes on their lockers, bad-mouthed them to the principal, and generally made their lives miserable.

Fariborz's situation was even worse than my sister's. He was a very smart and bright student but nobody wanted to acknowledge that, not even the faculty. His papers and his tests were marked down. When he raised his hand to answer a question, both the students and the teachers mocked him. His lab work was sabotaged as soon as he turned his back. To his classmates he was a terrorist.

Going to school every morning for Nazee and Fariborz was no less than walking onto a battlefield. But instead of wearing armor, they just developed a thicker skin. Thrown into a new city, with a new language, new school system, and hostile classmates, they had to adapt. Knowing they had no other choice, they developed new survival skills every day. Fariborz and Nazee persevered in their studies with a positive attitude.

My brother woke up every morning at the break of dawn, delivered newspapers to neighboring buildings for extra cash, came home, got ready and went to school. I was busy looking for a job for extra cash and applying to colleges. Nahid suggested babysitting. "It's easy money." I started putting signs up in the buildings around the neighborhood: "Fun and trustworthy babysitters at reasonable price." Taking care of kids was a pleasure for me, not a job. I loved kids and enjoyed being around them. I also went to random stores in Manhattan asking anybody and everybody for any position available.

Both efforts paid off. People called me for babysitting jobs, and I got a part-time position as a salesperson in a pharmacy/beauty product store on Madison Avenue and 74th Street.

On my first day at work, I woke up feeling nauseous. I was nervous, worried and insecure. The woman in charge of my department gave me a quick tour of the various makeup brands on the shelves and in the drawers. She sounded like an old record player, when the music is played on 78 fast forward.

"This section is Lancome. Lipsticks are here, blushes here, mascaras here and creams here. This section is Estee Lauder. Lipsticks are here, blushes here, mascaras here and creams here. This is Clinique. Lipsticks are here, blushes here, mascaras here and creams here. Here are the bags and wrapping paper. Get busy, look around, so you'll know what's where."

I turned red with the strain of trying desperately to take in what she was saying.

"Did you get it?" she asked impatiently.

"Yes, yes. No problem."

No problem, my foot! I opened each drawer one by one, trying to memorize the names and locations of all the products while my hands were shaking and my heart was racing.

She called out half an hour later. "Hey you—yes you—this lady needs help, she wants a Lancome lipstick."

Me? Is she talking to me? I thought.

"Why are you standing there? Help her."

"Hello Madame; how can I help you?" I asked.

"I need a red lipstick, please." My first customer looked very familiar. I had seen her before, but I couldn't remember where. "Yes, of course. You prefer red? I will bring you a couple of reds."

I went to the drawers, thinking, which one was for lipsticks? Where are they?

My boss yelled from the other counter, "What are you waiting for? Top right."

I opened the drawer and brought out a couple of lipsticks, praying one would be red. I rolled them out one by one and tried to be friendly and helpful.

My familiar-looking customer was very nice and patient with me. It was obvious that I was nervous; my hands were shaking as I showed her the colors. She looked at a couple of them and, thank God, liked one and asked me to wrap it for her. Now I had to charge her, and I had no idea how. I was sweating bullets. I went to my boss and admitted, in a shaky voice, that I needed help.

"Never mind, I will do it." She grabbed the tube from me and went to the register. She was not happy.

She collected the money and gave her the lipstick with a smile. As soon as the customer left she turned to me and said, "Do you know who that was?"

"No. But she looked familiar."

"She was Shelley Winters, the actress. She is a very good customer of ours."

Oh, that's why she looked familiar, I had seen her in the movie Poseidon Adventure! Here I had just arrived in New York, and my first customer was a movie star. *I love this country*, I thought. But getting through a shift at work wasn't easy. It wasn't the hard work or long hours of work that frightened me; it was the Godzilla breathing down my neck. She watched my every move, and if I wasn't quick enough, she stormed in and took over in annoyance.

I was very happy with the money I was making, considering how the dollar was getting more and more expensive back in Iran. I was happy I was with my family again. We talked about our day at the dinner table and laughed off all the negative things about life in this bewildering place. We knew adjusting and adapting in a new country was the most difficult part. From here on, things were going to get better. The future was in our hands; we had to try our best. Complaining was useless and a complete waste of energy. We stuck to the positive.

I had been working in the makeup department for about two weeks, and it was not getting any easier. A woman walked in and asked for a face cream that I had never heard of in an accent that I could barely understand (I later learned that it was "Southern.")

She kept on repeating what she was looking for, and I kept on helplessly repeating, "Excuse me?"

Once again, my boss walked forward and took over the situation. She found the cream, rang her up and handed her the small bag. It was the calm before the storm. At the end of the day, when the doors were closed, she lost it. She stood in the middle of the store and started shouting, "I can't work with this stupid girl anymore. She is not capable. She is driving me crazy. She doesn't understand anything. She is an idiot. Listen to me: you are fired. Yes, you! Pack up and go. Get out! I said, go! Leave. Out. NOW."

Tears started rolling down my face. I walked to the back, took my purse and walked out.

She was one hundred percent right, of course. Confused by the language barrier and the different names of the products, I wasn't fit for the job. I wasn't what she wanted. But I learned something during those two weeks. United States was the land of opportunity. I had no sooner arrived than I started making money. Okay, maybe Madison Avenue and 74th Street was not the right starting point. Maybe I was too ambitious for an immigrant. Maybe I was not yet capable, but it seemed that there was always an opportunity somewhere. This was the best country in the world. I fell in love with The United States of America.

How I Met My Husband

"Don't wait for the perfect moment, take the moment and make it perfect." —Zoey Sayward

Los Angeles, November, 1979

I was always to be found in the center of the dance floor. Wherever there was music, there was yours truly shaking, moving, shimmying and gyrating to one song after another. Iranian dance is sensual and seductive. The movements center around the hips and shoulders. You shimmy one part and shake the other, sometimes in slow motion and sometimes fast. In our dance neither the hips nor the shoulders ever lie!

Non-Iranians often watched our dancing with boggled eyes. "How, in such a conservative country, are women allowed to dance so sexy with no inhibitions?"

"This is a part of our culture," I'd laughingly tell them. "The movements come naturally to us!"

They had reason to stare. Authentic Iranian dance is fascinating, bewitching, and one of the sexiest dances on the face of the earth. Women rotate their hips while moving their shoulders and necks, looking at the people around them in a very flirtatious way to the beat of slow, seductive music. They move their arms in a fluid motion and put their hands in their hair, playing with it in a charming and enchanting way while gazing from the corner of their eyes. No one is judged on the dance floor, and

I was no exception. Every movement is allowed as long as it is in good taste—and Persian!

Music took me to the next level. It was a natural high, I was in a trance. I couldn't stop. I didn't want to stop. Music was my drug of choice, didn't matter what kind. I always wondered how people could stand still at parties when a good song was playing. Didn't the rhythm and every note go through their bodies, mix with their blood, move through their hearts and up to every cell in their brains? Didn't they breathe the music in and fill up their lungs with it? Didn't it cover them like a soft blanket and move them with the strength of an ocean? How could you *not* feel the music and move to the beat?

I was in my element, dancing at the wedding of a friend from high school in Los Angeles. Having been in New York for just a few months, the idea of being on the west coast was like a dream to me. I had been looking at pictures of Disneyland and reading articles about it since I was a young girl. I had seen pictures of the "Hollywood" sign on top of the hill. I had followed the lives of the stars and had Rock Hudson and Clint Eastwood posters up on my wall. Now I was there, in person, and could see everything up close. I could not have been happier.

The wedding was fun and I danced all night. Towards the end of the night, when most of the guests had gone, a short but well-built guy approached me, smiled and said, "Hi, my name is Moise. I am one of the bride's cousins. I wanted to ask you...would you go out with me?"

Back then, it was customary for Iranian guys to see girls at parties or social events and ask for their phone numbers and a date. Such gatherings were our Facebook page, and Jewish High Holidays in a synagogue our "online dating!" If a guy saw someone that he fancied, he, his mother, or his sister would approach the girl and ask for her name and family information—the old-fashioned way to "Google" her. It was a common practice. If you liked what you saw you would accept the "friend request" and release your information; if you didn't, you would come up with a sweet white lie. "I'm sorry, I want to continue with my education. I am not thinking of getting married now." In other words, if you didn't like what you saw, you swiped left!

In our community having a boyfriend just for fun was not allowed. If you wanted that kind of adventure, you had to find a way around the rules and hide the relationship as much as you could. Getting caught with a boy was a disaster. But going out with a suitor was not only allowed, it was encouraged.

"Of course, I will go out with you," I answered. "How is tomorrow? I have a great idea; let's go to Disneyland."

I am sure he was caught off-guard. I was obviously taking advantage of my suitors to get to the fun places that I so desperately yearned to see. He laughed and said, "If that's where you want to go on the first date, sure. Why not? Tomorrow at 10:00?"

Disneyland was magical. It was everything that I had ever imagined and more. I felt like a little kid. I bought Mickey Mouse T-shirts, fuzzy slippers, big round colorful lollypops, souvenirs for Nazee and Fariborz and took tons of pictures with every Disney character. It truly was "the happiest place on earth."

Moise kept following me from ride to ride, watching and laughing at my enthusiasm. It never took much to make me happy. It never took much to make me laugh, either. I walked around with a smile from ear to ear. I enjoyed watching a sunset, smelling a flower, touching the sand, playing with a baby, listening to music. I enjoyed everything and everyone. People were extremely interesting to me, each one a mystery and every life a story. I loved meeting new people and was curious about their experiences and struggles. The world and all its ingredients were fascinating to me. I was passionately in love with life.

Especially in Los Angeles—this sunny, beautiful place with new people, new stories, and new adventures. Sadly, Hollywood life came to an end after a week and I had to return home to Scarsdale.

My newly-married friend called me a few weeks later. "Soheila, we are coming to New York. My husband's friend saw you at my wedding and wants to meet you. We will all go out to dinner together next week if you are free."

We met in an Iranian restaurant in the East Village in Manhattan. There were about 10 people around the table. I was seated between my friend and my date for the night, an Iranian gentleman in a business suit who introduced himself as Jack. He was a touch taller than me, with a full beard, a thick mustache and glasses. *Why is the full beard and mustache in style everywhere?* I thought. *This look is becoming universal.*

Though we sat next to each other we didn't say anything other than the initial few words of introduction for the rest of the evening. I kept busy with everyone else around the table. We ordered dinner, danced, laughed at silly jokes, but he and I failed to speak, even though our shoulders were literally touching in that small, crowded setting.

I couldn't have cared less. I was enjoying myself. If he is not interested in me, I can't force him, was my attitude... not realizing that he was thinking, *Why is she carrying on non-stop with everyone else? Why isn't she paying any attention to me?* We went out as a group a few more times, and little by little he started having small conversations with me. The fourth night we spent together with friends he offered to drive me home to Scarsdale. I accepted. We failed to speak for the entire 45-minute car ride home! *What's his problem?!* I thought.

Finally, he broke the silence, just as he dropped me off. "Can I ask you out, but just the two of us?"

"Yes, of course," I replied. Why did I agree to meet him again when we were having such a hard time connecting? I don't know, but I did.

"I had never dated a Persian girl before," Jackie told me much later. "The night of our first meeting, I was very uncomfortable. I didn't know what to say. I didn't want to be rude so I was waiting for you to open up a conversation with me, but you never did!"

"And I was waiting for you to start the conversation with me, but you never did!" I replied.

He was a smart, funny, and hardworking man. He was full of stories, mostly about his struggles when he had just entered the United States.

His family had joined him just a few years before, and they all lived in a house that he had purchased for them in Great Neck, Long Island.

I didn't bother telling my parents who I was dating at the beginning. I didn't think anything would come of it. But as I gradually got to know the man behind the beard and glasses, I became more interested in him. "By the way," I told my parents one day, "I am dating a man called Jack Adelipour. His real name is David, but everyone calls him Jackie because of his Hebrew name, Jacob."

My father looked at me and said, "Is his father's name Yosef, by any chance? If it is, I know the family."

"That's funny, I think his dad's name is Yosef," I said.

"I know them, nice people... such a small world."

"What does he do?" An obvious question from any mother.

"He works in the garment district. He makes clothing for women."

Jackie and I started spending more and more time together, having fun with each other and laughing at each other's stories. I'd meet him around 7 o'clock under his office at 1375 Broadway, the heart of the Garment Center (which he called "Garbage Center" as a joke) after work or somewhere in the city on weekends.

In December of 1979, we were walking down Fifth Avenue enjoying the magnificent holiday decorations. I noticed the gigantic Christmas tree shining like a glorious mountain full of colored jewels on my right.

"Can we go and see the tree?" I asked.

"Yes, let's go. It's beautiful."

Obviously, I was once again taking full advantage of a "suitor situation" at that moment. The iconic Christmas tree with thousands of colorful lights looked like a dream. The gold statue of Prometheus by Paul Manship, the art deco skyscraper building dominating the center, the holiday angels on the promenade... where else can you see such glory and beauty? I didn't know the answer, but now that I was in New York City and so close to the extraordinary famous landmark, I had to experience it for myself.

"Let's go ice skating," I said to Jack. "Do you know how to skate?"

"Me? Yes, of course," he answered in a most convincing way.

"Fantastic, I am pretty good at it too. Let's go."

"You will be cold dressed like that," he said. "Let's go buy a thick sweater, you need one." He directed me towards one of the many stores around Rockefeller Center. We chose a warm blue turtleneck and walked back towards the ice skating rink. His kind gesture resonated with me.

Inside the rink, I put the boots on, helped Jack with his, made the straps tight and ran out to the ice. After a few minutes, I looked for him among the crowd in the middle of the rink. But he was nowhere to be found. I was beginning to get worried. Finally, I spotted him close to the entrance struggling to take a step. He was wobbling and swaying, trying desperately not to fall.

"Are you OK? Do you need help?" I yelled out.

He waved and said, "No, no, go ahead. I'm good."

I watched him for a few seconds. He was holding on to anyone that was in his vicinity and apologizing constantly. He was trying to keep his balance by using the innocent tourists as his cane. He went from Asians to Indians to Americans and I'm sure several European nations along the way to make it to the entrance of the ice skating rink. It was fun and funny watching him struggle. I had to give the man an "A" for effort!

I pretended I didn't see him and started ice-skating. I loved hearing the holiday music in the open air. To me everything about Christmas was beautiful and jolly. I was mesmerized by the decorations, the lights, the beautiful tree and of course the gifts. I had a couple of Christian friends back in Iran and had always envied them during their high holidays.

Now I was in the middle of one of the most iconic places in the world, the giant tree filled with little bright lights was towering over me, the wooden soldiers were framing the ice skating rink, and the music was filling up the air. I looked at the sky behind the tall and slick skyscraper and thanked God for making it possible for me to leave Iran. I was happy and thankful instead of scared and miserable.

I looked for Jack again among the people ice-skating in the middle of the rink but I couldn't find him. I went around and tried to locate him. I finally saw him three feet away from the entrance, hunched over, one leg bent in, one bent out, his chin almost touching the railing, holding on tight with both arms to the edge of the dividers. He looked desperate and helpless. He was trying to take a step but every time he moved one leg, the other slid out from underneath him, causing him to lose his balance and hold on even tighter. It was a scene out of a comedy sitcom. He was unable to move forward or back; he was stuck.

I didn't know what to do, it was obvious that he had never ice-skated before in his life. But I didn't want to scratch his ego either. No man wanted to be seen like that. He looked helpless and I didn't want to embarrass him. He was a self-made man who had entered the United States at the age of 16 with only $450 in his pocket—of which $300 had gone straight to an immigration lawyer for a student visa, leaving him $150 to live on. He started working in his uncle's men's store in an area in Brooklyn notorious for dangerous gangs and deadly shootings. He also registered in the local school and started learning the language. He missed home and had a tough time adjusting to his new life.

Before the revolution, sending young boys to America to learn a trade and begin advancing in the world was a common practice. The idea of a teenager living by himself with little or no money in a strange land with no language skills was widely accepted. No one ever questioned the practice. Boys were either sent to boarding schools in England, which was a horrible experience for each and every one of them, or to the United States to begin building a more promising future.

"If I made $25, I saved $30!" he said once. "I knew I had no other choice but to survive. Failure was not an option. I had to make money and build a future."

Jack worked hard and tried to catch up with school as well. Studying was at the bottom of his daily schedule, so when he enrolled in high school and was unable to make good grades he went directly to his math teacher with the only way he thought he could get one: a fresh $100 bill in his hand!

"You know, professor, if I do not pass this test it would look bad on my records. Maybe I can't keep the student visa anymore. What do you say to this?" And he slipped the $100 bill onto his teacher's desk. Money was so valuable to him that he never imagined someone would say no to that much of it.

"Are you trying to bribe me?" the professor asked.

Jack, not knowing what "bribe" meant exactly (his English vocabulary was very limited at the time) answered, "No, hmm yes, I don't know. Can I pass the test?"

The professor got up from his chair and pointed to the door and yelled, "Out, get out, I said get out."

"So that means you do not want my money?" Jack asked.

"I said, OUT!" he shouted. "Take your stupid money with you."

Jack took the crisp bill, put it in his pants pocket, and left.

The next day he was kicked out of school for good. He was relieved, but he didn't have the guts to tell his parents. He took advantage of his free time to work harder and longer hours.

Jack lived alone in a rented space in the basement of a house with no windows. "One evening I came home exhausted, I took a can of beans and put it directly on the electrical stovetop. I forgot to open the lid. I was too exhausted to think," he told me. He left the can to warm up and fell asleep while waiting. He jumped up to a huge boom. The can had exploded and the whole room was covered in beans. The ceiling, the walls, his bed... everything had red beans stuck to it. He spent hours cleaning the mess. It was a low point, but he knew that night he was so down that he had no other way to go, but up.

After couple of years working in Brooklyn, he thought he had collected enough money and experience to manage his own business. He found a small space in Queens and started selling men's clothing. He was only 20 years old. This marked the beginning of his financial success.

Fast-forward 10 years. This self-made businessman was slanted precariously forward on his ice-skating boots, desperately holding on for dear life to the edge of the handrail and apologizing to whomever he bumped or fell on. I watched him for a few minutes and decided not to embarrass him.

After 15 minutes, I approached Jackie. "Jack, are you OK?" I yelled from a distance. As soon as he heard me calling he tried to stand up straight and act in control of the situation. He was still wobbling.

"Yes, I am fine. Go on, don't worry about me," he yelled back. "I just need a few more minutes to get the hang of this again."

Again? I thought.

He was not fine; he was in agony. I think the blood had stopped flowing in his fingers awhile ago.

"You know something Jackie, it's cold. I don't want to ice skate anymore. Let's go have dinner."

"OK, but I have no problem staying," he said, trying desperately to keep his balance.

"I know, I'm done," I said.

"OK, then, let's go."

But how was he supposed to get to the exit of the rink and make his way back against the traffic? He had slid, skidded, slipped, fallen, glided, and scooted a whole 10 feet in the past half-hour.

"Let me go for one last round and then we'll leave," I said.

I skated to one of the people in charge of the rink. "Excuse me, do you see that gentleman there hanging on to the edge?"

"Yes, what can I do for you?" he asked.

"Please help him to the exit and position him on a bench," I said. "He is kind of stuck, I will join him soon. I don't want him to know that I have asked you."

"Yes, of course," he said.

I thanked him and skated to the opposite side of the rink. I took in the surroundings, the music and the magnificent tree for another few minutes and then joined him on the bench. "Where were you? I was looking for you?" I asked.

"I came here to take my boots off, I thought we were done," he said.

"Yes, we are. Enough ice-skating. Let's go eat."

That was the beginning of us dating seriously.

Living the American Dream

"It had long since come to my attention that people of accomplishment rarely sat back and let things happen to them. They went out and happened to things." —Leonardo Da Vinci

New York, 1970-1992

Jack's business partner, Joe Moinian, had come to the United States in 1971, when he was only 16 years old. His parents had decided, like so many other Iranian families, to send their eldest son to America for a better future. He arrived with a little money and rudimentary English. His father sent him Persian crafts that he sold for a small profit. His main source of income was from Persian rugs, which Joe rolled up, put on his shoulder, and carried from store to store until one finally made an offer that was acceptable to him. At night, he worked as a waiter in a diner called "Cozy Corner" where he met my future husband, his future business partner and brother-in-law.

Jack was eating a simple meal after a hard day's work, and Joe was working hard to make a living simply so he could eat. They became friends quickly; Joe was 5 years younger than Jack, but in the early 70's you held tight to any Iranian you met. There weren't too many in New York before the revolution, so if you happened to meet one, you kept in touch and never let go. Any Persian-speaking person meant home and safety. The two young men became each other's adopted brother.

They talked about their lives, their dreams, their struggles, and their ambitions.

Jack was happy with the money he was making in his men's store on Steinway Street. He had left basement life behind and rented a modest apartment in Queens, within walking distance of the diner. Both young men had big dreams, huge dreams, American dreams—and they were both hungry enough to go after them with teeth and claws. They talked about business opportunities and making serious money. They talked about the other immigrants who had come to the United States and made it big.

Joe had begun working for a Persian-Israeli guy called Chaim in the heart of the garment center. Chaim made affordable apparel for women, and Joe was observing him every step of the way. His number-one item was called the "tube top"—a strapless tank top made from a wrinkled stretchy fabric.

"He just cuts the fabric and sews the seams together in different lengths and colors and sells them by thousands," he told Jack one night after he was done with his work at Cozy Corner. "I don't see any talent in that, I see big possibilities. If you copy what other people are successfully selling, but at a cheaper price, customers will buy from you!"

Jack was doubtful. "I am starting to make good money in my store. I have looked at two other stores to expand. My income is great. I can't leave my business now."

Nonetheless, Joe pushed. "This guy just cuts the fabric and sews the seams. You should see the line. People are going crazy over it."

"I am doing well, Joe. I found the source for the Hawaiian print shirts. I sold 200 pieces only yesterday. My customers are fighting over them." Jack shook his head. "When I landed in New York and started working for peanuts for my uncle in Brooklyn, I never imagined one day I would be making so much money in my own store. My hard work is paying off. How can I let go? But retail is tough. Let me think about it."

After chewing on the idea for a little while they decided to go for it. They opened up a small office, ordered the fabrics and started producing "tube tops" in every color and size. They worked 8 days a week,

25 hours a day. Gradually they started adding dresses and blouses to their line. They searched high and low for a salable dress and design. Their number-one seller came during the success of the movie *Saturday Night Fever* starring John Travolta.

They designed a simple backless dress made of a shiny fabric covered in little sparkly beads called "cracked ice" in a variety of colors and sold out of them every week. They went to clubs and counted the girls who were wearing their "number" and started congratulating each other. They went to stores and switched their dresses with the ones hanging in front. They talked to customers and promoted their clothes. Soon enough, they became the success story that they had dreamed of.

Little by little they started looking into real estate. They didn't let their inexperience get in the way, but started investing in whatever they could afford. By the time of the revolution in 1979 and migration of the Iranians to New York and Los Angeles, Jack and Joe had become known as the duo that had made it in America and became the model for the newly arrived. Relatives, friends and strangers entered the garment district because of them and copied their path. Jack and Joe helped them get started and were there for any problems or questions. Jack's brother Eddie took over the men's store, and Joe's two brothers followed in his footsteps and started in ladies' apparel and real estate. They learned from the master. Jack and Joe each bought a house and moved in with their parents, becoming the patriarchs of their families. They were brothers at heart, then business partners. Soon enough they became officially related as well.

Joe fell in love with my younger sister the minute he laid eyes on her. He walked into my engagement party with his tall blond girlfriend on his arm and cursed himself for bringing a date when he noticed Nazee next to me. From that day on Jack and I could not do anything alone as a couple. The four of us traveled together, went to restaurants together, and spent weekends together. His friendship with Jack provided Joe an excuse to be wherever Nazee was. There was just one problem—Jack and I were newlyweds with no privacy!

Joe Moinian and Nazee were inseparable and in love. He proposed to her with 1000 red roses. I got busy working on her bridal shower. It was a happy time for both of us; she was a young fiancée in love and shining and I was a pregnant woman glowing... and vomiting. The day before her party I started having cramps and a few hours later bleeding started. I was scared and devastated. I called my doctor first and then Jackie at work. An hour later we were at the doctor's office. I sat there crying.

"I am sorry, you have lost the baby. You have to check into the hospital," my doctor said. "I have to perform a D&C on you."

"Why? I didn't do anything wrong," I sobbed.

He held my hands and said, "It has nothing to do with what you did or didn't do. Nature has a way of correcting itself around the third month. Maybe it wasn't a good pregnancy."

"Will I ever have a full pregnancy?" I asked. "Will I have a healthy baby?"

"You should be able to, you are young and healthy. But no one knows. Only time will tell," he answered. "For now, we have to take care of this one. I have to check you in."

"I'm sorry doctor, I can't now, not today or tomorrow. It's my sister's bridal shower," I sobbed.

"Soheila, you are bleeding," my doctor said.

"No doctor, not today. Please wait till tomorrow after the shower. I don't want anyone to know. I will greet the guests, act normal, and when it's over I will come directly to your office. It's a day party after all," I said, pleading. "Is there something you can give me for keeping the bleeding and the pain under control?"

"You want to go to your sister's party in this condition?"

"Yes, and I don't want anyone to notice."

I had decided to keep the devastating news to myself for the time being. I had planned an elaborate bridal shower for Nazee and refused to allow anything sad to overshadow the day of her happiness. I hosted the event and welcomed every guest with a smile. It was only when my friends placed their hands on my hollow belly, congratulated me, wished me a healthy baby and an easy delivery that I ran to the bathroom to cry my heart out. Then I refreshed my makeup, walked back to the party and continued smiling and dancing.

Joe and Nazee got married on Memorial Day weekend 1982, when she was only 19 years old. And despite my fears, I was soon pregnant again. This time, everything went smoothly. I was 7 months along when Jack and I decided to move out of the small apartment we had rented. We bought a house in Great Neck, Long Island where the Persian Jews had settled as they were migrating to New York. Nazee and Joe moved to a house down the block from us.

Zohreh had finally agreed to marry Jamshid, a tall, quiet, and reserved guy who had seen my sister at a party and from that point on never left her alone. He was the polar opposite of Zohreh. She wanted to be out partying, he was a homebody. She was talkative and full of opinions, he was quiet. She was into sports and outdoor activities, he preferred to sit and read. But my independent sister had changed by this point. She wanted to have kids and a family. She appreciated Jamshid's kind heart and his adaptability and flexibility towards any situation. Zohreh and Jamshid were married a week before I gave birth to our first son, Justin. When he was only 8 months old I became pregnant with another son, Stephen. Two months later Nazee was pregnant with her first son, Matthew.

Life was normal with everyday problems. We were busy managing our growing families. Meanwhile, our community in Great Neck continued to grow. We arranged playdates, took the kids to the park and set up carpools amongst ourselves. We raised our children collectively, and to this day they are each other's best friends. In that small town everyone knew everyone else. At times, it was suffocating. It felt like you were watched and analyzed for everything that you did or said. No one wanted an unnecessary rumor flying around. No one wanted to be the black sheep. We all knew the unwritten rules and we respected them. We all lived together in harmony in that small town.

Since the revolution and the migration of the Iranians to foreign countries, there were cultural issues in every household. My parents were no exception. My mother was a smart, capable and friendly woman. But there was no use for any of that, since she was home most of the time, keeping my father company and serving him. His old-school behavior at his age was considered normal and accepted.

The problem was my mother *was* an exception and did not accept her traditional role easily. She was hardly the typical obedient, passive, and subservient woman of her time. She was educated, she had an opinion, she had a voice, and she made sure she was heard.

My father (as was the case with most middle-aged immigrants) was the breadwinner and provider for the family. He sold whatever he could sell, bought American dollars in the black market, fled Iran and entered the United States. My mom was still the mother and the person in charge of the household—her role was not touched or changed—but my father was lost. He had lost his entire position in life. He woke up in the morning and had nowhere to go and no one to see. He took a shower, had his breakfast, put his suit and tie on and went to the supermarket with my mom. He had no one to order around and no decisions to make, so the home became his office; everyday life, his work domain; and my mother, his secretary.

The family's pride and joy and only son, Fariborz, graduated as an electrical engineer with the highest honors. He was hired by a Japanese company right out of school, where he was put in charge of creating new gadgets in the world of technology in the early 90s. He was making good money but not very happy with what he was doing. "What I do does not leave an impact on anyone," he used to tell us. "It is not satisfying to me. I need challenge, I need fulfillment. I need to come home thinking I made a difference in someone's life."

He worked as volunteer at a local hospital and found his passion. "These doctors change destinies. They save lives. They matter," he said.

Fariborz applied to and entered medical school. He was affiliated with Down State Brooklyn hospital in a tough neighborhood. This was back in the days before laws were passed prohibiting long hours for interns without sleep. After working at the ER for two days straight, a simple phone conversation required every ounce of energy from his reserves. He fell asleep wherever and whenever out of sheer exhaustion.

Each one of us was busy managing our lives. Nahid had moved to Manhattan and was working in Tourneau selling watches. Zohreh had opened her own architectural firm. I was in Great Neck with my boys and commuting to New York to finish my MBA in art gallery management. Nazee was busy with her kids and her studies in computer science. We saw each other regularly, on weekends and Friday night Shabbat dinners, but for the time being our brother was missing in action, stuck at the hospital. It was a price he was more than willing to pay; he was making a difference, and he was happy.

Then came the first dark cloud on the horizon. It started so simply.

"Everything is a Blur"

"Courage is a love affair with the unknown." —Oysho

New York, 1991

"Come, get into the car. I have to be back in Manhattan before two," Zohreh said from behind the wheel of her car.

I jumped in and asked, "Why? What is happening at 2?"

"I am not sure," she said driving towards the Queensboro Bridge. "I have an appointment with a neurosurgeon. There is definitely something wrong with me."

I looked at her in shock. "What is wrong with you?"

"I started having problems with my vision. At times, everything is a blur and dark, but it happens just for a few seconds. At the beginning, I did not pay much attention to it, hoping it would stop, but it didn't. I decided to go and see an Ophthalmologist yesterday. After he was done with his exam he sent me for a CT scan right away. He just called me and told me that he has made an appointment for me with a neurosurgeon at New York Hospital this afternoon."

I didn't know what to say. Why would one go to a brain surgeon? I had personally never come across one in my life. The only person I knew who was a neurosurgeon was our brother, and Fariborz had not yet completed his residency. When he'd told our father about his choice of specialties in the medical world, the response had been, "A brain surgeon? Who in the world has a problem with their brain? Why not a gynecologist? Women always have to give birth!"

Now my sister had to go and consult one. What could be that serious?

"I'm sure it is nothing serious," Zohreh continued, reading my mind. "I feel fine."

I looked at her. She was right, she was fine. She was driving and talking to me the same way she always did.

"Do you want me to drive?" I asked.

"I'm fine, thanks."

Jack and I had decided to renovate our house in 1990 after a major pipe burst on a cold winter night in our living room. We were away so nobody found out about the water damage until it was too late and half of the house was ruined. What started out as a simple renovation became a major reconstruction. Zohreh was our architect and interior designer.

We decided to move to Manhattan for the duration and found an apartment on East 51st Street in the area known as Beekman Place. I loved Manhattan. I loved the action. I loved the energy. I loved the idea of walking everywhere and being exposed to so many different options. I enrolled at Fashion Institute of Technology and received my Masters degree in Art Gallery Management. Justin was 7 and Stephen was 5; the boys thrived in the city.

Great Neck was a small village. Without a car, you were stuck in your house. In a snowstorm, you were stuck in your house. A branch of a tree fell in your driveway after a windy day and you were stuck in your house. Your choice of activities and events was minimal. People lived in Great Neck for two reasons only: the school system and the Persian Jewish community. No one expected or looked for much more.

During those wonderful years in the city, I got pregnant with my third son, Cameron, partnered with my friend Benny in an art gallery on 57th Street and spent my few free hours in the museums or the auction houses. Zohreh and I drove out to the house twice a week to check on the improvements. She was on top of everything and everyone. When it came to her profession, she was tough with no mercy. The job had to be done 100% right and on time. If not, God help the people who screwed it up. She cut them, diced them, grinded them, roasted them, and threw them in the dumpster.

This was supposed to be another ordinary day of our ordinary visits to the house. But it was far from ordinary; we were both scared and worried. "Zohreh, we don't have to go to the house today," I said. "They can do without us."

"It's OK," she answered, "time will go by faster."

I had never thought anything bad could happen to our family. The guardian angels were protecting us, I was sure. Why shouldn't they? We were good people. We never harmed or wished bad for anyone. Eternal optimist that I was, I said, "Everything will be fine, Zohreh, I am sure it's nothing serious." I sat back in the car and started talking about our ongoing project, the upcoming parties and the latest gossip.

We were at Dr. Snow's office at 2:00 in the afternoon. An athletic-looking young doctor walked in holding a set of images in his hand. He introduced himself and gave us a confused look, not knowing which one of us was the patient. Zohreh raised her hand and said, "I am Zohreh Zand."

"I'm her sister Soheila."

Dr. Snow leaned against the tall table and said, "I've looked at your CT scan. You have what we call in the medical world a Meningioma." He placed the images on the view box and continued. "You have a tumor in the front of your forehead. If you look at this area you can see it," pointing at the images. Zohreh and I turned towards each other in disbelief.

"The good news is," he continued, "the tumor is benign. However, you need to be operated on ASAP. When we take it out and after you have gone through the process of recovery, you will have a normal life, you do not need any chemo or radiation."

I held Zohreh and said, "Did you hear that? It's benign. Oh my God, Thank you. Thank you."

Zohreh showed no reaction. She looked the doctor straight in the eye and said, "If I can't live the life that I want to live, or have the activities that I want to have, I don't want to be alive. I want to be independent. I want to be able to go to my office. I want to be able to take care of my kids. I want to be able to continue to water-ski. I don't want to come out of surgery being incomplete and crippled. Please be honest with me."

"I am being honest with you," Dr. Snow answered. "You can have your normal life back. The great news is that it's not brain cancer—if it was, then I would give you anywhere between 6 months to 2 years, maximum."

"What is the next step, doctor?" I asked.

"Your sister has to go through some tests and make an appointment for the surgery as soon as possible."

After he was done talking about the procedure, we got up, thanked him and left. "Don't forget, you cannot postpone this surgery," he added.

Zohreh was deep in her thoughts, and so was I. It was hard to believe. *A brain surgery?* I thought. You go to an eye doctor with a question and 24 hours later you have a brain tumor! But thank God, it's benign. A lot of people sit in the same chair and are handed a death sentence.

She looked at me with cold and determined eyes and said, "We have to break the news to Fariborz and the rest of the family."

"That is not going to be easy, especially for Momon," I said. "What do we tell her? That her daughter is undergoing brain surgery?" She held my shoulders, stared into my eyes and said, "If anything happens to me, promise me you will take care of my children. Promise!" At that time her twins, Roya and Arya, were about a year old.

"Of course I will. You know I will. But nothing will happen to you. Our guardian angels are watching over us," I said. Zohreh called Fariborz with the news.

"Where did you find this doctor?" he asked, trying to stay calm.

"My ophthalmologist sent me to him," Zohreh answered.

"I will find you the best neurosurgeon for meningioma in New York. Different doctors have different specialties. Give me a couple of hours." And he got to work right away. The news about Zohreh's brain surgery got out in the community, fast. Everyone was shocked at first and then amazed—once they talked to her—by her courage and strength. She was all smiles, "a temporary condition, an uncomfortable situation, a bump in my road, but nothing that can't be fixed," she told everyone.

After numerous tests and doctor's visits, the day of the surgery finally arrived.

Zohreh was ready to go into the operating room. My mother was standing in the corner, crying. I walked towards my sister on the hospital bed just as she was ready to be rolled away and said, "Listen Zohreh, remember in Iran, in high school, we had to learn and memorize the Arabic poetry; ANALDEEKO MENAL HENDEE?"

She looked at me as if I had gone crazy and said, "Yes, why?"

"When you are out of the surgery, in the recovery room, I will recite the first part and you give me the second part, which is?"

"JAMEELA SHAKEE VAL GHADEE!" she replied.

"Yes, exactly. If you remember that, then we know that your mind is in perfect shape. That will be our code. Are you OK with that?" I asked.

"Yes, Fariborz, please bring Soheila in first after I am done." She smiled, "I will see you soon." And she was gone.

Time went by very slowly. They had to prep her for the surgery and shave her head completely. Nahid and Nazee were trying to talk to our parents to keep them occupied. My mother looked like a helpless child, her face filled with sorrow. It broke our hearts watching her sob like that. Our father was sitting on a chair staring out the window. Fariborz was pacing the waiting room back and forth.

"What am I doing here?" he said suddenly. "I should be by her side." He took his ID out, attached it to his shirt and walked in the OR. (He was traumatized for a long time after that. He witnessed the doctors peeling back the skin of his sister's forehead, breaking her skull, taking the tumor out, replacing it with a plastic part and then sewing her back up.)

Several hours later he emerged from the operating room. "She is fine. The surgery went very well. She will be in the recovery room soon." My mother collapsed on the chair and started crying, this time from happiness and relief.

"When can I see her?" I asked.

"Not too long, maybe in half an hour. I will take you in when she is ready. I want to go back in to make sure everything is fine with the post-op."

"Thank God Fariborz is here," I told my sisters. "What would we do without him?"

He walked out again after an hour and said, "It took longer than expected. Don't be shocked when you see her. Her head is full of stitches, but she is fine. They had to make sure they have drained her head from fluid buildup. She will be in the recovery room soon." And he disappeared again.

Half an hour later he walked into the waiting room and said, "You can come with me." My mom got up to join us. Fariborz stopped her and said, "Sorry Momon, one person at a time." I turned towards her and said, "I am sorry, but she asked me to go in first and ask her a question. I will just be a minute." I walked out with my brother.

That was my first experience with washing hands, putting on a hospital gown, wearing a surgical mask, and walking into an ICU. The room was cold and impersonal. Almost everything was grey; the walls, the curtains, even the lighting was depressing. Beeping noises in different tones could be heard from every corner. Nurses were busy running around and attending the patients almost robot-like. There was no window or natural light. It was a scene from an old black and white science fiction movie.

Zohreh was on a bed, her eyes closed, her face swollen, her head wrapped in a turban, IVs and tubes sticking out of every part of her body. I wouldn't have recognized her if Fariborz hadn't pointed towards her direction. She had rolled in that morning as herself and rolled back out as a nightmare version of herself.

I took a deep breath, got close to her and whispered in her ear, "Zohreh, can you hear me? Listen to me, 'ANAL DEEKO MENAL HENDEE.' Did you hear me? Talk to me, ANAL DEEKO MENAL HENDEE."

Zohreh tried to open her eyes, but she couldn't. She said in a low and weak voice, "JAMEELA SHAKEE VAL GHADEE."

98

I looked at Fariborz; tears were rolling down our faces. It was a miracle. Her mind was perfect. I squeezed her hand and said, "Ain't nothing wrong with you, sister!"

She smiled a faint smile and tried to nod. "Everyone wants to come and see you. I will be back soon," I told Zohreh. I ran out of the ICU towards the waiting room and yelled out, "She is fine. Her mind is intact. She answered correctly. Momon, go in and see for yourself."

My mom got up and ran towards the ICU. "Only one at a time, Fariborz is standing next to her!" I shouted.

"Poor Momon, she is going to be shocked when she sees Zohreh, she looks terrible," I whispered to Nahid and Nazee.

She remained in the ICU for a week. Zohreh's spirit was high and she was very positive about her recovery. She was not able to open her right eye, but her doctor assured her that the nerves were traumatized as a result of surgery and would soon be normal again.

We were busy keeping her company and taking care of her kids. She didn't want any visitors besides her family members so people sent their good wishes and love. She was happy to get home with her kids and into her own bed. Her head was bald, her scalp stapled from the top of one ear to the other in the shape of a headband, her forehead swollen, her eyes bruised. It was sad and depressing to see her like that. She didn't look anything like herself. But her character and her strength were the same. "I will be 'new and improved' Zohreh," she repeated. We had purchased two wigs before her surgery. But it was too soon and the stitches too fresh for a Cher moment.

Little by little she gained her strength back and was able to walk around and leave the apartment for short periods of time wearing a bob-and-bang wig and oversized dark sunglasses in Anna Wintour's style. Her right eye was still closed and she didn't want anybody to notice that. We were told to massage the lazy eyelid every day, and we did. A month had passed by and there was no change. We were all getting worried, but we never let Zohreh feel it.

"The nerves need time to heal. It takes at least a couple of months," we told her. She started going back to work and socializing with her newly acquired look. "If the editor of *Vogue* magazine can walk around and go to parties like this, so can I. I own that look for now." She was happy she was alive and well enough to take care of her kids and hopeful her eye would heal.

Months went by and still there was no change. Her doctor suggested an eye surgery to lift the eyelid. Zohreh was upset and angry. "No one talked about a damaged eye before my brain surgery."

"Zohreh, please look at the big picture," Fariborz pleaded, "you are alive and well enough to be with your young kids and go on with your everyday life."

"My vision is horrible, I can't drive. I am a designer and I can't see three dimensional."

She underwent a painful surgery to fix the eye. It helped, but not 100%. The eye opened, but not 100%. Zohreh was better, but not 100%. She could see with both eyes, though they didn't look even. She learned to fix that issue with the magic of makeup. But her eye and her vision would remain her biggest challenge in the years to come.

Our Changing Lives in the United States

"I grew up with six brothers. That's how I learned to dance—waiting for the bathroom." —Bob Hope

New York, 1997-2006

I took a deep breath and said, "Guys, I have news for you, I am pregnant. You are going to have another brother or sister."

Justin, Stephen and Camy turned and stared at me in shock. The three boys were in the back seat of my Suburban; Justin and Stephen on either side and Camy in the middle. We were on our way from Great Neck to Manhattan to spend the day with the cousins and have lunch at the famous Jekyll & Hyde restaurant. I'd been watching them in the rearview mirror, waiting for the right moment to break the news.

They were busy talking and Stephen was teasing his 6-year-old brother as usual. It was his favorite pastime. He played practical jokes on him, taught him curses, tickled him and wrestled with him. Camy was Stephen's favorite toy and punching bag.

"Camy, how many bad words do you know?" he asked while poking him.

"Stephen, stop! Mom, tell him to stop."

"Camy, c'mon, tell me one. I will give you your Gameboy back if you say one."

"Mom, it's my Gameboy!" Camy yelled.

"One word," Stephen said. "One curse word."

While most parents would threaten to turn the car around or ask them to keep quiet, I took it in and enjoyed what I was looking at. To me any interaction was better than no interaction. There was an undercurrent of love, attention, and connection there underneath the teasing. It made me smile, but I didn't let any of them see it.

When Stephen heard the announcement he stopped tickling his brother, looked at Justin from the corner of his eyes, placed his hands over his mouth and said with a mischievous smile, "Justin, that means mom and dad had sex."

"Why did you have to get pregnant again?" Justin said, shaking his head in disbelief.

I ignored Stephen's comment and said, "I really don't know why, Justin."

"Is it a brother or a sister?" Camy asked. "When will it come? Can I bother him the way Stephen bothers me?"

"I don't know yet. We will find out soon, Cameron."

Justin shook his head and looked out the window of the car, probably thinking, *My parents are crazy, having a baby at this age.* Justin was 14 going on 34. He was an old soul. He never did anything without thinking it through, weighing the situation thoroughly, and relying on his common sense. He was a perfect student and a serious teenager. He approached everything and everybody with a kind heart. If it didn't make sense to him or it wasn't the right thing to do, he was not interested.

Stephen was 17 months younger but in a completely different world. The two brothers were day and night, black and white, north and south. Stephen was easy-going, a free spirit, a daredevil and a funny boy. He was the clown of his class. He was open to any suggestion or idea. He had a way with connecting with people. He made friends easily and had fun with everyone.

Our house was a hangout place for all his friends. There was a constant traffic of teenage kids throughout our house, which I loved. The constants were Stephen's friends Brett, Benji, and Roxy. Stephen and Brett were inseparable; they did everything and went everywhere together. Brett had learned key Persian words which he used on a regular basis at our house.

Cameron was only 6 years old. He was a cute boy with a round face and a headful of curly hair. He looked like the male version of Shirley Temple. He was a stubborn boy and wouldn't give up until he got what he wanted. Everything around him was a source of curiosity. He jumped from one question to another. At times, I had to bribe him to stay quiet so I could get 10 minutes of much-needed peace.

I was happy and content. With all three kids in school full-time I had some much-needed freedom after years of having small kids at home. The idea of being pregnant at age 38, then changing diapers and going through sleepless nights again, was a nightmare. The thought of looking for playdates at age 40 was ridiculous to me and not something I looked forward to.

My newfound freedom had been short-lived. I felt miserable with my all-day morning sickness. What was I supposed to do with an infant? I have been there, done that, three times, in my early 20s and 30s! Never thought I would do it again in my early 40s.

For 9 months I walked around depressed and counted down the days. Until New Year's Eve of 1997, when Jordan was born. He was a beautiful baby with deep blue eyes. He brought happiness with him and became everyone's new toy. I started my long sleepless nights of feeding, changing diapers, and buying formula again. I hired help at home, continued on working in the city part time and rushing home every day to do the carpools and be with the kids. Justin, Stephen and Camy played with Jordan after school until I got home around 4.

I was not ready to give up the feeling of professional achievement followed by the side order of satisfaction from my work. I needed that extra dose of adrenaline and connection with people outside of my immediate household. I was convinced I could do both and keep a balance. *So what if I am a bit exhausted*, I thought, *It's worth the challenge and the great feeling of accomplishment.* But it wasn't easy.

My husband was busy at work and didn't see any reason for me working at the stores. His mindset was: If I wanted to be out of the house and working I'd better be ready, willing, able, and prepared. It was my decision to work. We didn't need the money, he was a good provider after all. It was on me to handle the household and juggle everything.

Justin and Stephen noticed my balancing act, how I was running around taking care of everything and trying to keep everyone happy. They wanted to make it easier for me, they wanted to help. They decided to get involved and took charge with their younger brothers. They played with Jordan and helped Camy with his homework when I was not around. They became my understudies when I was absent.

Evenings were my favorite part of the day. We were all in the den, everyone doing their own thing under the same roof and in-between the same four walls. One was studying, the other busy with a project, Camy was watching Nickelodeon, Jordan was playing with his toys and I was in and out helping them while preparing dinner.

Every Sunday afternoon and Monday evening it was time for Jackie to sit in the den in his usual spot, directly in front of the TV, on the corner of the brown leather sofa with a large glass of fresh-brewed Persian tea and a plate of sweet dates next to him and watch the football game with the boys. By half-time the testosterone level at our house reached its peak. Justin and Stephen picked Jordan up and used him as a "human ball" in the den, throwing him to each other and running around with him. This drove everyone crazy (especially my father, if he was there). But I was surprisingly comfortable with it. I loved watching them in action. With every throw Jordan burst into laughter.

"It's my turn, it's my turn. Let me throw him. Justin, please, my turn!" Camy begged while running after them.

On family vacations we either went in tribes, with 10 other families, or just the six of us. Either way we had fun. When we went away in a large group, each kid ended up having friends his or her age and they played and had fun together all day. At night, we usually took over a local restaurant and came in with our own playlists of music, turning a quaint place into a nightclub. There was no age barrier; toddlers, kids, adults, everyone danced with everyone else, on the floor, on the table, or on the bar. We included all the guests and the employees. It was a big party and everyone was invited.

My love of dance made me the DJ, in charge of music. When it was time to change the CD, I stood back and separated myself from the crowd, watching and taking it all in. I looked at my boys and their happy faces, dancing and jumping up and down with their friends, and thought, *This must be heaven. This is heaven. Why do people want to die and then see the paradise? It's all here, right in front of us. Nothing could possibly feel or be more beautiful or perfect than this.* Looking back, those busy years were my happiest.

Fariborz was never included in any of our family vacations. He was working hard. We were all proud of him. Our mother's face would light up when she talked about her son. "He has excelled in whatever he has touched," she said with pride. "Wait and see, he will be one of the best neurosurgeons in the country." The only son was her greatest source of happiness.

When he was ready to settle down and start a family, my mom's friends sent frequent messages to her in hopes of match-making. He dated a few girls with very little success until he met Jennifer on a blind date. He liked her right away, and she fell in love with him at the first hello. Jennifer was an American girl from Virginia. She was skinny, tall with fair skin. They started seeing each other frequently. She was working in a trading company as a stockbroker and he had two more years of residency. After a few months, he broke the news to our mom. "Momon, I want to arrange for a dinner or lunch for you to meet my girlfriend Jennifer."

"You are serious about her?"

"Yes, very serious."

"But you know very well that the Persian mentality and an American one do not mix." She was clearly disappointed. "The result is never good. It never works."

"But you can't say that without meeting her. You will like her if you give her a chance."

"I have seen enough to know. Look at my brother's wife," she sighed, referring to a troubled marriage that had caused much gossip in the community. "Everyone told him not to marry her. Look at what happened. She divorced him with five kids after cheating on him."

"You can't use your brother as an example. She was up to no good from day one."

"I am not happy with this match. You need to marry a Persian Jewish girl. Birds of the same feather flock together."

My father stayed out of it; he didn't want the headache. Fariborz didn't give up; he was in love and wanted her blessing. It wasn't just Momon; we all tried to talk him out of it. We had seen enough divorces to know that the two cultures were not fit for each other.

Fariborz felt at ease with Jennifer and loved her unconditionally, so he persisted. He took us out to dinner with her and tried to prove to us that she was the one, that she had all the qualities he was looking for, that she was as good as any Persian girl. Jennifer learned a couple of key sentences in Persian, she was full of compliments, and was very kind to my mom. Most importantly, she made Fariborz happy. Even though she wasn't a bird of the same feather, she was a bird after all.

My brother proposed and they got married on October 25th, 1997. Jennifer was now one of the sisters. Our new sister worked on Wall Street and our brother was affiliated with Lenox Hill Hospital. He became a star surgeon in a short time, the one everyone respected. He was known as the doctor with a heart. He never gave up on a patient or treated any of them as a case number. His philosophy was, "As long as there is a breath left, there is hope."

His friends all entrusted their families to him. Phil, one of his best friends, came to him with his mother. She was in extreme pain and no doctor wanted to touch her case. Fariborz operated to remove an encapsulated tumor at the base of her brain and gave her 5 more years of healthy life. A few years later he operated on Phil's back and removed a degenerative disc, which allowed him to walk and work out with no pain. The most amazing case was Phil's cousin; Fariborz operated on his spine through his mouth when everyone else had given up on him.

Where the rest of the surgeons saw an operation as pointless, my brother proved them wrong. He performed surgeries on people that were left with no hope and had been rejected by every other doctor. Most of the time they ended up in a rehab facility instead of the morgue.

"A life is a life. You can't put a value on it based on their bank account. Any person in agony should be able to wake up in the morning and live a pain-free and meaningful life with his or her family."

The staff at his daughter's school, neighbors, doormen, relatives, friends—all came to him for consultation or any medical concern. When a child needed simple stitches his number was the one they dialed first. They knew they would get immediate attention.

"I want to be able to sleep at night," he used to say, "knowing that I have done my absolute best."

He was respected and loved by the staff, the nurses, the interns, the janitors, the receptionists, and the physicians at the hospital. He treated them all the same, with respect and kindness. He was, in fact, a real-life Dr. McDreamy in that hospital.

He diagnosed Zohreh with meningitis when her own doctor overlooked it. In the 15 years since her first frightening surgery, our sister had undergone several more operations and tons of procedures and tests in between. Her tumors grew randomly, like mushrooms. Her brain was a minefield; no one knew what was hidden, where. The scary and devastating phrase "We have to cut open your skull" had become as routine as "Let's do a blood test" to her.

A week after her fifth and last brain surgery, she was complaining of a severe headache. Dr. Sicktine (we chose that name for him), the neurosurgeon who had performed the surgery, told her as we sat in his office, "Of course you have a headache, what do you expect? You just had a major brain surgery! Go home and relax."

"But I am in agony," she insisted.

"There is not much I can do. Take a painkiller," he said and walked towards the door.

I ran to stop him and started yelling, "You are not a doctor, you are a heartless and cold-blooded man. You don't deserve that white uniform. Help my sister, she is suffering."

He took a step back in shock and said, "Please leave now."

That same evening when Fariborz came to visit Zohreh at her apartment, he noticed that her balance was off. "This is not normal, she is wobbling. By now she shouldn't have a headache either. Something is seriously wrong."

He grabbed her and rushed to the hospital. She would have died in 24 hours from meningitis in her spine had she stayed home and "relaxed" that night.

And that wasn't the only time he saved one of our family member's lives. He was next to our father at every one of his visits to the doctor for his health issues and, later on, his dementia and eventual diagnosis of Alzheimer's disease. He stayed next to our mother at the hospital day in and day out when she fell and broke her spine. He adored our mother and had great respect for her. He took care of her and fussed over her constantly. He named a rose garden in his Connecticut home after her and made a beautiful sign dedicating the flowers to her. My mother was overjoyed with pride. She looked at her only son with admiration and gratitude, hugged him and kissed him with tearful eyes.

Fariborz was on his way to a great future. His reputation and practice were expanding. He found a beautiful townhouse on East 78th Street with the help of his good friend Dr. Diego Herbstein, a neurologist. He started negotiating, financing, renovating, and designing the space with Zohreh's help.

He loved what he did and did what he loved. He had partners in his practice but he was in charge of most of the decision-making. His colleagues trusted him, listened to him, and followed him. Everyone loved the new office space, which Zohreh had done a great job designing and decorating. Fariborz entered the new location every morning as if he was entering the White House, with pride and hope for a better day for every person who walked in to be treated.

Though Fariborz was working long hours, he was also involved in his kids' lives. He encouraged Alexa to play tennis at a very young age. Jennifer was an excellent tennis player and she became a side coach. He always made it to her tennis matches. He cheered for her and after the game they dissected every forehand and backhand with "love."

Ava was three years younger. She was an active baby, the kind that couldn't sit still. As she grew, her vigor translated into a love of gymnastics. She cartwheeled her way around the apartment, the sidewalk, the park, or any flat surface. Fariborz's life consisted of taking care of his patients, his family and people that he loved.

The years were flying by, with everyday joys and problems.

During Justin's college years in Michigan the number-one thing my kids missed the most was our Sunday family dinner ritual. Justin and Stephen kept it up by texting each other during commercials while watching *The Simpsons* or football games. They discussed the episode and went over every stupid but fun quote—especially those by Homer.

Stephen joined Justin in Ann Arbor for the major football games, while Justin flew out to see his brother and meet his new friends at Boston University. "Mom, you don't understand. We were sitting at the bar and we couldn't finish one conversation. We were interrupted every 10 seconds. People walked over to say hello, shake his hand, say a few words, have a few laughs—then they hugged or gave each other high-fives and left."

"Stephen loves people," I said.

"And people love him. It was amazing. I was thinking who is the older brother? Him or me? I should learn from him."

"It's very simple, most people want to be approached," I said, "because it is difficult and intimidating for them to be the approacher. It's out of people's comfort zone. If you are able to break the ice, and make the first move, almost everyone would welcome you," I said. "He just naturally does that, and it feels genuine."

"Yes, he is the Big Man on Campus. The one everyone wants to hang out with," Justin continued. "When Stephen introduced me to his friends, they told me stories of how they met and how nice he was to them. At parties or get-togethers, Stephen walked over, introduced himself and included them in his group and their conversation."

"See, you don't need any skills for that," I said.

"We really had the best time together. Stephen owns BU." He said, "I am glad I went."

It was January of 2007.

During Stephen's sophomore year at Boston University, I decided to legally change the spelling of his name. I had chosen his first name when I saw a book in Barnes and Noble by Stephen King, not realizing that the "ph" would be pronounced "V" and not "F" in the United States. Almost everyone called him "Steven," and nothing annoyed him more. He wanted to be called "Stefen," and he corrected everyone on every occasion.

"If I wanted to be called Steven I would have spelled it with a V! It's pronounced *Stefen*," he told everyone. I knew how adamant he was, so I applied to officially change the spelling of his name. I called him the day I received the proper documents.

"Guess what? You are officially Stefan from now on," I said over the phone.

"What do you mean mom?"

"It's changed legally. I just received the papers for it. The name on your graduation papers will be Stefan Adelipour, and you will be starting your job and your life with that name. No one will ever call you Steven."

"That's great, thanks!" he said with excitement. "Mom, just wait and see, I'll work so hard and be so successful. I'll build skyscrapers and name them after our family. If anyone Googles me, pages and pages of information will come up. I can't wait to graduate. I have so many plans for my future, so many dreams. You will be proud of me." He took a deep breath. "Thanks, I love you, mom."

"I have no doubt in my mind that you will be successful. You will graduate soon, keep in mind that sky is the limit for you. This is the best country in the world. It is the land of every opportunity," I said. "*Ghorboonet Beram* (I sacrifice myself for you). I am proud of you already. By the way, I changed your name legally to 'Stefan,' but you will always be 'Stephen' to me."

Family trips remained our favorite and it was much easier now that Jordan was almost 5. The most memorable one was during the summer of 2003 when we rented an old villa in a small village called Montespertolli in the suburbs of Florence. The charming villa had a terrace overlooking the vineyards and olive trees. The owner of the house, Anna, was a lovely and warm Italian woman. We became good friends almost the minute we met. She hardly spoke any English and back then, I only knew a bunch of Italian phrases. *I should pick Italian up besides my French lessons so I could communicate with her*, I thought. Her family owned 12 villas and acres and acres of vineyards and olive trees from generations back. The compound was called La Gigliola. It was exactly what you would see in the movies and post cards. We were indeed "Under the Tuscan Sun."

Every evening we watched the magnificent sunset behind the hills of never-ending rows of grapevines. The tall and proud Cypress trees surrounded the driveways and villas. The scent of lavender and earth filled up our lungs when the gardens were hosed down. The roosters crowed at the crack of dawn and the birds chirped all day. We sat with our newfound Italian friends and sipped Anna's house wine after dinner.

It was so heavenly that I grieved for each day that passed. *If I could only put a stick inside of the clock of this world so it wouldn't move forward so fast!* I thought.

Early in the morning, I walked to *il centro* of the small town and bought freshly baked bread, sweet red tomatoes, and homemade cheese. I unwrapped everything on the wooden kitchen table, played my favorite Italian music, and started making breakfast. The aroma of the ripe tomatoes mixed with the warm bread filled up the kitchen.

Next I had to get my eggs from the chicken coop. I tiptoed to the chickens with my basket and apologized to each and every one as I took their future babies away from them. "So sorry, *mi dispiace*, I am so so sorry my dear chickens, but you will have more tomorrow morning. It is not that you had to carry them for 9 months! Laying eggs is not so bad, is it? I mean you guys have it easy. Look at us! It would have been so much easier if we could give birth while our children were safely in an aerodynamic container with no labor pain. Don't you think? You will get over it soon. You can't tell them apart anyway. Your babies all look the same! I am so sorry, forgive me. One more egg and I am done."

I set the table on the terrace and made a heartbreaking but delicious omelette. We sat and talked around the table and enjoyed every bite of that one-hundred-percent fresh and organic breakfast.

Jack returned to New York after 10 days. I had invited Nahid and Zohreh to join me. We drove to nearby towns and villages through miles and miles of sunflower fields on an almost-daily basis. We cooked with Anna or went to local restaurants in the neighborhood.

On one of those trips to Forte Dei Marmi, a charming town on the water, one of Anna's friends, Michele, started singing Italian love songs while driving. I looked around at my kids in the car and then at the magnificent view surrounding us, turned to Zohreh and said, "Zohreh, do you realize where we are? Do you see how perfect everything is? Look at the field of flowers, listen to that heavenly voice, take in the fresh air, can it get any better than this?"

The years had taken a toll on Zohreh, with the threat of tumors constantly hanging over her head. Still, we were happy with the fact that they were benign, and Zohreh could go to her office and take care of her kids and live a normal life after a few months of fearful pause. For now, she was tumor-free and there were no surgeries in her immediate future. I was happy she was there to enjoy the beauty of life and we could see a smile on her face. She looked at the sunflower fields from the window of the car and said, "I was thinking the same thing."

"I am telling you, this is as good as it gets. Take it in, bottle it, engrave it in your brain."

"My brain has been engraved upon on numerous occasions already!" she replied with a smirk, watching the view. Nahid and I looked at each other from the corner of our eyes. She was right. She didn't have it easy.

We drove to the beach, swam and had a delicious lunch in a restaurant on the beach facing the beautiful water. We sipped on local wine and took bites of the homemade desserts while our feet were touching the warm and soft sand. The tables and chairs were painted in a bright and deep shade of blue. They were placed in the middle of tall canopies complete with sheer white curtains. With each breeze the curtains flew up and started a dreamy dance against the blue sky and the ocean.

It was a gorgeous day… but all too soon we had to leave and return to regular life.

My sisters and I left for New York together, but we left our hearts with Anna and La Gilgiola. Those three and half weeks in Italy with my family are among the most beautiful and magical times of my life. At home, we woke up to normal problems every day, the ones we could handle or dodge.

For his semester abroad Stephen decided to go with his friends to Australia. "How come Australia, Stephen?"

"I want to go to places that I have never been and seen. Australia is different and interesting. Plus, it will be warm there while it's cold on the east coast and in Europe."

"I guess you are right. I always wished I had a few years on my own before being married. I would have liked the opportunity to experience life free of obligations and limitations."

"A bunch of us want to go to Australia. When I am done with my semester, I will travel to Cambodia, Vietnam, Thailand and whatever other country I can get my hands on."

"By yourself? Why?"

"No one else can come with me. I don't want to miss out on the opportunity. I'm on that side of the world anyway. I'll get the special package for students and take the train everywhere. Mom, what are the chances that I'll end up on that side of the world again?"

"I don't know, 'plenty,' as you always say. Stephenjoon, get someone to go with you, please."

"I will try, but if I can't find anyone, I am going regardless."

He left for Australia in January of 2006. He emailed us on a continuous basis. He brought tears to my eyes with one specific email, thanking us for being great parents, allowing and trusting him to travel and do as he wished.

"By giving me wings and trusting me, I do not have the urge to do anything behind your back. There are kids here trying any drug they can get their hands on, or they get so drunk that they pass out on the street. I watch them and think to myself, I don't have the urge to do any of that stuff, I don't feel like I have gotten out of captivity. If I do or don't do something, it is because of my love and respect for you guys and then love and respect for myself. Thank you for trusting me."

I read that email numerous times and thanked God for giving me a mature and wise boy. *This one, I do not have to worry about,* I thought.

He came back from those trips with tons of stories. He had talked to anyone that could put two English words together. He asked about their lives, their jobs, their families. He sat next to them on the sidewalks, benches, coffee shops and just talked.

"Mom, I look at life differently now. I don't take anything for granted. We are very lucky to have this life, each other, and our health. People are so *badbakht* (miserable) it breaks my heart."

"Very true."

"They live and die without knowing what happiness or even a good meal is."

He was passionate and curious about people, it didn't matter if it was his own brother or a homeless person on the sidewalk.

"They need validation and significance as much as they need food and shelter," he would tell me when we passed the homeless in the streets of Manhattan. He was famous among his friends for leaving them and sitting next to a less fortunate person and carrying on a conversation with him or her, asking questions and showing himself genuinely interested in their lives.

For the Christmas holidays of 2006 and New Year's of 2007, we traveled to St. Martin with our friends, Zohreh and her two kids. We spent days by the pool and nights dancing to my playlist on the tables at the restaurants. Our pictures from that trip speak of happiness and laughter. Justin, Stephen, Camy, and Jordan were jumping up and down with their friends.

It was a short-lived happiness. When we returned to the hotel, Zohreh pulled me aside and said, "Come to the bathroom with me."

"What's wrong?"

"You will see."

We walked back to her room and as soon as we stepped into the bathroom she put her fingers into her hair and then opened her fist in front of me. I looked at her hand in horror. A thick piece of black hair was resting in her hand. She slid her fingers again and another bunch came out. I looked at her head and saw bald spots in random places. In a matter of a few minutes the sink was full of black hair that only moments before had been on her head.

I couldn't hide the horror on my face.

"Oh my God, why is this happening?"

"I don't know, it started a few hours ago while we were dancing. I wanted to put my hair up in a bun and I saw that it is coming out in bunches. I got so scared I stopped touching my hair until we got back here."

"It's too late to call Fariborz now."

"I know, I'm going bald. Please don't tell anyone, I don't want to ruin this vacation for everyone. The last thing I want is worried eyes staring at me. I will wear a hat for the remainder of the trip."

"It must be a side effect of one of your medications."

At that moment, in the bathroom of our hotel room, looking at the sink filled with long black hair and her balding head, I was beyond sad; I was devastated. This could have happened two days later when she was home and her vacation was over. But the universe had to test her again. She was happy to be away with her kids and her friends. She was enjoying every minute of those glorious days in St. Martin. But now she was reminded yet again, "Hey, don't get too comfortable, your battle is not over yet. We have other challenges for you, major ones. Get ready to receive some serious punches, the kind that would knock you out completely."

She started the New Year with a newfound fear, but the next day Zohreh and I both tried very hard to put on a happy face. We avoided groups, found a secluded area, sat on the beach and watched the waves. We both knew that she had another major challenge ahead of her. She had called Fariborz and he had told her that as soon as she was back she had to go for an MRI. Zohreh was worried and scared.

That trip was a short preview of what was coming next. God had planned it very well. Talk about efficiency and being sneaky—he not only ruined the vacation for Zohreh and me, he took priceless time and memories away from me being with my son. Soon after everything changed.

Tragic News

"When we are no longer able to change a situation—we are challenged to change ourselves." —Viktor E. Frankl

February, 2007

When the third week in February rolled around—the annual winter break in New York City public schools—our vacation destination choice was obvious. We were going skiing in the picture-perfect snowy town of Megeve in France and to meet Anna in Florence afterwards. My husband was not a big fan of skiing and cold weather. He decided to stay home.

I picked up Cameron and Jordan from school Friday afternoon, called a taxi, placed the luggage in the trunk, made sure I had everything, stood in the doorway of the empty and quiet house, smiled, closed the doors behind me, and headed towards JFK airport. I had a policy: before every trip, I tried to take care of every loose end, pay off anyone to whom I might owe money, and call each of my kids and siblings to say goodbye. First I called Justin, who was at work at Goldman Sachs, "Hi Justin, guys—say hi to Justin," I said to Cameron and Jordan.

"Hi Justin," they shouted into the speakerphone.

"Are you on your way to the airport? How nice. Sorry can't talk much, I am stuck at work. Have a great time. I'll miss you guys," he said.

"We will miss you too Justinjoon, I wish you could come with us." Next was Stephen. "Hi Stephen, guys say hi to Stephen."

"Hi Stephen!" they shouted in unison.

"How are you Stephenjoon? How is school?" I asked.

"School is always good. But skiing in Europe sounds better. You know, I could have come with you, I have couple of days off," he said.

"Why didn't you tell me earlier?" I asked.

"I didn't even think about it. I didn't realize it was Washington's birthday. Now I have nothing to do, what a big mistake," he said.

"We could have been together."

"Next trip. Have a wonderful time. Love you mom. Love you guys," he said.

"Yes, there will always be a next trip," I said.

"Love you, Stephen," the kids shouted, then I broke the connection without realizing there would never be a "next" anything with him. That was the last time we heard his warm voice.

We landed in Geneva early Saturday morning. It was a sunny, cold, but comfortable day. We took a cab and went directly to our hotel in Megeve. We got to our room, took our clothes off, and went to bed. The room was small and cozy with a charming fireplace. Every wall, shelf, table and chair was carved out of massive pieces of dark brown wood. The view from the small window framed a pure winter wonderland of pine trees covered in snow. After four perfect, beautiful days of skiing, it was time to go to Florence on the overnight train.

We arrived in Florence early the next morning, walked to our hotel with our luggage, and checked in. The kids wanted to watch cartoons in Italian, but I could not wait to go and sit in a cafe and order cappuccino and cornetto and do some serious people-watching. We did exactly that. We sat there and analyzed and dissected every moving object in front of us. I called Anna and made plans to meet her for dinner.

On Saturday morning after breakfast I decided to go to a boutique a few blocks from our hotel and buy the beautiful Python bag that I'd been eying for days. I looked at my watch. It was exactly 11:00 am local time. "Camy, Jordan, wait for me right here at the hotel, I will be back in no more than thirty minutes," I said. They were glued to the television, watching *Sponge Bob Square Pants* in Italian. "Did you hear me?" I demanded. "Camy, take care of your brother."

"OK, mom." Several minutes later I entered the store, placed two Python bags next to each other on the counter and examined both minutely with extreme excitement. I finally chose one and took my prized possession back to the hotel. We hit the streets again, bought an Italian gelato, watched the street artists paint on the sidewalks, listened to random people singing beautiful Italian love songs, and bargained with the vendors on the streets.

At the end of our day I sent an email to Justin and asked him if there would be someone at the airport to pick us up the next day. "Can you or dad come?" I asked.

"Someone will be there." His answer was short and brief. Almost too short and too brief. I sent longer emails to him and Stephen describing our trip. Justin answered with a "yes" or "no" or "great;" Stephen didn't respond at all. It was out of character for them both. But total optimist that I was, I thought, *They are probably too busy.*

For our last night in Florence, I had invited my Italian friends to a dinner in a local restaurant. We talked, ate, drank and laughed until late.

The next day we were on our flight back to New York. I was in my window seat as always looking at the blue sky, thinking, *It was a beautiful trip. Too bad I have to wait another year to do this again.* We watched a couple of movies on the plane, ate our Swiss chocolates, talked about the trip and school, and took a nap until we landed in New York. It was an ordinary flight.

The plane pulled over to the gate slowly and stopped. The passengers stood up at once and started looking for their belongings in the overhead compartments. The flight attendant opened the door and before anyone could leave the plane, an announcement came over the speakers:

"Miss Soheila Adelipour, walk to the front please. Miss Soheila Adelipour, walk to the front please." And life as we knew it ended in that instant.

Camy looked at me and said, "Why are they asking you to go to the front? Something bad has happened."

"Don't be negative, Camy. Nothing bad has happened. They probably have a question."

"Mom, something bad has happened. I know," he said.

"Miss Soheila Adelipour, please walk to the front of the plane and introduce yourself," the announcement came again.

"Mom, I am worried," Camy said.

"Don't worry, Camyjoon," I said, "let's go and find out." The three of us walked to the front of the plane.

"Hi, I am Soheila Adelipour," I said.

"Hello, these two gentlemen are waiting for you," the flight attendant said, pointing to her right. I turned and saw two uniformed police officers standing by the airplane door. Camy grabbed my arm and said, "I told you mom, something bad has happened."

"Can I help you, officers?" I asked.

"Hello Mrs. Adelipour, can you please follow us?" one of them said in a very kind voice.

"Is there a problem?" I asked.

"We are here to escort you out," the other officer said.

"But why? Why do I need to be escorted out?" I asked.

"Give us the stubs for your luggage please, we will take care of the bags for you," he continued without addressing my questions. I looked for my boarding pass with the stub for the luggage attached to it in my purse and handed it over. My heart was pounding. I could not understand why I couldn't go through immigration and collect our luggage myself.

"Now can you please follow us?" he said.

"Follow you where?" I asked in confusion.

"You have to go through immigration, right? We will make it quick for you."

"Officer, why are you here? Please answer me. Why do we have to be escorted out?" I asked.

"You know, ma'am, your brother has been there for us whenever we asked for his help. He has been there for the NYPD whenever we needed medical attention; he has even been there for our families when they had health issues. Now it's our turn to pay him back for all his kindness. He asked us to assist you and walk you quickly through customs and that's what we are here to do."

It was obvious that they were not going to give me any further information, so we just kept quiet and walked the long corridors behind them. We reached the passport control area, where the room was packed with people. Long lines snaked in every direction. It reminded me of a box of worms, each one crawling and moving on top of the other in harmonious speed. The two police officers went straight to the last window, avoiding every line and every tired passenger. We followed silently behind them.

"Can I have your passports please?" one of them asked.

"Yes, yes, of course." I reached in my bag and handed him our passports. He took the three passports from us and handed them to the immigration officer.

The officer didn't look up. He took the stamper and without comparing our faces to the photos, without asking any questions, without saying a word, stamped our passports while avoiding our gaze and handed them back. *He is avoiding us. He didn't look up,* I thought. At that moment I knew for sure that something horrible had happened. Whatever it was, they all knew and we didn't. My knees started trembling. I did not take another step forward.

"Please tell me what's wrong," I begged.

"Your son is waiting for you outside." The cop pointed towards the exit sign and started walking. We had no choice but to follow. We walked by the luggage area, past the exit to the street, towards the elevators. "Mom, what is wrong? Why are we going this way?" Camy asked.

"I don't know, Camyjoon."

There was Justin, standing by the elevators. I ran towards him and said, "Justinjoon, what is wrong? Why are these police officers here?"

"Nothing, mom, I had an accident and Khaleh (aunt) Nazee had to come and get me. It is a long story. Let's go up, I will tell you all about it."

I knew he was lying, he was avoiding my eyes. "Where is up?" I said. "Why up?"

"Mrs. Adelipour, this gentleman will collect your luggage for you," one of the police officers said, and gave the tickets to a man in a black suit. I was watching Justin from the corner of my eye. He was taking deep breaths and was extremely nervous. He had tears in his eyes but was fighting to keep them back. He was pale as a ghost. I had never seen Justin like that. We all walked into the elevator, got off the next floor and walked towards a dark room.

I had never known there were chapels at airports.

We stepped inside to face an unimaginable reality. I looked in confusion at my brother, my sisters Nahid, Zohreh and Nazee; my niece and nephew Roya and Arya; all dressed in black, sitting on the benches, crying. They all stood up as soon as they heard us enter. "What's wrong? What is happening? Somebody, anybody, say something," I begged, my eyes going from one familiar sad face to the next.

Fariborz walked towards me and held me tight. I thought to myself, *Our father has probably passed away. That is why they are dressed in black. But why are they here?*

Fariborz started crying out loud. Between breaths he said, "Soheilajon, Stephen is not with us anymore." I looked around me and then at Camy and Jordan. They just stared at Fariborz. None of us understood at that moment what that phrase meant. I saw Roya take Jordan's hand and together they left the chapel.

Justin threw himself at me and started sobbing on my shoulder. "Mom, Stephen is gone. He died yesterday morning." I looked at Nahid, then Nazee, then Zohreh for an explanation, or maybe for correction. But all I saw was confirmation in their sad faces. I fell to my knees and screamed, "No, NO, what are you saying? It can't be. It can't be."

"Mom, Mom, please, please," Justin pleaded, "don't do this. Mom, he is gone. Stephen is gone." He was shaking and crying.

I kept hitting the floor with my fist and crying out loud, "No, no, Stephenjoon, my baby, it is not true. Stephen, *Ghorboonet beram*, where are you?" I got up and started running hysterically around the room and screaming "Where is he? Where is Stephen?" My brother followed me with a syringe in his hand. He grabbed me and held me tight.

"Justin, help me." Justin held my arm and pulled my sleeve up.

"Leave me alone, leave me alone, I want to see Stephen!"

"Soheilajon (my dear Soheila), please calm down. This will help you. Please stay still," Fariborz said in his kind voice.

"No, it's not true," I cried, "Fariborz, tell me it is not true, Please, I beg you. Stephen, where are you?"

My brother held onto my arm with Justin's help and injected me with the drug. They were both shaking and sobbing, but wouldn't let go of me. I was sandwiched in between them and little by little started feeling numb.

While they were keeping me still, I saw Camy on the chair with his head down, crying. I turned to Justin and looked into his sad eyes. *My poor kids. My poor, poor kids. This is not fair to them,* I thought. I shook loose from my brother and Justin's arms and walked slowly towards Camy. I knelt down in front of him, asked Justin to come close, held on to their hands, took a deep breath, gathered all my courage together and said, "Listen to me, stay strong, we will get through this. I promise you. Life goes on. Camyjoon, look at me, we are still a family."

Justin held me tight and started weeping again. "Mom, I love you, thank you for saying this. Mom, I love you."

Camy didn't make a move.

"No Justinjoon, I am still here. I am your mom and I am telling you; we will get through this together." We sat on the floor, cried together and held on to each other. For how long? I had no idea.

It seemed as if everything was moving in slow motion and a thick fog had blurred my view. The world was in shades of grey and black. Even outside, on the busy sidewalks of JFK, things were moving in a strange way. I looked around me, thinking, *This is a nightmare. I will wake up soon and sigh with relief when I see I am still in my bed and this whole thing has been a bad dream.* My sisters were crying, Fariborz was crying, but I had stopped. I refused to believe that this was my reality.

My kind, handsome and perfect son is gone forever and I never got to hug him and say good-bye to him. He disappeared. He vanished. He ceased to exist. I can't touch him anymore. I can't kiss him anymore.

I can't hear his voice anymore. Every mother carries a baby for nine months, goes through labor pains, gives birth, suffers through sleepless nights, puts his needs in front of hers, takes care of him day and night, fusses over him, cries when he cries, kisses his booboos away, loves him to death, all in hopes of raising a good human being. I was lucky, I achieved that goal—but in a second he was taken away from me. Gone forever.

We got into Nazee's car and pulled away. No one said a word. I broke the deafening silence, "How did it happen?"

Fariborz took a deep breath and said, "There was a fire in his building, around five yesterday morning." *My God, fire? He burnt to death? My beautiful Stephen was burnt to death?* I thought but did not verbalize. I did not want to create a permanent image in my kids' minds. Whatever that injection was had taken care of every ounce of emotion in me. I just sat in the car for the ride back home and visualized him in the middle of a fire. What had happened to my handsome son and his beautiful smile? He must have been so scared, scared and helpless. And no one was there to help him. He was trapped and he knew he was going to die. No, this is a nightmare, it can't be true. Still, I could not cry. Justin held on to me the whole ride back. Camy did not say a word.

The car pulled into our driveway. Fariborz held me as I was getting out of the car. I walked towards the entrance thinking, *Why can't this be like every other time that I've entered my house? Free of heartache and pain.* The driveway was filled with cars, cars I had never seen before. My sisters opened the door and I walked inside. I had left that empty house with a smile and now it was packed with people, dressed in black, sad. They looked at me but no one stepped forward. My mother saw me, ran towards me, threw herself into my arms, and started howling. I didn't make a move, I just looked at her and then looked at my sisters. They walked forward and pulled her away from me. I could still hear her sobs.

My husband was sitting on the couch covering his face with his hands. I couldn't take a step forward, I couldn't say a word. If I did, that would make it all real. I looked around the room—my in-laws, their kids, my nephew and nieces, my friends, Stephen's friends—everyone was dressed in black. They were either crying or trying to calm another family member. *This is not my home, and these people are not real,* I thought. *This whole thing is a bad dream, a horrible dream.* People walked over one by one and held me tight. I could feel their moist skin against mine. *If this is a dream, why do they feel so real?*

Nothing made sense. *This is not reality. It can't be reality. It is too final to be real,* I thought. I walked over and sat on the staircase, looking aimlessly at the crowd in front of me. Elysee, one of my closest friends sat next to me. Roxy, my son's classmate from childhood, whispered in my ear, "Stephen was my best friend, a unique and rare gem."

Was? I thought, *Past tense? We will use past tense from now on next to his name? After 22 years, he will be remembered and talked about only in past tense. What a waste of a young life.*

Brett, his closest friend, walked towards me. His eyes were swollen and red. He had probably been crying all night. He stood in front of me, held his head down, and then hugged me tight. "Oh Brett, what are we going to do? How can I go on living without his smile?"

"I miss him so much," he said, "We were inseperable. It is hard to believe. We can't have our laughs anymore." Roxy and Brett sat next to me. My heart ached for them.

I stayed motionless and emotionless on the staircase while people came forward one by one to pay their respects. No one knew what to say or what to do. But they tried their best. This was a tragedy for everyone in the community.

Justin was standing next to me and watching my every move. "Where is Camy?" I asked.

"His friends are all here. He is in his room. They are keeping him busy."

"Could you tell me, what exactly happened?" I asked.

"Mom, I don't want you to get more upset than this, I love you but I can't see you like this," he said as tears rolled down his face.

"But I have to know, Justinjoon," I said, "what happened?"

He wiped his tears with the back of his hand and said, "Stephen and his friends returned to their apartment from a party, apparently around three am. There was no electricity in the building. The water and power company was checking on something or fixing something in that area. They lit candles and stayed in. They hung out for about an hour, Stephen called a cab for the girls, made sure the cab was safe, said good-bye to them, came back up and went to bed. Apparently one of the candles fell over and the apartment caught on fire around five am. The roommate and his girlfriend were pronounced dead at the scene but they revived him, he is in the hospital now."

Five am? Five am in New York is eleven am in Italy, I thought. What was I doing at that time? I wanted to know if I felt anything, or saw a sign anywhere, when he passed. I thought back. I was at the bag store. I bought a python bag. No, I did not feel anything at 11am. Nothing seemed different. It was just a normal day. My son had died and I did not feel any disconnection or sign of his departure.

"Where is Stephen now?" I asked.

"Mom, please, I can't talk to you like this. Dad has been howling and sobbing all day yesterday. Don't…"

"Justinjoon, where is he? I have to know."

"They have transferred him here. He is in the funeral home." He started crying. "The police called dad on his cellphone. He was playing cards with his friends. He was so devastated that they had to drive him home. They called me, and I called your sisters and Fariborz. They have been here since yesterday. The news traveled fast. Everyone came here to help. They didn't know how to break the news to you." He took a deep breath and said, "We were afraid you would listen to your messages on your phone as soon as you get off the plane. Fariborz came up with the plan that the police officers take you directly to the chapel and calm you down with medication. We called the phone company and begged them to disconnect your services."

I looked around me. Fariborz was sitting on a couch, watching me while tears were rolling down his face. I smiled at him and sent him a kiss. He smiled a sad smile in return and stared at the floor.

My husband and my mother were weeping on opposite corners of the room. "Justin, please tell Nazee to come here." Nazee's face was covered in sorrow. We had never seen each other like this before. We had never faced a tragedy like this before.

"Nazee, please tell Momon to either cry in silence or take her to a different room." My sister knew exactly what I was talking about. Our mother's crying was a long, loud, sorrowful howling. The women of that generation would raise their hands and hit themselves in the heads or their faces for days when grieving. It was heart-wrenching and disturbing to see, and I was not able to deal with my pain and witness that too. I was trying to hold tears back and keep it together for my kids. That screech was daggers in my heart. Nazee, with Nahid's help, held our mom's arms and walked her out of the living room. Her cries grew fainter as she was led away.

Zohreh, meanwhile, stayed quiet in a corner. She had undergone her fifth brain surgery early in January—a week after we'd returned from our trip, which had been the last time I saw Stephen. He'd come to New York for Matthew's (Nazee's son's) birthday party. He stayed only for the weekend, I had stayed at the hospital both days. He called me at the hospital Monday morning.

"Mom, I am leaving for Boston early afternoon," he said.

"Oh no," I said, "I didn't even get to see you. I was with Khaleh Zohreh the whole time."

"Don't worry mom, I will drive to the city, spend half an hour with you and then leave," he said.

"Are you sure?" I said, "I don't want you to drive in the dark. Please leave the house earlier then. See you soon."

"I will. See you."

Zohreh was weak; the only thing she could do was talk. She jumped from one subject to the next. An hour later Stephen called me from the hallway of the hospital.

"Mom, I'm here. How is Khaleh Zohreh? I am scared to come in and see her. How does she look?" he asked.

"Half of her hair is shaved and her forehead is swollen but she is OK. You can come in," I whispered into the phone. Two minutes later, he was standing in the doorway, all smiles.

"Hi Khaleh Zohreh. How are you?"

"Hi Stephenjoon, I am good. Nice to see you." Zohreh said with a beaming smile.

"I like the new, cool hair style. Very edgy," he said.

"Yes, that's my style for now, 'edgy meets punk,'" she said.

We talked for a short time, mostly about school and life in Boston. Then it was time for him to leave. He got up, picked up his backpack, hugged and kissed me goodbye, sent a kiss and waved goodbye to Zohreh and left. I walked with him to the door and watched him walk to the elevators. That was the last time I touched my son.

Now, a month and half later, Zohreh was still not her old self. She wasn't confident when she spoke, so she kept quiet. For years, we had been worried sick about losing her every time she went under the knife. Then, in a second, we lost a young and healthy 22-year-old boy. What a cruel game.

Our friends and family stayed over till late hours. I was exhausted. I wanted everyone to go away, to disappear, but none of them had the heart to leave our grief-stricken family and return to their safe homes. Each one volunteered to help in different ways. One took Jordan to their house for a playdate, one went shopping at the supermarket, one was washing the dishes, another one was serving tea and coffee. I was on that staircase, frozen, looking but not seeing. I knew my smallest gesture or move was being watched by everyone. I gathered my energy and walked to my bedroom, closed the door behind me, sat on my bed and dialed Stephen's number. His warm and friendly voice came on, "Hi, this is Stephen... Please leave a message and I will call you back as soon as I can."

"Stephenjoon, I love you, my love, call me back. OK? Please. I beg you, call me back."

I kissed the phone and lay down on my bed, pressed my face in the pillow and wept. I had never felt such desolation. I was sobbing hard and rolling back and forth on my bed, calling out, "Stephen, Stephen, where are you? *Ghorboonet beram.* Come back. This whole thing is a lie. Come back, *Ghorboonet beram*, my love. Please, Stephen, please." I cried, howled, screamed, wailed, yelled, but deep down I knew it was useless. Nothing would bring him back.

I felt a gentle touch on my back. I looked around. It was my kind brother. I reached over and hugged him and we both started crying on each other's shoulders. He kept on repeating one phrase over and over—that night and for years to come, "I am so sorry Soheilajon, I am so sorry."

Existing

"The wound is the place where the light enters you." —Rumi

February, 2007

According to the Jewish law, the funeral should be held the day after the loved one passes, but since I was away and my family did not want to give me the news over the phone, Stephen's service was postponed until Monday morning. Our friends and family were on the phone calling the funeral home, the cemetery, the Rabbi, the flower shop...the flower shop! *I should have been ordering flowers for his graduation, not this,* I thought.

As that first interminable day wore on, our home became more and more crowded. Everyone in our community had heard the tragic news, but not everyone thought that coming to our house was allowed under the circumstances. They had reached out to close friends and family that were already in our house, gotten approval, and found the courage to come and share our pain. They felt much more at ease being there, with us, instead of waiting helplessly in their own homes.

Our friends wanted to be a source of support, they wanted to comfort us, do something, anything, but they also knew there was nothing to be done. The absolute worst had happened. A young member of the community had lost his life. Stephen was well-known in that small town. He was loved and respected. And now he was gone forever.

His friends from Boston University had chartered a bus and come to New York with one of their Deans, Mr. Daryl Deluca. He was supposed to graduate with them in less than two months. But instead of a diploma they had made a large collage with his pictures. Pictures of him in a Halloween costume, pictures from his travels abroad, pictures of him hugging his friends. They handed me a notebook filled with their fondest memories of my son. I walked towards the giant framed collage and touched and kissed each picture one by one.

I asked his friends to share their memories with me, "Guys, please tell me stories about him. Whatever comes to your mind."

Benji was one of my son's oldest friends. They had been classmates from kindergarten all the way through college. "He was the most popular guy on campus. He thought of everyone and was always there for you when you needed help," he said.

Rich, his roommate, added, "When we came back from our friends' birthday party Saturday morning around 3am, I told Stephen, 'My girlfriend has invited me over, but I can't go.' He asked me, 'Why can't you go?' I said, 'I don't have enough money for a cab.' He put his hands in his pocket and said, 'Here's a twenty, go, have a good time.' I took the money, called a cab and left. Had he not insisted on me going and given me the money, I would have been trapped in that fire as well. He saved my life indirectly by just being caring. By just being Stephen."

His good friend Eric from BU chimed in. "If he noticed a homeless guy, he would always buy a sandwich or a chocolate bar, sit down on the sidewalk next to him and start talking to him about his life. He loved people no matter who they were."

The stories went on and on. At times, we would laugh. But the sad part was that the conversation was, incredibly, all in the past tense. He had ceased to exist.

Brett and Roxy came forward and handed me a notebook. "We were looking around in his room and found this on his desk." Brett said, "Read this page."

It was Stephen's handwriting. It was a journal entry. I touched the words on the two pages gently and started reading it. He was talking to us from the other side,

> This entire trip from AUS working in a Restaurant + Hotel, then Viet, Camb, Thai. Nothing I ever have will be taken for granted. Everything will taste, feel, smell etc. better. with more thought as well. I realized family + friends is everything. Without them you can't enjoy anything from a view to a nice dinner. Doing shit alone all the time just sucks. I can't wait to tell them that. I was also thinking the other day to try to get something awsome for john's Bday but I can't think of anything. All I can think about is this speech in my head about an unspoken bond b/w us and how during his bar mitsvah my speech meant nothing b/c when you care about someone and
>
> that you love them you don't know what love is at the age of 12 I was just saying it because it sounded right. But now I know we were born still being raised by our parents still living in the house. But I learned it truly counts when your away from home, when you can truly rely on someone for help at anytime of day

It was the most heartbreaking thing I have ever read. How many twenty-two-year-olds would show such an outpouring of love for their brother?

"How did you find this?" I asked.

"We were just looking through the stuff on his desk. Not for anything in particular, whatever reminded us of him. We came across this page in his notebook. He must have written it when he was away in the far east." I took the notebook and kept it close to my heart all day.

Later, in the evening, Fariborz gave me a pill and said, "Take this, it will help you."

"What is it?" I asked.

"Xanax."

"Fariborz, you know I don't take drugs," I said.

"I know you don't take drugs, but you need help and this will calm you. I gave one to Jack as well. These are not normal circumstances. I will give you one every night, but just for 10 days. Xanax is addictive."

He placed the pill on the palm of my hand and handed me a glass of water, kissed me on my forehead, shook his head in disbelief and walked away. That was my first introduction to prescription drugs.

I went to bed and cried in silence. That was the beginning of many nights to come that I found refuge in sleep. I used to wake up from a bad dream and take a deep breath, happy to be awake; now I woke up to a horrible reality and couldn't breathe. There was no escaping from my real-life nightmare. I had peace of mind, some relief, and my life back, only when I was asleep.

The next morning felt like I was in a twilight zone. I didn't remember the events from the day before. Either I was confused, or what had happened was so horrifying that I refused to believe it as a reality. Our story had become people's worst nightmare. I walked around the house aimlessly. The picture collage was still leaning against the wall. I felt a sharp pain in my heart. *It is true, he is gone.* My knees started to shake. I collapsed on the cold floor and started weeping.

My sister Nahid and her daughter Lisa had stayed over our house. They ran towards me, held my arms and tried to pick me up from the floor. But I refused to move. I didn't want to. If my son was going to be buried that day, I wanted to be on the floor, on the ground.

I looked up at them. "He is gone, and I am still here? I was supposed to go first, then my children. He was such a good boy. How could this world be so cruel?" Tears were rolling down their faces, but they had no answers. No one did. It was indeed a cruel world.

They dragged me to the couch. "Soheila, don't do this to yourself," Nahid said, "you have to be strong for your kids, they need you. They look to you for strength."

"Today is a difficult day for all of you. Please Soheila, at least not in front of your kids," Lisa said.

Even in my daze I was conscious of the fact that my kids needed me as their rock. I knew they were looking at me for strength. I had known that even when I was under the influence of drugs the day before. I saw the horror on their faces. I felt their fear. I witnessed their broken hearts. But in these early hours of the morning, with no one around, I wanted to mourn for my son. I wanted to cry so hard so my gut would burst out. I wanted to punch the floor so severely that the earth would move. I wanted to howl so loud that the Gods could hear me. Why? Why such a good boy?

I went upstairs to his room. "Mom, don't you think it's a bit too late for redecorating my room?" I heard Stephen's voice in my ears.

I had bought a new bedroom set for him only the previous year. I wanted to surprise him. On one of his trips back home, he went upstairs to his room, saw the new furniture, and yelled from the top of the staircase with a big laugh, "Mom, don't you think it's a bit too late for redecorating my room?"

"Why do you think it's too late?" I yelled back.

"Well," he said, "I have news for you, I'm not moving back home after I graduate. Sorry to break it to you, mom." He started laughing. "I will move to the city."

"Stephenjoon, you can take it with you wherever you decide to go," I said, "It's yours."

He was right, he didn't move back.

I walked towards his closet, opened the door, and started touching and smelling his clothes. He loved to dress up. He took his best picks to Boston. *They are probably burnt too*, I thought. I took out one of his shirts, looked at the collar, hoping to see a ring. His collar ring. I did not want a freshly washed and pressed shirt.

"Mom, it is so inexpensive to make custom shirts in Thailand."

"How many did you buy?"

"Not enough," he answered with a smile.

I took my top off and put his shirt on. It felt right. I felt close to him. I sat behind his desk and touched his pen and his notebooks. I laid down in his bed and tried to imagine what he was looking at when he was in his bed. I walked into his bathroom and touched the half-used soap on the sink. I opened his book on Machiavelli, and started reading the parts that he had underlined.

I heard Justin calling me, "Mom, mom, where are you?"

"Upstairs Justin, I will be down soon," I answered.

I kissed Stephen's book, where I imagined his fingertips had been, and walked downstairs.

"Is that Stephen's shirt? Mom, don't do that to yourself," Justin said.

"It's OK, Justinjoon, I can handle it, I'm fine." He hugged me tight and started crying.

"Listen to me, we will get through this. Life will be normal again, but a new normal. We will have happy days again. I promise you," I said into his ear.

"Thank you, mom, for saying that. I needed to hear that."

"Life never stays the same. It's full of challenges. Unfortunately, this one is the most difficult one."

"I miss him. I can't believe he is gone," Justin said.

"Neither do I, neither do I." I kissed his face and said, "We have a very heavy day ahead of us. We better go and get ready."

"Mom, I want to speak today at the funeral."

"In that case, I will be standing right next to you while you speak."

We were moving around the house like ghosts, in slow motion and in silence. No one spoke unless they had to. My husband held his head low and didn't say a word. We were preparing to go to our son's funeral. How many times had we walked out of this house? How many different places had we gone when we left this house? How could we ever have imagined that one day we would be walking out those double doors to go to a funeral home for our son?

It was a short drive. Justin was quietly crying. Camy was still quiet. Jordan kept on hugging me, kissing me, and cracking jokes. He was trying his best to bring a smile to my face.

I watched Camy from the corner of my eye. He didn't look up or say a word. He refused to speak, show any emotion, or share his feelings.

"Camyjoon," I held his knee and said, "We are not the first one, and unfortunately we will not be the last one that tragedy has hit, but we will try to survive it and move forward. We still have each other."

He looked up at me with tearful eyes, "It's not fair. It's not fair. Why did he have to die? He was such a good person. What kind of God would do such a thing? There is no God. If there is, he is a cruel God. Stephen didn't deserve to die young." And started crying.

"Leave God out of it," I said. "He doesn't go around and decide who lives and who dies. It was a horrible accident. Life is not fair. So many people die every day for no reason. We must be strong for each other."

I was giving him a speech that I did not believe. I was preaching, but I was not practicing it myself. I was angry at God too. This world would be a better place with people like Stephen in it. Nazi officers, criminals, dictators, and drug dealers lived well into their 90s and he leaves us at age 22?

After the heart-wrenching couple of hours at the funeral home we drove up the narrow road inside of the cemetery and the car stopped next to a hole that was freshly dug. The last time I was in that miserable place was years ago when my father-in-law had died at age 90. I looked at the giant hole and thought, *Lucky him, he had his children, his grand-children, and his great-grandchildren next to him when he died of old age. What else could you ask for?* It was unimaginable that I was here for my young son.

We got out of the limo and walked towards the plot. People followed us. The Rabbi walked to the top of the plot as the men of the family and Stephen's friends walked towards the hearse to get in line to carry the coffin to the graveside. It was a tragic and heartbreaking scene. Almost everyone that was at the funeral home had come to the cemetery, wanting to be there for support.

I walked over to the coffin, knelt on the ground, put my hands on the cover, and started kissing it. I finally started crying and couldn't stop. They were going to bury my son. The one that I thought had figured everything out for himself. The one that I was sure I didn't need to worry about. Justin walked over and helped me stand up.

And it was done. My son was buried. My beautiful son gone, and our lives changed forever. I went down on my knees and put my face and hands on top of the fresh dirt. I whispered, "I love you Stephen. I will miss you forever. *Ghorboonet beram."* I was picked up and led towards the car.

The crowd started to scatter; some were getting into their cars, some walked towards the gravesite, some started having small talks in groups. I looked at the pile of dirt on top of my son and walked towards the car. On a normal Monday, our friends would have been at work, but nothing about that day was normal. Most of them followed us home. It was a heartbreaking day for everyone in our community.

Stephen was famous for his smile. His full lips were his signature piece. Even if it was a mischievous smile, he wore it in the cutest way. As a young boy, he was a handful. Justin had been a conservative and quiet boy, and Stephen was the absolute opposite. He bothered Justin all the time. He broke his Legos, ripped his paintings, took away his toys, then stood in a corner with that devilish smile of his.

One day, after hours of hard work on Justin's part, making a perfect Lego town, Stephen walked in with authority and smashed it with a kick. Justin was five and Stephen was about three and a half. I ran towards them and saw what was left of Justin's hard work: Lego pieces all over the floor.

"What happened?" I asked.

"Mom, Stephen broke my Lego town. Look!" Justin cried.

"Why did you do that? Don't you love your brother?" I asked. He just looked at me with a sparkle in his eyes and shrugged his shoulders.

"OK, go to your room, right now. If you don't know how to play, you will stay there until you learn." I grabbed his hand and walked with him to his room. He sat on his bed with his head down. His long straight hair covered his face and his big lips poked out.

"Think about what you have done." I closed the door. I came back and helped Justin pick up the pieces.

"Mom, I love Stephen, but only when he is sleeping. Because then he can't bother me."

I started laughing out loud and said, "Wait, you will be the best of friends. Let him grow up a little."

Five minutes later, Stephen walked out of his room. He stood there in the opening of the den holding a bottle of red nail polish. I saw the wicked smile on his face and screamed, "Stephen, put that nail polish down. Don't you dare!" He moved his arm back and in a sudden move threw the bottle. The bottle shattered into hundred tiny pieces.

I yelled, "No Stephen, no, don't do it." But it was too late. There was red nail polish all over the floor. I took his hand, "Now you really did it. Wait until dad comes home. You have to explain to him." I carried him to his room and closed the door behind me.

After about 10 minutes, I started to get worried. I opened the door and saw another disaster. Apparently when I left him in his room for some "quiet time," he had pulled his pants down and peed all over the room. The walls, the cabinets, the bed, everything was wet.

"Did you pee in your room?"

He just looked at me from the corner of his eyes, trying to hold his smile back, and shrugged his shoulders. At that moment, I had to turn around so I could hide my laughter. I was laughing so hard in silence that tears started rolling down my face. How could such a young child think of that? In his mind, he had gotten back at me.

I had to walk away, because every time I attempted to say something to him I would burst into laughter again. He felt it, because he still had that cute smile on. I told him, "Look what you made me do. Now I am crying because you made me so upset." In truth, I wanted to pick him up and kiss those delicious full lips. And I should have. He was just a boy, an adorable boy, a creative boy!

How I miss those days. The days when I didn't have a minute to myself. When I used to complain about how difficult it was to raise two boys back to back. Now I was pressing my face into the pillow so no one could hear me, "Stephenjoon, I miss you. What happened?"

My friends came to the bedroom door one by one to make sure that I was OK. I walked back down with them. I was still wearing Stephen's shirt. It felt right. It felt soothing. I noticed everyone was wearing black from head to toe. A sad and heartbreaking scene. My sisters were sitting next to me. "Nazee," I said, "please tell whoever is here not to wear black from here on in my house. Tell them to wear any other color they wish, but not black. I don't want to remember my house like this. This used to be a happy house. We can still have wonderful days here."

Nazee told our close friends about my request, and asked them to get the message across. That was the last day that people walked into our house wearing black. Most men came directly from their work. They were tired, drained, and hungry, but that did not stop them from staying and supporting a heartbroken family.

Justin walked over and hugged me every once in a while and said "Mom, I love you. I love you."

I whispered back, "I love you more. We will get through this."

"Thank you, mom, thank you." The fact that I was sitting there with everyone, and not 100% drugged in a dark bedroom, under the covers in my bed, to him was enough.

We got through the first day. The last person left around eleven o'clock.

The next day our friends walked in one by one. They had to get their kids ready and drive them to school before coming to our house. No one was in black anymore; brown, grey, dark blue, even dark green had replaced the color black. They had brought coffee, bagels, sandwiches, cut fruits, and they were begging me to eat.

They could not have been more loving and supportive. Still, I wanted to yell out and ask everyone to leave. I wanted to lie on the floor and mourn and cry. Alone. Why was I sitting on a comfortable chair in a warm room while my son was in a wooden box in cold February weather? The thought of it was killing me. And so many times I wished it would.

A Desperate Move

"Life is like riding a bicycle, in order to keep your balance, you have to keep moving." —Einstein

May, 2007

Our once-happy home in Great Neck was filled with sad faces all day long. Our friends were still fussing and watching over us like hawks. I was floating and looking in on my life from a distance like a spectator. Nothing made sense. *This can't be our reality, it's a lie, it's a joke, a vicious joke,* I thought. If this was a wrestling match, I was pinned down by grief.

Weeks went by and with profound sadness in my heart I still smiled and kept up a strong front. Jackie was a different story. I was dealing with the tragedy head-on; he avoided it. He went to work during the day and played cards with his friends at night. I created a foundation in our son's name two weeks after losing him; he didn't want to know about it. I talked about what Stephen liked or did with the kids, he would change the subject immediately. When a stranger asked us how many kids we had, I replied 4, while he replied 3 at the same time. Jordan was only 8 years old, Camy 15 and Justin 23. Very soon when they wanted to talk about their sadness, they would only approach me.

I would do anything to finish another day, another week and another month, faster. I sacrificed my everyday for the following day. Sleep was my escape, my solace, my savior. I left my bed every morning counting the hours till it was time to go back. "Thank God another day is behind me," I told myself each night.

I wanted days to go by and weeks to go by and years to go by and my life to go by so I could go and see my son again and tell him how much we loved him and missed him. How sad everyone was now that he wasn't around. I wanted to ask him why he didn't escape the fire. I wanted to make sure that he didn't suffer. I wanted to touch him and kiss him and see him smile again. I wanted to hear his voice again. I wanted him to tell me how much we were alike again. I wanted to see his mischievous eyes again. I wanted my son back again.

I continued with my everyday chores. I took my kids to school and birthday parties. I went supermarket shopping. I cooked and talked to my friends. But I was just a pale shadow of myself. It was me but hollow. I walked around with a heavy heart and distraught mind. I envied almost everyone. If I saw a homeless guy, I stared at him thinking to myself, *I would happily switch places with this guy.* If I heard of a friend going through chemo, I thought to myself, *I never had the luxury to get ready for a departure and have closure or a second chance.* I wanted to be anyone but me. Me, was torture. Me, was pain. Me had become a horror story. Living was difficult, existing wasn't.

My friend Shirin called me from Los Angeles. "You need a change of atmosphere, why don't you come and stay with me for a few days?"

I had traveled to LA many times with my family; the Persian community there was much bigger than the one in New York and we had made a lot of friends throughout the years. Looking back, I don't know why and I don't remember how I decided to travel.

I flew to LA, maybe because I had no idea what else to do to make the time go by faster. Maybe it was a distraction, or maybe I was just not thinking again. I don't remember, but that trip changed the course of my life. On a beautiful sunny afternoon, one of our friends asked, "I am going to see a beautiful house for sale. Why don't you come with me?"

I was willing to do anything to keep busy. So off I went to see "a beautiful house for sale." The agent opened the front door and we entered a bright and sunny room with high ceilings. The walls were painted a warm, pale yellow and the ceiling was covered with images of the beautiful sky. The bright California sun was shining through the arched windows of the living room. Lush curtains framed the view of a huge palm tree and the hedges. I stood under the sun facing the view in that delightful living room and felt a certain warmth and ease.

I don't want to go back to dark and cold New York. I want to stay here, I thought to myself. New York was miserable and grey in winter and hot and humid during the summer. Those beautiful golden rays of sun filling that room lifted my spirit for the first time in two months. The view of green mountains and cypress trees brought a smile to my face. The landscape was unfamiliar and new and that's what I needed. This scenery was free of any memories.

We took a tour of the entire house. My friend had been right, it was beautiful. For the rest of the day I couldn't stop thinking about that sunlit room that held no sad story. I didn't want to return to our house in New York. I called Jackie. "I saw a house that's on the market today."

"Why?"

"You always wanted to live here, you've been talking about it since the day we got married. You can see the house through the virtual tour on your computer. I am emailing you the info as we speak. I fell in love with it. It's beautiful," I said.

And that was the entire conversation. *It is a crazy idea,* I thought, so I stopped thinking about it. My husband loved our house and life in that cozy town. The idea of moving from Great Neck to Manhattan, a distance of only 25 miles, was absurd to him. Now I was expecting him to move more than 2500 miles away? What was I thinking? Obviously, I wasn't!

Jackie called me back the next day. "Soheila, I'm in love," he said.

"In love?!" I asked. "With whom?"

"With the house! I looked at the website three times," he said.

I was shocked. I had been begging my husband for years to move out of that suburban town and into the city but he was always against it.

"Alright, what do you want me to do?" I asked.

"Make an offer!" *What? Make an offer?* I immediately looked around for a few flying pigs, but there were none in sight!

"OK! Will do." I hung up the phone, called the broker and told her we were making an offer. I never seriously thought that it would be accepted. I think, deep down, I must have thought, *I will try, they probably will say no, or Jackie will change his mind and then we will all continue with our lives in New York.* Still, the idea of beginning a new life and having a fresh start was very appealing to me. For the first time in more than two months I put makeup on and wore my own blouse, not my son's shirts and sweaters, and went with the broker to meet the owner of the house. Five minutes into our conversation, she held my hand, looked into my eyes and said, "Honey, I can only see you in my house. The house is yours, I will take it off the market."

The house is mine? I looked up, searching for Stephen. I was convinced he was responsible for this. He knew how badly I wanted to leave Great Neck. He was behind it all, he was helping me. I called my husband and told him that our offer had been accepted.

I hadn't mentioned anything about the house to my parents or any of my siblings. I had no idea how to break the news to my kids. "Kids, I went to Los Angeles for 5 days and bought a house so hey, guess what? We are all moving there." It would be shocking to everyone. We belonged in New York. Our closest friends were there, our families, my parents, my sisters and my brother.

I was sure something would come up and the idea of starting over would remain just an idea. Even the broker said, "Promises mean nothing, until it's signed on paper. Whoever pays more gets the house." A few days later I got a call on exactly that subject. "There is a higher offer on the table from another interested client, what do you want to do?"

"But she said the house is mine!" I said.

"Money talks, there is a lot of interest in this house."

"Let me think about it," I said. I called the owner.

"Yes honey, it's true," she said. "I've been told that I have a higher offer. But as I promised before, the house is yours. I want to see you live in that house. The contract is almost ready." Again, I looked around for flying pigs. Couldn't find any. I looked up the forecast for hell on the weather channel. Nope, no sign of it freezing over, still above 1000 degrees! Now I was absolutely convinced that Stephen was behind it, and I became adamant about moving into that house.

I broke the news to my kids at dinner back in Great Neck. Justin was shocked. "But mom, I don't want to move. My friends are here. If you move our family will fall apart. There is no unity anymore."

"I will travel back and forth, I promise," I said. "Please understand, I can't live here anymore. It's eating me up like an uncomfortable and itchy wool sweater. It is torture for me. You know dad will never move to Manhattan. If I pass on this opportunity I will be stuck in this town and in this house forever. It would be slow death for me."

Tears were rolling down his face. "Justinjoon, you are 23 years old, old enough to live your life without my supervision. I must do what I have to do to survive. I will be back every month. Please understand." He was heartbroken and disappointed, but said he would try to understand.

Camy was devastated. He didn't take the news lightly. He started crying and pacing back and forth in the room. "No mom, no! You can't do this to me. What is in LA? Who do we know? I don't want to move. Please mom, change your mind. I beg you. I don't want to move." It broke my heart to see him hurting so much. He had just turned 15, and he was set in his own world. His friends had been keeping him busy. Those friends were the only thing that kept him going, and now I was taking that away from him too.

In hindsight, I should have never moved out of New York, but at the time moving out meant moving on for me. Those who know me well know that I have always given up what I wanted in favor of other people. I would happily give up my wishes and change my plans if I knew it would help someone else. But this time was different. I don't know how I found the strength to go on with the move, in spite of seeing my kids so sad and heartbroken. I probably thought it was Stephen's wish and plan for me.

"You will find new friends, Camy." I said. "You already know a couple of people there. Make an effort, please."

"No, I won't. Those people are not my friends. My friends are here. Our home is here. Our family is here." He sobbed. I sobbed with him. But I didn't change my mind.

My sisters and brother were equally shocked. "New York won't be the same without you," Fariborz said. "I will miss you."

"I will miss you, too, but I can't stay here. Jack liked this house and it's my only chance to get out. I can't breathe in this house. It's torture for me. I pass by Stephen's room and my heart races so hard it feels like it wants to burst out and land in the middle of his room. I don't think I can survive here." I started crying.

Fariborz hugged me tight; he was sobbing too, "I am sorry, Soheila. I am so sorry for you. I will miss you here. It will never be the same without you. But I promise I will arrange for an annual trip to Los Angeles so we can be together."

Nazee and Nahid both understood my need to escape from New York and wished me luck. "We just have to add Los Angeles to our itinerary from now on."

Zohreh was not happy with my decision. "What do you mean you are moving? You belong here," she said. "Are you seriously moving for good?"

"Well, I am moving for now! I am not so sure if it's for good."

On August 18, 2007, six months after losing my son, we moved to Los Angeles. Zohreh stayed with me for a few weeks after our move.

The new house and new surroundings kept me busy and somewhat distracted for a while. Physical work was therapy for me. If my body was in motion, I was in better shape mentally. "Soheila, you are like a wave, you should always move, and move forward. The minute you stop you cease to exist," a friend told me once. She was right. I always find something to do, doesn't matter if it's for me, or someone else. I tried to avoid my pain by keeping busy and organizing shelves and closets.

I planted flowers in the backyard. I started decorating the kitchen. Anything that could possibly distract me I would do. But it wasn't much of a help. I was heartbroken. In hindsight, if I had known what was waiting ahead of me and how upset Camy was I would have never moved.

Camy was suffering. A few months passed and he was still miserable in Los Angeles. He came back from his new school, returned to his new house, went directly to his new bedroom and started crying. He wanted his old friends, his old neighborhood, and his old school back. "Mom, I want my life back. I just want my life back," he said while pressing his face into his pillow.

"Camyjoon, I want my life back too. What do you think? I am happy here? I want our lives back as much as you do. I want Stephen's life back most of all," I said, sitting next to him on his bed. I had run away from the four walls that held so many memories. We were in this gorgeous house in this beautiful city and we were miserable. Had I made a huge mistake? Had I scarred my kids for the rest of their lives? Justin was alone in New York, Camy was depressed here and Jordan kept to himself and never complained because he saw how sad I was.

What have I done? How can I fix this? I looked at Camy sobbing on his bed and felt a sharp pain in my heart, sharper even than the constant pain I felt for losing Stephen. I had acted selfishly, thinking only of myself, I didn't foresee the consequences. This pain was caused entirely by me. This one was all my fault. This was a huge mistake. "Please mom, let's move back to New York. Let's go back to our home. This is not our home. Let's go back to our old life. Please, mom." Every word felt like a dagger, and every time it went deeper and deeper.

Camy had always been a fun boy, a good boy, going through his teenage years without a care in the world. He was now sad, heartbroken, hurt and angry at the world. He had been very close to his brother. He looked up to him. He spent a lot of time with him and his friends even though they were 6 years apart. Now his brother was gone. His home was gone. His friends were gone. The life that he knew was gone, and he was begging me to give back to him what was still possible.

He had given up on the idea of me moving back, but he was still working on the idea of me sending him back. I knew I would never hear the end of it. I knew he would never give up. I knew he would eventually come to hate me for keeping him away from Great Neck. I gave in; I arranged for him to move back.

My husband's brother Eddie and his wife Kathy lived next door to our house in Great Neck. We had put the house on the market but it was not yet sold. I asked my mom to stay with Camy in the house and Kathy and Nazee to help with everyday needs, such as shopping or transportation. After a few months Camy moved to Kathy's house.

With Camy safely installed back in Great Neck, I was more depressed than ever. We had been a happy family of six around the dinner table at the beginning of the year. Now, in November, we were downsized to Jordan and me as Jack spent many evenings with his new friends in LA. It was difficult for me to carry the burden by myself. I was alone most of the time. But I thought, *If that's what's helping him forget about the loss, then let that be.* I wished that I, too, had an outlet or an escape. Unfortunately, Zohreh would soon require much of my attention.

"My vision is failing me, it's declining more every day. I am worried," Zohreh said. Her voice trembled over the phone line. "Every morning that I wake up I feel the difference from the day before. I can't see so well, everything is blurry. I'm scared."

"Did you talk to Fariborz?" I asked.

"I did. He has already made an appointment with a specialist."

It was summer of 2010. Even though I traveled to New York quite often, I called Zohreh several times a day from LA. My poor sister needed a break and she wasn't getting one.

She had an axe hanging over her head. All the while, as she did her best to go about her life, those damn growths kept creeping up on her. She knew another dangerous operation was around the corner. She'd had five brain surgeries over 20 years and now it seemed another was imminent. She knew the symptoms all too well. When she felt tired or dizzy or her vision was blurry, she couldn't brush it off and think, "Oh, it's nothing serious, I must be overworked or stressed out. I need a vacation." In her case, it was always something—something very serious!

Fariborz sent her to multiple specialists. The results came back worse than we could have imagined. The tumor was positioned in a spot more dangerous than ever before, and we were more worried and scared than we had ever been. The tumor was attached to the optical nerves deep in her brain, an unreachable and sensitive area. Zohreh had two horrible options. First: to let the tumor be. In that case, it would grow bigger and eventually end up killing her. That was unthinkable. Second: Do radiation and Gamma treatment, which might burn the tumor into nothingness but would likely damage other parts of her brain as well.

None of us knew at the time that the first option was (comparatively) a walk in the park on a sunny spring day and the second option would lead my sister to a tortured life in total darkness and silence… and eventually an agonizing death. At the time, it was "Forward, march." We pulled together to do our best for our sister. "Zohreh has to go either to Mass General in Boston or Loma Linda hospital an hour away from Los Angeles," Fariborz said on one of our many conversations about her condition.

"Why don't you arrange for her to get the treatment here in Loma Linda?" I asked. "I can drive her there and back every day and be with her."

"She wants to be home on weekends. She doesn't want to be away from her family for two whole months."

"But what other choice do we have?" I pleaded with Fariborz. "The idea of me traveling to Boston and going to Mass General every day is agonizing. I lost Stephen there. How could I go back to that city… it's too painful."

"Get it out of your head, Soheila. I would never let you go back there," he said. "We will find a way."

In the meantime, he was doing his research to find the absolute top person at Mass General and organizing the treatment for her. I flew to New York every month, doing my best to keep a balance on both sides of the country. When I was in LA, I dropped Jordan off at school early in the morning, picked him up at 2:30 and spent every minute with him until it was time for him to go to bed. Traveling back to New York was always an issue with his schedule. There was no public transportation available at his school. The school buses dropped off and picked up at certain stops, which for me was useless. He was only 11 years old and he needed an adult to pick him up from the designated stations. I needed someone to drive him to school and back while I was gone. With Nazee's help, I hired an au pair from Italy.

Her name was Assunta, and she was kind and caring. She didn't speak a word of English, but I spoke Italian so communication wasn't so difficult. She was a godsend, allowing me to spend one week out of every month in New York without worry. Camy and Justin were living there, and Zohreh wanted more of my care and attention. Assunta drove Jordan to school and back and spent her mornings in an English school.

It was getting closer to Zohreh's treatment in Boston and we still had no one to stay with her. "Maybe we can divide the weeks, what do you think?" I asked Fariborz.

"I told you, I will not allow you to go to Boston," he answered. "That would leave Nazee and me, and I can't take time off from work every other week."

"This is horrible, we have to come up with a plan soon," I replied.

I hung up the phone and went to the gym as usual. I couldn't stop thinking about my phone call with Fariborz, replaying the conversation over and over inside my head. *There must be a way*, I thought. In the middle of punching and kicking, it came to me! Assunta can stay with Zohreh in Boston! Why didn't I think about it earlier? Zohreh is fluent in Italian and Assunta is young and energetic. She can take care of her and be with her. Problem solved!

I ran out of the gym and called Fariborz. "I got it, the Italian girl will go with her. She can be in Boston 5 days and explore Manhattan on weekends," I said.

"Are you sure she would agree?" he asked.

"Yes, one hundred percent sure, she has told me many times she wished she had enough money to go see New York. I will buy her the plane tickets and she can stay with Zohreh in the city."

"Great idea, I will get to work now," he said.

He got busy taking care of the logistics. Assunta left for New York the following week. For 8 weeks, the two of them took the train to Boston Sunday nights, stayed in a hotel next to the hospital, went for Gamma and radiation treatment every day and took the train back to the city Friday afternoons. Assunta spent each weekend walking around and exploring Manhattan, which was a release and extremely exciting to her.

The treatments were taking a toll on Zohreh. Her memory and her speech had been badly affected, and she had become weak and fragile, but Fariborz assured us that it was only temporary. "There is no other option for her condition. Let's keep our fingers crossed and hope for the best," he said. "Give it some time, her body will restore itself. Radiation was her only choice and she is done with it. As long as the person is breathing you have to try every possibility."

It was a cold and miserable winter in New York. Zohreh was home most of the time. She was disoriented. Her brain was foggy. She was a cross between Anna Wintour and Forrest Gump. Same hairdo, always well-groomed and presentable, but completely lost in her world.

"Hey, why don't you come to LA? It's sunny and beautiful here. Come and stay with me for couple of weeks?" I asked her.

"I don't know," she answered right away.

Her response wasn't because she wasn't sure of her plans. She wasn't able to focus enough to give me an answer. She couldn't gather her thoughts together. I insisted, "Zohreh, just get on a plane and come." Which she did with her daughter's help, Roya. Zohreh was changed. She jumped from one subject to another unrelated one. She lost track of time by hours. She forgot where she left her things. She was confused but happy to be in sunny Los Angeles.

Little by little she got better until after months she became nearly her old self again. We thought she had done the impossible by pinning down the opponent and forcing it into submission. She had won that round, but the enemy would soon get up with newly-acquired energy and a new master plan, ready to attack again, this time with no mercy. The worst was yet to come. Her real and dark nightmare was just beginning.

In the subsequent months and years Zohreh made the rounds of various doctors. Her vision eventually became worse every day. She started using magnifying glasses to look at things or read. She made the fonts on her computer as large as possible and added a special keyboard designed for people with poor eyesight. She held our arms to walk around and asked us to describe everything to her. She was scared but hopeful, hopeful but in denial. "There must be a solution for my condition. Some doctor somewhere should have an answer for me. I will not give up. How can I? Live the rest of my life as a blind person, in complete darkness?" she pleaded. We visited every doctor from UCLA and USC when she came to visit me in LA.

At the same time, I was organizing a small party for Jordan's Bar Mitzvah in Israel. I was depressed and angry at God and the whole world that Stephen was not with us. I realized that after a tragedy, what should be the happiest moments in life become the most painful ones. The days that people think should take your sorrow away are the ones that weigh the heaviest on your heart. I talked to the caterer and cried, called a DJ and cried, designed the invitation cards and cried. *Jordan deserves a happy event*, I thought, therefore in front of my family and friends I tried to be my old self.

Zohreh stayed close by most of the time. "You know I am going blind," she whispered in my ear while watching a beautiful sunset in Israel. "I know we are looking at a sunset, but I can see only parts of it."

I didn't know what to say. "Try to be positive, maybe the medication works. Let's hope for the best."

While walking arm in arm, she turned around and asked, "Is it beautiful here? I bet it is. You know I am going blind. Pretty soon all I will have is darkness."

I was in pain already and her comments, though she kept up a very strong facade in front of everyone else, were killing me. What could I do for my sister besides stay next to her, giving her my love and undivided attention and accompanying her all the time?

Her remarks were constant. I tried to be understanding and patient, until the night of my son's Bar Mitzvah ceremony. She came in while holding onto her husband's arm, walked directly towards me and said, "I would have told you everything looks beautiful if I could see. But I'm almost blind."

The me that was patient and compassionate 99% of the time vanished, replaced by the 1% filled with anger. "You know, Zohreh, with everything that has happened in my life, I think you could have kept that comment to yourself, at least for tonight. I wouldn't have said such a thing to you if I was lying on my deathbed," and walked away. She stood there for a while gazing at nothing in particular. I was disgusted by my own behavior. She kept her distance the whole evening while I was trying to put a happy show on and dance as always. But the comment that I'd made to her was eating me up throughout the evening.

Back home in New York, people quickly moved out of our way when they saw a well-dressed woman walking with a cane, wearing dark glasses, with us guiding her. At restaurants, we cut her food and placed it in front of her. She tried catching a piece with her fork and most of the times the food fell off halfway to her lips. She was embarrassed when her lips touched the empty fork. It was aggravating for her and heartbreaking for us. She searched for her glass of water with her hand with extreme caution and we tried to slide it towards her fingertips, hoping she wouldn't notice.

Unbelievably, the noted architect and the interior designer, the athlete and the artist, the world traveler and the girl with the most joie de vivre was now a completely dependent and helpless being.

One Perfect Day

"Life is so ironic, it takes sadness to know what happiness is, noise to appreciate silence and absence to value presence." —Unknown

Connecticut, September, 2014

I t was one of those perfect days on the East Coast. The skies were blue and clear, not a cloud in sight, no sign of humidity, just a pleasant breeze and wonderful weather. It was a beautiful day to have an outdoor party.

Fariborz had purchased his house in Connecticut for two reasons only. The first was to have a place to go to on weekends with his family where they could enjoy the great outdoors. The second was to hold Alexa and Ava's Bat Mitzvah celebrations there.

The beautiful Georgian Revival-style house was situated on a hill, surrounded by green grass and massive trees. At the bottom of the hill in the distance was a lovely lake, with rows of old willow trees, their long green stems touching the water, making it a picture-perfect place for the seagulls, ducks and geese to hang out.

Fariborz had renovated and fixed the house to perfection, and it was time to enjoy the fruits of his hard work. The day he had dreamed of, Sunday, September 12th, 2012, Alexa's Bat Mitzvah, had arrived. It was a beautiful day.

As soon as we pulled into the circular driveway, I saw my brother in the doorway of his house wearing a radiant smile and greeting his guests. He was handsome and charming and beaming with joy. He was dressed in a white pants, white shirt and a light blue blazer. With his hair oiled back, he looked like an Italian movie star from the 60's.

"Fariborz, can you believe this weather, who do you know that I don't?" I yelled out from the car. He raised his hands, looked up at the sky and laughed out loud. He ran towards us like a little boy, hugged and kissed us and said with enthusiasm, "Unbelievable, right? Come on, let's go take family pictures before it gets too crowded." We walked to the side of the house and took tons of pictures. Friends, family, work associates arrived one by one. Everyone was happy to be there.

It was time for the Bat Mitzvah ceremony and Alexa's and Fariborz's speeches. We took our seats in the front rows reserved for family members. Alexa spoke with confidence and grace. She was only twelve, but she spoke and handled herself like a mature adult. After the Rabbi said a few words, it was time for Fariborz's speech. We all knew his words would be emotional. He loved and cherished every minute that he spent with his wife and kids. To him family was sacred and needed to be protected at all times.

He choked up before he started, took a deep breath, faced Alexa, and gave a beautiful and touching speech. Tears started rolling down his face; he was overcome with emotion. At times, he had to stop, take a breath, and start again, as if he knew deep down that he would never get another chance to pour out his feelings to his daughter, ever again.

A Father's Pledge

Alexa my love, on this important day when you make your transition from childhood to adulthood, and where we celebrate your metamorphosis into a Jewish woman with all its rights and responsibilities, I would like to welcome you to our community—the Jewish community.

On this day, it is customary to talk about your accomplishments—sing you accolades, possibly lecture you a bit about how you should conduct your life. We all know your accomplishments but in your tradition of being completely understated, unassuming, and unpretentious I would not speak of them. Furthermore, I would not even lecture you on how to be and how to conduct yourself since if I had half the innate qualities you already possess I would have been a successful rocket scientist.

Instead I would like to make a Pledge—a Father's Pledge— My Pledge to You, that I would hold for the rest of my life:

I pledge to guard you and protect you for as long as I am physically and mentally capable

I pledge to be by your side whether you would need my assistance or not, so that you wouldn't have to look far

I pledge to treat you as I have always led my adult life—with honesty and truth as my guide

I pledge to remind you about the importance of having common sense and sound judgment

I pledge to support you in all your endeavors as long as they are done with conviction in your heart

I pledge to tell you when you are being lazy or selfish (which has not been very often) and when you might consider a different approach

I pledge to be just

I pledge to have my arms always open to embrace you so that your worries would melt away

I pledge to listen intently with patience whenever you pour your heart out to me

I pledge when asked to give you my opinion in earnest and only to help you reach your goals without my self-interest in mind

I pledge to always love you no matter what, even when you are grim and grumpy

And I pledge to you that I would NEVER EVER turn my back on you.

In reference to one my favorite books "The Giving Tree"—In return all I ask is that you would play in my tree, swing from my branches, take shelter under my protective shade, use my fruits, leaves, and trunk to build a better life... And when the time comes, lean on my stump, rest on the deep roots I have laid for you and reflect on the values I have instilled in you—so you could get your strength back to carry on.

He kissed Alexa's face and hugged her tight. Jennifer and Ava walked forward and held onto Fariborz. They stayed there, oblivious to the crowd watching them, the four of them as one. He didn't want to let go, he was inhaling the moment. Most of the people had tears in their eyes as they got up to leave the ballroom.

We walked towards the patio, marveling at the beautiful scenery and the flawless weather. The open white tent protected the guests from the sun, while the breathtaking view of the green hill and the blue lake with a crown of willow trees was still visible from every angle.

On that perfect day, Zohreh, though completely blind, tried her best to talk and mingle with everyone. At times when the DJ played her favorite songs she asked whomever was close to her to take her to the dance floor. She stood in the middle of the crowd and started dancing, not knowing that a human shield was being created around her.

We all tried to make sure that the unfortunate scene would not put a damper on our brother and his family's mood. He had done everything possible for Zohreh for the past twenty years. Not much more could be done at this point. Just love, unconditional love, and tons of it. That was the remedy for her condition now, and she was getting it in huge doses.

The party was going on full force. Fariborz was proud and happy. His guests were walking around admiring the view, dancing, drinking, mingling, laughing, having a wonderful time. It was a perfect day. This was what he had been dreaming of since he was a young boy: to make it on his own, and share his success with people that he loved and cared for. His dream came true that day. It was a testament to his hard work. He was grabbed and pulled constantly by his friends, either to dance, take a picture, or just make small talk.

I kept on repeating, "Fariborz, can you believe this unbelievable weather? Do you know someone up there that I don't?"

He laughed and said, "I told you, we have a guardian angel watching over our family."

"I hope she keeps on watching," I replied.

That had been our belief for years, but since the tragic fire, I had given up on that idea. *The guardian angel was either asleep or has found another family to watch over*, I thought to myself.

The party lasted till 6 pm. My mom called out, "Let's talk for a few minutes before we head back home." Momon had found a new-found freedom now that our father was in an assisted living home. Our father's dementia had become a full-fledged Alzheimer's at that point. He wanted to leave the house and go to the bank in the middle of the night. He didn't recognize the doormen and thought they were there to steal his belongings. He couldn't remember where he lived. It had become an impossible task to take care of our father and Zohreh at the same time. We decided to place him in an assisted living home. One day our mom came back from visiting him, trying to hold back her laughter while speaking. "You won't believe what happened! I cooked lunch and went to see your father. As soon as I sat down in the dining room, I saw him walking in, hand in hand with another woman from the center. They sat down in front of me, he took a piece of the chicken that I cooked and fed the woman. She smiled at him and he did it again. When lunch was over, they got up together and walked towards the garden. I followed them. The woman picked flowers and handed them to your dad and he smiled a loving smile." She started laughing and said, "Guys, your dad is in love! He didn't recognize me at all. Just so you know, he is very happy where he is. At least I don't have to worry about him." We all started laughing.

It is amazing, I thought. *Your mind can go, your legs can go, your entire body can go, but your heart still has the ability to fall in love!*

Nahid, Zohreh, Nazee, my mother, my brother, Jennifer and I sat down and recapped the party for about fifteen minutes. That, for us, was always one of the best parts of any party.

We gossiped and we gossiped well, until it was time to go. The weather had started to change. Dark clouds were moving in slowly and covering the blue skies, and the wind was picking up. The staff started collecting and placing everything inside. We hugged, kissed, said our goodbyes and drove away.

Leaving Fariborz's beautiful home, we had a 15-minute drive on local roads before we reached the highway entrance that would take us back to Manhattan. The minute we got on the interstate, the skies turned black, winds began buffeting our car, and hail started falling. This was not a storm; it was a monsoon. Visibility was close to zero; we crawled along the dark highway in slow motion, straining to see in front of us. We sat, silent and tense, until the storm eventually passed and returned to normal rain. I immediately called my brother.

"Did you see the change in the weather? It wasn't a normal storm. It was bad, Fariborz, and scary," I said.

"Yes, the wind almost took the tent away," he said with a laugh.

"It was perfect timing," I said, "Great sunny and dry weather all day, and the minute everyone left it became a major storm. I can't believe it. What are the odds?"

"Apparently plenty, as Stephen would say. I told you, Soheilajoon, our guardian angel was watching. The patio is a mess. It doesn't look anything like what it was an hour ago," he said, and started laughing.

"It was a great day, the way I always envisioned it," he continued.

"It was. It was. I hope your sky is always blue and sunny. You deserve it," I said. "Tell Jennifer she has done a great job."

"I will, and how great was Alexa? Did you see how composed and confident she was? I am so proud of her."

"And you should be, Fariborz. By the way, loved your speech. There was not a dry eye in the room. Thank you for a perfect day."

"I meant every word. It came from my heart."

Everything that he had worked for, wished for, prayed for and dreamed of was squeezed and concentrated into that one perfect day. Little did we know that the dark clouds were inching in slowly but surely.

We had stayed close to Roxy, Stephen's friend from school. It was a happy day when she announced her plans to marry. We all loved both Roxy and her husband-to-be Ben, and the whole family was invited to the wedding in Los Angeles in October of 2012. Zohreh had said that she wanted to come with Roya. I knew it would be difficult for her and Roya both, she was getting weaker every day, but none of us had the heart to tell her not to come. As it got closer to the date of the wedding my sister started doubting her decision and her strength.

"I am sending Roya," she said. "I will stay in New York. It's easier."

"Are you sure?" I asked.

"Yes," she said, "very sure. Tell me all about it as soon as you can. I want to know everything, most of all how Roya looked."

Zohreh had stayed with me in Los Angeles many times after losing her eyesight. It was a welcome distraction for her but not easy on either of us. My house was unfamiliar territory, so getting around and using the staircase was not only challenging but extremely dangerous for my sister. I tried to be with her from the moment she got out of bed until she returned to it. In between I had to watch her every step and move. It was embarrassing to her and the people around her when she fell and created a scene. We spent days at various doctors' offices waiting and hoping one of them would say something remotely promising, but none ever did.

"What will happen to me, Soheila? Will I die a slow and agonizing death?" I had no answer for her. I couldn't even lie and make something up. But we continued on our rounds, going from one doctor to another. She held my arm and we went together to restaurants, coffee shops, stores, friends' houses, the beach, even to shows and the movies while I reported and whispered what was going on in her ears.

On one visit, I snuck out to the gym early one morning, thinking, *She'll still be asleep by the time I'm back.* I bought her a coffee after class and drove back home. I got to Sunset Boulevard and saw the streets were blocked because President Obama was in town. I kept on begging the officers to let me drive through, saying that I had a sick sister at home, that it was a matter of life and death. But it was of no use. I was worried sick. No one else was home, and if she got out of bed by herself there was nobody there to help her. I didn't want to call and tell my sister, "Don't do anything until I get back!"

Frustrated and angry, I started crying behind the wheel and cursing at the whole world. I felt completely helpless. Finally, I picked up the phone and called some friends, asking them to call her and keep her busy on the phone for as long as possible. They did. When I finally made it home after an hour-long delay Zohreh said, "It was the strangest morning. I must have had fifteen phone calls. Everyone had decided to call me at the same time!"

To that I responded, "They love you, Zohreh. They love you and they are worried about you."

But this time it was different. Another trip for her was not in the cards. She was getting worse and she knew it. She stayed in New York and her daughter flew to Los Angeles.

Roya had a wonderful time at the wedding. She was glowing. It was another world away from the suffering she was exposed to on a daily basis. Everyone welcomed her and made her feel at home. Nazee and my dear friend Sima walked towards me at the end of the party. "What do you think about the idea of Roya living with you in Los Angeles? She looks very happy here," they asked.

"That's funny you said that. I was thinking about the same thing," I answered. "Why not? She just got out of college. She can find a job here. Jackie's niece has been living with me for a year already, she can move in too."

I called Zohreh the next day and gave her every last detail, especially about Roya: her gown, her hair, her dancing. At the end I added, "Zohreh, what do you think if Roya stays here with me? I will take care of her as if she was my own daughter. You know I would."

Silence hummed over the phone lines. I understood the enormity of what I was asking my sister. Finally, she answered. "You have been the guardian in case anything happens to us. I think it is a very good idea. I will tell Jamshid. There is not much I can do for her. I am handicapped in the worst possible way."

Roya loved the idea. She had already found new friends. She loved the beach, the sun, the outdoor coffee shops and the relaxed and carefree lifestyle. She cancelled her return ticket, asked her father to send her clothes and started her new life in Los Angeles.

I flew back to be with Zohreh more often. On November 19th, Stefan's birthday, I held my yearly fundraising event for my son's foundation in New York. Fariborz fussed over Zohreh and me, knowing it was difficult for both of us. For me there was the emotional pain of talking about the loss of my son; for Zohreh it was a physical challenge being among a big crowd and not being able to see. Nazee and Nahid watched over her as if they were two private bodyguards, shielding her from the overwhelming crowd.

As always, friends and family lined up to say hi to Zohreh and kiss her before the event started. People stood on line to talk to her. They were amazed by her strength. She had lost her vision and her hearing had been failing for quite some time, but not her spirit. She still dressed up and showed up wearing her dark sunglasses. She was a living example of bravery and courage. She felt their love and loved the feeling.

On New Year's Eve of 2013, Zohreh's situation got worse. Only six weeks later at a small get-together, as our friend Shifra was trying to talk to her and keep her busy, Zohreh covered her ears with her hands and begged Jamshid, "Let's go home, please. I can't take it anymore. The noise is killing me." They left the party, and that was the last time anyone saw her in public. She decided to stay in her apartment and stopped socializing as of the next day. She lost all sense of hearing almost immediately; by mid-January she was deaf.

I flew back from Los Angeles and stayed in her apartment. I sat next to her all day and spelled out "yes" or "no" or other simple words on the palm of her hand while she talked. It was sad and heartbreaking. I had read Helen Keller's story as a kid, and now I was living with a similar one. Zohreh's world was dark and mute. She talked non-stop, even though she couldn't hear herself. I think she wanted to make sure someone was next to her when she felt the touch of our forefinger on her hand.

I told Fariborz on one of his visits, "People die all the time, but this process of death is scarier than death itself."

"She will die in a couple of months." Looking at her with sad eyes, knowing she was unable to hear him, he added, "The gamma radiation has caused permanent damage to her nerves. There is nothing left. We just have to make sure she is as comfortable as possible."

We all stood there and looked at her not knowing what to do.

My mom moved into her apartment. She was free to come and go as she wished with our dad being cared for, happy and in love. He didn't know anything about this series of unfortunate events. He was deep in his own world, thinking he was still living in Shiraz, Iran. The one suffering from Alzheimer's was happy and free of any emotional pain. The rest of us were not.

Day in and day out I sat on the bed while Zohreh talked. Every day after work, Nahid, Nazee and the kids came to visit her. They held her hands or massaged her body.

One morning she woke up, held her usual large cup of coffee with both hands and said, "Last night I had the most beautiful and colorful dream. We were all by the beach, it was probably one of our many trips together. The ocean was the color of emerald and turquoise mixed, the sky was powder blue, we were surrounded by palm trees. The music was playing and we were all dancing on the beach. I was able to see again. I saw Roya and Arya's faces and their smiles again. I saw color and heard music again. I was able to be me again, but only in my sleep. I will be able to live again, but only when I'm dead."

I looked around the room, at the sofa, the nightstand, the shoes in the corner, the dog next to the bed, her clock radio, the crack on the wall, the sun shining through the window. What I was looking at so casually had become her impossible dream. She woke up to complete darkness and absolute silence. Death should be more pleasant than this. Why couldn't she just die while under one of her many brain surgeries like normal hospital malpractices? Why didn't she get hit by a car while crossing the street? Why didn't she die when she hit her head on the side of the bathtub and fainted a couple of months ago? God, why do you have to make it so torturous that I wish for my sister's death? Why such a long and drawn-out process of dying? Why this?

"I do not want to live anymore," she continued. "I am inviting the angel of death to come and take me with her. Enough suffering."

I wrote "NO" on the palm of her hand. She pulled her hand away and said, "Yes, I want to die."

I kept on writing "NO," but I didn't mean it. I understood her and agreed with her deep down. In fact, I wished I could do something to expedite it for her, but there was nothing that I could do. She didn't have much of an appetite and swallowing food had become difficult for her. It was getting harder every day, and she soon stopped eating altogether. My mother panicked and begged her to take a bite, pushing the spoon to Zohreh's mouth, but she held her lips tight together and refused.

"What will happen to her?" my mom cried, "She can't survive without food."

"Survive what, Momon?" I asked, "You want her to live like this?"

"Don't say that! Don't say that!" She sobbed. "She can't die. She is my daughter."

I looked at the "Do not resuscitate" sign posted on top of her bed and told my mom, "Look, she signed this paper years ago. How many times did she tell us that she didn't want to be alive if she was not a complete person? We have to respect what she wanted now that she is not capable of communicating with us."

"But she is my daughter, how can I accept that?"

By March, Zohreh was down to her skin and bones. She never ate, hardly spoke, mostly slept. Roya flew to visit her every chance she got and hugged her on her bed. Arya held her hand and talked to her constantly, knowing very well she couldn't hear. Zohreh caressed Roya's hair with her bony fingers and smiled a painful smile at Arya. The last two weeks she just laid in her bed with her arms crossed on her chest.

My brother's visits became fewer and fewer. He had his own demons to fight and dark days to face. Zohreh faded away in front of our eyes.

"My sister"

My free-spirited sister is still in bed
in the same position she was in this morning,
the same position she was in last night,
and the day before,
and the week before.
Breathing, but still not dead
Little by little, she is fading away,
down to skin and bones,
arms crossed on her chest,
head tilted to the side, and rest
eyes closed, bones squeezing]
pushing out of a skin that's now grey
She's been in that bed for months
blind and deaf and thus
she's been helpless but she fought.

God, why do You turn your back to us?
You're pushing us, trying to see
how much punishment we can take and still be.
It's a cruel joke, God, a cruel game.
And we have no one else to blame—
We can only feel her breath.
Then why prolong her death?
You should have taken her life
when she was still under the knife,
before she entered the darkness,
before the perpetual silence.
My sister was never afraid of death,
but she was terrified of the process of dying.
and you made sure she went through it, marching
Step
By step
By step
My sister is still
in bed, in the same position she was in this morning,
in the same position she was in last night
and the day before,
and the week before,
but tonight,
she's not breathing,
no, not anymore.

Photo Gallery

Newlyweds, mom and dad.

My young mom with Nahid
and Zohreh, in Ahwaz.

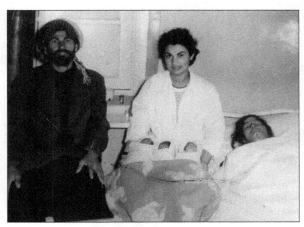

Momon in her 20s, helped a woman
give birth to triplets, single-handedly.

Stephen when he was 8 years old.

Justin and Stephen ready for mischief.

Justin, Stephen and Camy.

Justin, Jordan, Camy and Stephen, Club Med.

My hand-
some Stephen,
our last trip
together,
January 2007.

Stephen and
Jordan, New
Year's party.

Stephen and Roxy
Italy, summer of 2005.

With his close friend,
Brett Boskoff.

Stephen with long hair with Ben,
Mickey, Josh and his cousin, Matthew.

Alex, Roxy, Stephen, and Justin.

Sharon, Roxy, Nicole, Stephen,
Justin and Dan, Saint Martin
January, 2007. His last trip.

College years, Lauren,
Stephen, Eyal, and Benji,
his very good friend.

Stephen with his close friends from childhood, on vacation and at parties. He loved his friends and was loved by them.

"My favorite color is rainbow!" Susan, with Eric and Stephen.

Bahamas, Danny, Dan, Stephen, and Johnny "To the pool!"

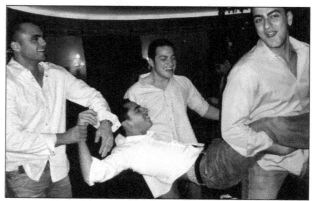

Halloween, Gideon, Stephen and Justin.

Stephen's 20th birthday, with Jordan and Camy.

Justin, Roya and Stephen.

Halloween, as his favorite personality, Ali G.

Traveling alone in The Far East.

Paris, following the path of
"The Da Vinci Code."

I cherished every second of
being with my family.

A scrumptious organic breakfast with the view of Tuscan
Hills. Summer 2004.

Megeve, three days before hearing the devastating news. February 2007
Life was normal with everyday problems, till then.

My "Four
of a kind."

Nahid, Zohreh, Roya and me, in Tuscany, summer of 2004.

My boys,
Florence, 2004.

New Year's party, 2007. Our last picture together. Zohreh showed me her balding head at the end of the night.

Justin and Stephen, Germany, The World Cup, 2006.

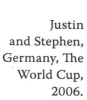

Three sisters exploring Tuscany. Summer of 2005.

Our many trips to La Gigliola and staying with Anna.

Justin's engagement to Setareh, how we wished Stephen was there.

Roya and Arya's graduation,
with Zohreh and Jamshid.

Professor Elie Wiesel as a speaker
at 'Stefan Adelipour for Life
Foundation' fundraiser.

Momon, Fariborz and
me, happy times.

Me, Nazee, Nahid and Zohreh after her many surgeries.

From right, Jackie, Stephen, Justin, me,
Camy and Jordan, June of 2002.

Nazee and Joe's summer party 2012, From top right, Joe Moinian, Mitchel, Justin, Roy, Roya, Camy, Zohreh (with dark glasses), Philip, Nahid, Me, Fariborz, Alexa, Jordan, Serina, Michaela, Nazee, Caleb, Setareh and Linda.

Zohreh at her kids' coming-of-age party.
She was the happiest on that day.

His beautiful cleft chin.

A 22-year-old buffed Fariborz with Zohreh.

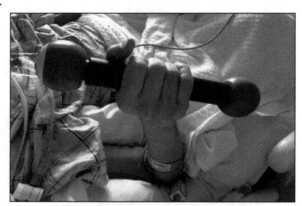

Fariborz as a cancer patient.

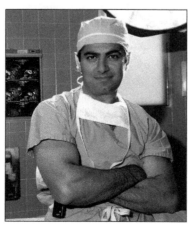

Fariborz as
Dr. McDreamy.

On "a perfect day," our friends were there for
our brother and his last day.

A proud Fariborz, center, with Jennifer, Alexa and Ava surrounded by family members. A perfect day.

Family picture, from right, Philip, Fariborz, Jennifer,
Zohreh, me, Liza, Linda, Nahid, Nazee. My mom and
dad, seated. Liza's engagement party to Roy, 2001.

My family now, from right, Cameron, Jordan, me, Stella
(my granddaughter) Justin, Setareh and Jack.
January 2018.

Cytoxan, the Queen of Chemo

"Abandon all hope, ye who enter here." —Dante, Inferno

March, 2013

Mount Sinai hospital is an impressive structure. The building stretches from Madison Avenue to Fifth Avenue on 101st Street in New York City, with elevators and exits on both sides. I got out of the cab and stood frozen on the sidewalk. I could not take a step forward. I dreaded walking in. I looked up at the massive building, thinking, *Is this true? Is my brother a patient here? A patient on the 11th floor, Oncology!?*

How many times had my mother told us, "There is no history of cancer in our family. If you look at my seven siblings and their kids and grandkids, then look at your father's side of the family with their kids and grandkids, there is not one case of that horrible disease in the whole tribe." She was right. There had never been one, but now there was. Her son was the "chosen one!" The apple of her eye, her pride and joy, the reason for her smiles...was the first-ever cancer patient in the family.

It was February of 2011 when the phone rang. "Hi Soheilajon, how are you?"

"Hi, Fariborz?"

"I want to tell you something, but you have to promise it will stay between us."

"Of course, for sure, what's wrong?"

"Remember I asked you and Nazee to come to the hospital for a doctor's appointment last month?"

"Yes, why?"

"You guys had some blood tests done and I told you I just wanted to know who is whose match genetically so, God forbid, if an emergency comes up we are prepared."

"Yes."

"Well the 'God forbid' part has come up. I have a blood condition called Polycythemia Vera. My blood creates too many red cells, white cells, and platelets; as a result, it is thicker than normal. I was short of breath most of the time because oxygen can't travel easily. I consider myself lucky that I didn't have a stroke from a blood clot."

I held the phone to my ear, not believing what I was hearing. My hands started to shake; I could feel the throbbing of my heartbeat in my head.

"But I am fully aware of my condition now and I am on top of it. I must drink a lot of water, exercise, and remove a pint of blood every month so it becomes more diluted. However, you might want to know how it relates to you? You and I are a 100-percent match; Nazee and I zero. Statistics show that 6% of people with this condition suffer from Acute Leukemia but at a later age, usually after the age of 60-65. To make the long story short, keep yourself healthy and alive for more reasons than one, please. You are my insurance policy. Someday I may need your bone marrow."

I was speechless. I was stunned. I was trying to understand, process, and digest every piece of information he was giving me.

"Soheila, can you hear me? Are you there?"

"Yes, yes, I am sorry, that was too much information at once."

"I'm sorry, but I had to break it to you."

I tried not to sound worried and distressed. I took a deep breath and said, "Don't be sorry, but let's think, you are in your early 40s, you have a long way to go till 60... plus 6% is not such a high statistic. And you have me as a backup plan, so let's not worry about it now."

"Statistics doesn't mean anything. When it happens to you, any percentage becomes a perfect score, one hundred." He took a deep breath and continued, "Once you enter a hospital you need luck by your side."

"You said you are on top of it. Let's make a deal: you take care of yourself and I will keep myself alive and healthy, I promise."

"You know Soheila, I knew you and I were a 100% match, I had no doubt. We have a special bond."

"Then why am I not smart and accomplished like you? Why did I get the crappy genes?"

"It doesn't work like that."

"I know, I was kidding, when will you be in Los Angeles with Alexa?"

"Like every other year, in March."

We talked about his annual trip to Los Angeles and his plans a bit more and tried to pretend that everything was going to be fine.

"Great, love you, Fariborz. Take care of yourself, all will be well, I promise."

"Please do not mention my situation to anyone. I mean *no one*. Except for Stephen. Tell him I am not ready to see him, not anytime soon."

"Of course."

I had kept the secret for two long years, while worrying about it day and night. Worrying about crossing the street, getting on a plane, walking in the streets late at night, or even catching a cold. I was my brother's insurance policy. I started searching for institutions to freeze my bone marrow in case anything happened to me, but I couldn't find any; I even approached hospitals in foreign countries with no success.

Now the worst had happened. It was March of 2013 and the 6% probability of leukemia in patients over the age of 60 had become 100% in one patient at the age of 47. We were on the Oncology floor at Mount Sinai hospital to treat Acute Leukemia in our brother.

I took a deep breath and walked into the vast lobby, a mixture of a central station, a temple, and a modern museum. Half of the crowd wore crisp white uniforms and the other half was a cross-section of every color, race, gender, and age group under the sun. Doctors, nurses, and visitors all doing their best to get to their patients or loved ones as quickly as possible.

Everyone was in a constant rush, either holding a cup of coffee, talking on their cell phones, or reading a chart. The never-ending line for Starbucks was in the shape of a massive snake, twisting and curling, moving forward slowly. Behind it, a large glass wall exposing the garden and in the middle, an imposing modern sculpture towering over busy and tired bodies. The lobby was bright and open. Chairs and tables were scattered around with worn-out and exhausted figures leaning on their elbows, dozing off or filling up on much-needed caffeine.

I looked around for the closest elevator, ran to it, jumped in, pressed the button for the 11th floor, and waited for the doors to close. People kept on walking and squeezing in every time the door made the smallest attempt to close. My heart was pounding. I was short of breath. I had no idea what was ahead of us. I had been told that he was undergoing a very potent chemotherapy, the queen of them all, "Cytoxan." After his treatment was complete, they would check to see if there were any more blast cells (cancer cells) in his body. Best-case scenario, Cytoxan would kill them all (in the process getting rid of all the white cells as well), and we would go ahead with the bone marrow transplant. That was the plan. Sounded simple and straightforward, but it was neither simple nor straightforward.

The elevator stopped at every floor. Some got off and new people pushed in. It was the longest elevator ride of my life. I finally got to the eleventh floor and ran to the reception area. "Good morning, I am looking for Dr. Noban's room."

She looked at the list of the rooms and pointed to her left, "Room 1101, in the corner."

I thanked her, rushed towards the room, opened a door, and entered a small area with computers on one side and a nurse's station on the other. "Good morning, my name is Soheila, I am Dr. Noban's sister."

"Good morning, Dr. Noban is in the room to your left."

Three doors opened to that small area. "Please wash your hands, put on a hospital gown, and wear hospital gloves before entering."

"Of course." I did as I was told, then opened the door slowly. My heart was pounding. I put my head through the door and said, "Hi baldy!"

He had taken a selfie and sent it to us the minute he shaved his head. His eyes were filled with tears and sorrow in that picture, almost apologizing with his sad smile for sending such an unthinkable and dreadful image. He had become an official cancer patient then.

"Hi, Soheilajon, welcome to New York," he said with a faint smile. Nahid, Nazee, and Jennifer were already there. I entered his room, walked past them, and headed directly towards Fariborz. Nahid whispered in my ear, "He was waiting for you." He was leaning against the windowsill, with a view of a small park on Madison Avenue as his backdrop. I did not know if I was allowed to touch, hug, or kiss him. I stopped, took two steps back and said, "How are you? How do you feel?" He looked at me with sad eyes and said, "I feel fine, a bit weak, but that's a given. I am waiting for the chemo to arrive. It was supposed to be here an hour ago."

"How long of a treatment is it?"

"Four to five days. I can't wait for it to be over, till then, keep yourself alive and healthy for me, please. You are my only hope. All my bets are on you."

I bowed down and said, "It is a promise, my lord!"

We tried our best to keep him entertained and busy until the queen of chemo arrived. We talked about everything and anything. We gossiped, discussed politics, and talked about the latest fashion trends. Any subject was allowed and welcomed but the sad ones. As the time went by he became more and more restless. He kept on looking at the round clock on the wall from the corner of his eyes. The queen of horror wanted to build up some unnecessary suspense, anxiety, and tension mixed with our fear, panic, and revulsion by showing up late.

The Cytoxan did not arrive until late in the afternoon. The nurses got busy putting the line in Fariborz's arm. He looked at us from in between the arms in uniform while his veins were being examined and said, "You get it, right? The word Toxin is on this shit?"

What chemo does to a body is inhuman. While the patient is hoping that the poison invades and kills the cancer cells, it ruins, damages and destroys a lot more. The side effects and the viciousness that come with the poison is as bad as the disease. They are evil and bloodthirsty twins, separated at birth. Cancer is a heartless serial killer and chemo a vengeful executioner. When one falls short, the other picks up the pieces and runs with them. I am sure at some point in future "chemotherapy" will be considered a thing of the past; a barbarous, brutal, destructive, and sadistic approach. The collaboration of the two Cs, Chemo and Cancer, create a heartless and wicked exterminator that affects and butchers every organ in sight.

However now, at this moment, today, in this hospital room, chemo is considered a trusted friend. A friend that will hopefully give a helping hand and walk my brother out of this nightmare, slowly but surely. A villain turning hero. We were relying on *The Royal Highness* one hundred percent. The queen of horror was here to help.

"Consider this 'shit' a friend and let it do what it's supposed to do, and that is kill the cancer cells. Toxin or no toxin! You can't kill those damn cells with kindness!" I said.

We all stayed in the room for a couple more hours. Jennifer, Nahid, Nazee and I were the only four people in the family and the community who knew about his condition. We kept it secret from our mom too. Having a terminally sick daughter was horrible enough. Zohreh was on her deathbed, and everyone knew about her grave condition. How could we possibly drop the second bomb? How could we break the news about our brother? Everyone would be devastated by the news. Hopefully, and with God on our side, Fariborz would be done with the chemo and the bone marrow transplant soon and would go home without anyone finding anything out.

If only it was that simple! How little we knew! Somewhere up there, God was getting himself prepared for the upcoming wrestling match.

My sisters and I left to go see Zohreh. We had been missing in action the entire day, which was very much out of character for us. Jamshid, Zohreh's husband, and my mom were wondering what could have possibly kept us away from our sick sister for so long.

We entered her apartment and immediately felt the sadness and the sorrow. My mother was sitting on a couch, hunched and defeated. Grief and anguish had changed her; she had aged visibly. My brother-in-law sat across the room from her, his elbow leaning on the arm of the sofa, his face in the palm of his hand. Arya, my nephew, was in his room with the door locked. My mom looked up and just shook her head in lament and despair, *What are we going to do?* Nahid sat next to her and held her shoulders.

Nazee and I went straight to Zohreh's room. She was a dreadful and depressing sight. The figure on the bed did not look anything like our sister. In her place lay a human skeleton covered with cellophane-like skin. Her eyes were sunk deep in their sockets. Her teeth and jawbone were sticking out. Her long and skinny arms were crossed on her chest. "When a patient stays in that position it means they are waiting to die," I remembered Fariborz telling us. I uncrossed her arms and placed them at her side. She made a slight move and tried to bring them back to her chest. I held them down, but it was useless. I let her be.

Then it was time to try to feed our mom. She had no appetite. She just cried. We gave her half a Xanax and took her to bed. My mom and I were sleeping in Zohreh's apartment; it was easier for everyone. She did not have to go back and forth to her place, which took about an hour, and I stayed with Zohreh as I always did when I came to New York. I kept my sister company and helped my brother-in-law as well.

The next day, we went to visit Fariborz again. Before entering his room we were reminded to wash our hands and wear the hospital gown and the plastic gloves. He was on his bed, attached to an IV containing "the poison" aka "his friend." Drop by drop, little by little, the solution was entering his veins. The battle had started, and he was ready to put up a big fight. Being a physician, he knew every fact about his disease, and he knew the odds were against him. It was not going to be easy; he knew his opponent was difficult to beat.

But we were the lucky ones! He has me as a backup, as an insurance policy, as his lifeline. He can bank on me. It is a long and difficult road, but everything will be fine, I told myself.

Jennifer and Nazee were standing by his side with worried faces. I said, "Hi Fariborz, how are you doing?"

"Weak, very weak," he said, "but besides that I am OK. I can't wait for this shit to be over."

We all sat around his bed and started talking again. The subjects were so random that now, when I think back, I can't remember any of them. But one thing was for sure, we were there to support him, we were there so he was not alone. He did not want to be alone, ever. He did not need to say it; we all knew that about him.

"How is Zohreh doing?" he asked.

"The same."

He shook his head, looked away, and said, "The poor thing."

"Fariborz, you did whatever you could do for her and more, for the past 20 years. There is nothing else left to do. It is time for you to think about 'you' now," Nazee said.

"This is a fucking nightmare," he said.

There was no point talking about Zohreh. She had just a few more days to live. He was right, it was a "fucking nightmare." The worst kind of nightmare, the kind that you wake up to, the kind that continues day in and day out. The only time you get a break is when you are asleep and the few seconds right after you wake up in the morning. The few seconds that you are still disoriented, the few seconds that you are in twilight, the few seconds when you are not completely awake, in-between your dreams and your harsh reality. Those few seconds were the most peaceful time of the day, until we were faced every morning with the existence of our perpetual nightmare.

"We will put this, as you put it so nicely, 'fucking nightmare' behind us soon. You have to think positive thoughts about the future," I said. "Let's play some music." We started searching for songs on our iPhones and continued talking about new ideas for his house in Connecticut.

The next day, when we entered his room, we were all shocked by what we saw. Fariborz was not himself; he was weak and his color was gone. His skin was dark grey. It was obvious something was wrong, but we thought it was the side effects of having a killer friend called Cytoxan.

"Guys, I don't feel well. I have difficulty breathing. I think I have pneumonia," he said with a weak voice. We all stood up and approached his bed. "Tell the nurse to call Dr. Isola right away. Tell him it is an emergency." Nazee ran out to call the nurse. Dr. Isola showed up after a couple of hours.

"Doctor, I am pretty sure I have pneumonia. Please order a bedside X-ray machine. I do not feel well."

"But Dr. Noban, chances of that with patients under treatment with Cytoxan is minimal. I have never seen a case personally."

"Please order an X-ray machine, I assure you I have pneumonia. Statistics will not help me when I'm dead."

Soon it was confirmed. Pneumonia was all over his lungs. Had he not noticed that himself, the combination of the chemo and deadly bacteria would have killed him in no time.

Dr. Isola stopped the treatment right away. His body had shown an extremely unusual adverse reaction to the poison. It was not safe anymore. It had never been safe to begin with, but in his case the treatment would have killed him way before the leukemia got the chance.

Fariborz was disappointed. This was a huge setback. He had his heart set on the "queen of no hearts," "the most potent chemo of them all," to save him. The one that was supposed to kill his blast cells. But instead "his friend" had tried to kill him.

His white cell count was very low. He had to be quarantined in a hospital room. No one was allowed to get close to him without a mask, as his body was not strong enough to protect him from germs and bacteria. Cut fruit from the stores was not allowed. Food from a public place was not allowed. Drinking from a glass was not allowed. The drip for the chemo was replaced with a drip for the antibiotics. His hope was replaced by despair.

"This will postpone everything," he said. "The chances of anyone developing pneumonia as a result of Cytoxan are close to zero, yet I fell in that small percentage. I told you, when you enter a hospital, you need luck on your side.

"Look at the positive side, Fariborz, if you had not diagnosed it yourself, you would have had no chance of survival. A normal patient without a medical background was doomed to die. A few weeks here and there doesn't make much of a difference," I said.

He just looked down and shook his head.

Dr. Isola instructed Fariborz to stay at the hospital for 6 days and then return to his apartment when his lungs were completely clear. He was under strict rules. With his low white cell count, his body was an open house to the tiniest virus or bacteria. He was told not to touch, hug or kiss his kids at home. All visitors or family members were instructed to wear a face mask and wash their hands the minute they entered his house, until he was clear from the deadly pneumonia.

Maybe someone had rung the bell for the wrestling match. Maybe they had to take a break. Maybe God was reconsidering his strategy. Whatever the reason, we looked at this as a temporary setback, a bump in the road, a small defeat. Maybe even a lost battle, but we all agreed that he would have been dead if it wasn't for his prognostic abilities. He was alive and he was home with his family.

Momon Finds Out

"Life is not a problem to be solved, but a reality to be experienced." —Soren Kierkegaard

May, 2013

On the 8th day after Zohreh's passing, I flew to Los Angeles with my mother. Her favorite spot in the house was our open and sunny breakfast room. It was everyone's favorite spot.

With the three glass walls, one could see the city of Los Angeles, the sun setting over green mountains, and the neighbor's vineyard: an image of the Tuscan hills at one glance. Momon relaxed in that bright room, leaning back in a chair with her legs resting on a stool, taking in the view. On a good day, she'd browse through a magazine or read a book, and on a better day she'd knit. Most of the time, though, her eyes were frozen on the landscape. Emotionally she was in better shape now, better than when she first arrived. She cried less. She was away from the constant reminders of her daughter's suffering and death.

If she was not in the breakfast room, she was busy gardening. It was her preferred activity; it brought her joy. Nothing changed her mood like getting busy with plants and flowers. She whispered to them while pruning their branches, digging up a hole or taking out the weeds. You could see her smile when she saw a new bud on the side of a lemon tree, or a frown between her eyebrows when the wrong branch climbed the wrong tree. It was "off with their heads" and the poor branch fell lifeless on the ground. Nature gave her some much-needed peace.

She had regained some of her energy and started welcoming visitors and friends. The new environment was helping her. She needed the sun and the sea breeze, not the four walls of her apartment that held so many painful memories. But I could tell she was worried about Fariborz, who was still at home recovering.

She called Fariborz every day, and every time she asked the same question, "When are you going back to work?" In her mind, if he'd gone back to his office, then he was fine and his life was back to normal. She was sold on the idea that he'd had pneumonia and that was why he'd been missing in action during Zohreh's funeral and the week of mourning. We couldn't tell her the truth.

It was not easy keeping the secret; still, everything had gone according to plan until the day that my mom and I were leaving for Los Angeles after Zohreh's memorial. I wanted to see Fariborz before my departure. He was still in quarantine at his home.

Nazee and I walked in, put on the surgical mask and gloves and sat on a chair a few feet away from him. He was seated on his favorite leather sofa against the window. His head was bald with just a few strands of hair here and there. We sat down and talked about everything, while keeping our distance from him. He simply couldn't take the chance of getting close to anyone that might carry any bacteria, have a common cold, or even a simple cough.

"I told the driver to pick Momon up and come here so you can go to the airport together," Nazee whispered to me, "but he will call me when they are close."

"OK, if she doesn't see Fariborz looking like this, we can buy some time."

We were busy making small talk until we heard the buzzer. "Who is it?" Jennifer asked.

"Your mother-in-law is coming up," the doorman replied.

"OH NO!" Jennifer gasped. "Guys, Momon is coming up."

Fariborz ran for his baseball cap as we sat there stunned. "Idiot, he was supposed to call me, now she will see Fariborz. She is not stupid, she will figure it out," Nazee said.

We took off our masks and gloves and a minute later Momon stepped into the living room and walked towards Fariborz.

"Hi, Fariborzjoon, I couldn't wait to see you. Why are you wearing a hat? Take it off, let me see."

Fariborz stepped away, holding onto his baseball cap. "It's OK, don't worry Momon."

"Why are you bald? What happened to your hair?"

"I decided to shave it all. It will grow back."

"But why? Tell me the truth, what's wrong?"

"I have pneumonia, that's all. I will be fine in couple of days."

"Momon, you will miss your flight," Nazee said. "You better go."

"I will, first I have to know the truth," reaching out for the baseball cap.

"I was not feeling well, I went to the doctor and I was told I have pneumonia, a very dangerous one, but now everything is under control. I lost my hair because of one of the medications. That's all."

My mom looked at Fariborz with intense suspicion and said, "I think I should stay in New York."

"No Momon, you go to L.A., I will keep you posted," and he escorted her to the door.

"Soheila, let's go. You will miss your flight," Fariborz said, while trying to keep his distance.

Momon tried to argue, but Fariborz wouldn't give her the chance. "Please go and enjoy Los Angeles, I will be fine. I promise you."

I had left with my worried mom for LA on April 16th. Now, more than a month later, my mother and I were sitting in the breakfast room looking at the beautiful sunny scenery as usual when Fariborz called. I picked up my phone.

"It's time to fly back with Momon," he said. "I'm checking back into the hospital tomorrow." I looked at my mother, hoping she hadn't heard his voice, hoping she hadn't noticed the blood leaving my face, hoping she hadn't read her son's words in my expression.

"One second," I answered. I left the breakfast room and walked to the front yard.

"Can she stay here a little longer?" I asked in a low voice, thinking of giving her a few more days free of torture.

"They're starting with another dangerous and potent chemo," he said. "A lot of shit could go wrong. She should know the truth. She should be here. We can't hide it from her anymore."

I wanted to bargain with him and extend her stay for a few more days, but he was so adamant I decided to keep my wishes to myself. "I understand, I just wanted to protect her, but of course you are right." I continued, "Nothing will go wrong. I have my bionic bone marrow ready for you. Top of the line! Can we fly in the day after tomorrow?"

"Yes, the day after tomorrow is fine." Fariborz had a commanding baritone and it was a pleasure listening to him speak, but I could hear the tremble of fear in his voice. I could tell he was holding back tears.

"I wish I could believe that nothing would go wrong, but that is not the case when one enters Oncology," he said in a sad voice. "For now please take care of yourself and don't do anything dangerous. Remember, you are my insurance policy. By the way, you still have my 'Just in case' email, right?"

My brother sent an email to me on January 1st of each year, listing all his financial information and his assets so 'Just in Case' anything happened to him, I would have all the necessary facts and instructions.

"Fariborz, I love you," I said. "We will all be there for you. I am here for you." Like a fool, I continued, "I promise you. Everything will be fine. I will not need your 'Just in case' information." I held back tears of my own. We were both trying to sound strong over the phone. "Good luck to all of us."

I heard him sigh from thousands of miles away. "Soheila," he said, "You have no idea how much of that luck I need right now and what a big role it plays in my life. I told you, when you enter a hospital you need luck to stay by your side."

I had never believed in luck. Unlucky was my least favorite word. I disliked that word with passion. Did it mean if someone was lucky, then someone else could be the opposite? Unlucky meant one was chosen and destined to suffer, without knowing, without deserving it, without being able to resist. Was one just unlucky? No, these were just events, coincidences, situations—not a permanent condition.

"Fariborz, we have each other. There is a reason we are a 100-percent match. I love you, don't worry, please."

"Remember, tell Stephen I don't want to see him anytime soon."

"I will, I will."

I hung up the phone and walked back to the breakfast room with the weight of a fresh disaster on my shoulders. *How can I tell her?* I thought. *How do I break this news?*

"Momon," I said. "I have to fly back to New York the day after tomorrow to meet Zohreh's lawyer and sign some papers. Do you want to come with me?"

She jumped from her chair, not at all like an 82-year-old, and said, "Yes! It is about time! I will go pack."

Even though she was enjoying life in Los Angeles, she wanted to break free from the invisible chains that held her there. She had to see Fariborz healthy with her own eyes.

"But wait!" I said, "You have plenty of time!" She was already rushing to her room.

"No, no," she said, "I have to get ready and get my luggage together." She was anxious to see him, to make sure that he was fine so she could stop worrying. I retreated behind my computer to buy return tickets to New York. My mother, meanwhile, was already downstairs packing.

The flight from LA to NY takes about 5 hours, plus the 3 hours lost to the time difference. By the time the plane lands in New York, the whole day is gone. I watched people as my mom and I were walking slowly towards our gate. Almost everyone was rushing to their planes, holding onto their bags with one hand and their kids with the other. I wanted to stop them, look them straight in the eye, and tell them, "Enjoy these moments, enjoy your family trips, enjoy these carefree days when the kids are young and with you. Go make memories and cherish them." Instead I just watched in silence and envied their state of mind.

Momon kept fidgeting in her seat on the plane, grasping at my hands, asking how long it was before we landed. I tried to be patient and answer her repetitious questions, but I was on pins and needles myself. Now that Fariborz's lungs were clear from pneumonia he was allowed to resume with a new chemo treatment.

I decided to offer her a glass of wine. To my surprise, she welcomed it with a look of relief. Soon after, she was asleep. I placed a pillow under her head and a blanket over her. I ran through various scenarios throughout the flight, trying to figure out how to break the news to her, but I realized there is no easy way of telling a mother her son has cancer. One thing I was sure of—after losing Stephen and my sister, nothing bad could happen to Fariborz. God understood, he knew we'd already had our fair share of tragedies. We'd filled our quota. We had paid our dues. *He'll be fine,* I thought. *He'll go home healthy and get old.*

I looked out the window. The thick clouds and the enormity of the sky made me feel closer to God. I remembered a line that played over and over in my head from the movie *Fiddler on the Roof,* when Tevi complained to God about the series of unfortunate events that was happening to him: "I know, I know. We are your chosen people. But, once in a while, can't You choose someone else?" That line would become my mantra over the long weeks to come. I could not help but wonder, wasn't there a terrorist out there somewhere who was more deserving of cancer? A serial killer? A pedophile?

We landed in New York around 7 pm. Nazee's driver was waiting at the curbside to take Momon home. I kissed her goodbye and promised I'd call the next day. "Let's meet at Fariborz's apartment," she said. I was at a loss for words. "Yes, we can do that," I said, knowing very well my brother wasn't in his apartment anymore. I pulled myself away from her to hail a cab to Nahid's and called Fariborz at the hospital as soon as I closed the car door.

"Can I come see you now?" I asked.

"No, Soheilajon. It's late. You're tired. Go relax, take a shower. I'll still be here tomorrow." I knew that he wanted to spare me an extra night in the hospital, but I wanted to see him. Everyone else had been with him while I was in LA with my mom, and I envied the time they got to spend together. Besides, I knew he didn't like to be alone. He always wanted company.

"But I have not seen you for more than a month."

"Go to bed, you had a long day."

"Whatever you say," I said. "I'll be there early tomorrow morning." I stared out into the night for the rest of the taxi ride, thinking, *This can't be our lives. But if this is a horror story, why can't I put the book down? If it's a nightmare, what's taking so long? If it's a bad movie, why can't I walk out?*

The next day I was in his room bright and early. Fariborz was trying to smile and put up a courageous front. I wanted to jump from the doorway and touch him, kiss him, feel him alive.

"Can I hug you?" I asked.

He shook his head. "No," he said. "Any stray germ could destroy me."

I stepped back. Everyone had masks and gloves on but him. Jennifer was standing at the side of his bed and Nazee was massaging his feet. I could see they were bent under the pressure of his suffering. "I told momon, Fariborz is here for a couple of tests, and a driver is coming to pick her up," Nazee whispered to me. We all worried how she'd take it. Fariborz sat halfway up in the bed, an IV sticking out from his left arm, the poison entering his body drop by drop. I stared at the bag attached to his IV and thought, *This poison is not our enemy. This one is not going to cause more harm. This one is our best friend. This one must save my brother's life.*

"Do they have any idea when we're going through with the bone marrow transplant?"

He shrugged. "If I didn't have a negative reaction to Cytoxan, you and I would've been done by now. They switched me to a cocktail called

7 + 3. This one should take care of the blast cells, but again, it's another potent and dangerous chemotherapy, a lot of things could go wrong."

The driver called Nazee. They were close. In only a few minutes, they'd arrive. We looked at each other in horror. Nazee left at once, she wanted to speak to our mother before she entered the hospital. She was about to see her only son lying in a hospital bed, IVs sticking from his body, no hair, no eyebrows, no eyelashes.

I wondered if God was paying attention. Maybe he was asleep. Maybe he was busy. Maybe he had just turned his back on us. Whatever he was doing, we were not part of his agenda in that hospital room.

The door creaked open and Nazee walked in with our mom. As soon as she saw her son, she heaved out a sigh, raised her hands in the air and then slapped them against her face. She ran her fingernails down her cheeks, leaving red, bloody lines on her skin, and melted down. She fell to her knees and started sobbing in the doorway.

Nazee had already told her part of the story, that I was a 100% match, that this process would be the worst part, that he'd be fine after the bone marrow transplant. She kept screaming, "Why God? Why? Why my son? God, leave our family alone." We gathered around her, rubbing her back, trying our best to comfort her. Nazee held a glass of sugar water to her lips.

"Momon, I'm his match, all will be well." She looked up with pleading eyes and asked in a trembling voice, "What would happen if you weren't a match?"

"No sense in going there now," I said. "I'm here, and I'm a match. That in itself is a miracle."

After half an hour, she managed to calm down. Every so often, she'd fall at the foot of Fariborz's bed and cry, "Why, God? Why are you punishing me? What wrong did I do? I tried to be a good person. Why him? If you want to take someone, take me. I have lived enough."

She was right; Fariborz was selfless, giving, kind, devoted to his friends, his family, his patients… and so was my mother. What lesson was there to learn in all this suffering? Why did God want to pin us down and show his victorious face to us? We didn't know, but one thing was for sure, one thing we knew for a fact, that the love we had for each other as a family should be and would be stronger than any other force against us. I hoped God was paying attention to that small detail and taking notes.

The Man Who
Would Beat Cancer

*"When the world pushes you to your knees, you're
in the perfect position to pray."* —Rumi

May, 2013

I knew that going to the gym each morning for my hour-long work-out was crucial. If I could keep up my regular routine, I was happy. Exercising for me remained my medication, a therapy, an antide-pressant. I needed to create endorphins naturally and stay positive. Even though I wanted to be in the hospital with Fariborz every possible minute, the fear of sinking back into depression was frightening and very real to me. It had taken me a long time till I got into the daily routine of working out and free from the "happy pills!" Lexapro had created a zombie out of me. I was on those pills for 7 months. My doctor had suggested them when he noticed how depressed I was at the beginning of my move to LA. But with those pills, I switched from feeling depressed to not feeling at all. I spent most of my time in bed, staring at the ceiling, not knowing that every emotion in me was drugged. And now I would do whatever it took to keep that darkness at bay.

I decided to go to the gym early each morning before going to the hospital. With my workout done, I could stay with my brother for the whole day until late at night. Jennifer arrived each morning after the girls left for school and left in the afternoon. Nazee was there all day, and Nahid, the nieces and nephews, and my boys all came after work. My mom, my poor mom, was at the hospital almost all day, every day. That was our routine: wake up, head for the hospital and keep him company for as long as needed.

Nazee arranged for evening prayers for the sick; our friends and family members started gathering at sundown. Matthew, her son, was by her side praying and begging God to save his uncle. They stood behind his door and prayed for his health every night. I stayed at my brother's side till 11 pm and watched TV with him or talked about everyone, especially Alexa and Ava. It was not an inconvenience for me. Jordan was at school in LA with my husband and since I had no one at home waiting for me in New York, I stayed until it was Fariborz's bedtime.

"Soheilajon," he would say, "would you please close the shades (so the room stayed dark) unplug the refrigerator (too noisy), move the chairs to the side (so he wouldn't trip while trying to go to the bathroom in the middle of the night holding on to the pole with IVs hanging), call the nurse (for his sleeping pills) and go home, go rest." I did each of those small tasks every night before leaving his room. I prayed for a better day while leaving the hospital.

We posted a calendar on the wall right in front of him and crossed out the day that had just passed. His stay there was a prison sentence. We were anxious to see the last cross on the date that his chemotherapy was supposed to be over.

The rest of the bare walls of his room were covered with fly fishing posters brought in by Linda, Nahid's daughter, and Philip, her husband. Fly fishing was my brother's passion and his love was the great outdoors. "As a surgeon, I spend most of my days inside hospital walls, it's important for me to be in touch with nature. I need to see and feel the beauty of this world," he often said. He traveled long and far to be in the right location to fly fish and savored every second of it.

The empty spaces in between the large posters were covered with family pictures from happier days. Days when life was normal, when we all smiled freely, when he had a full head of hair. Alexa and Ava made personal cards for him and posted them on his walls. Liza, Nahid's daughter, knitted soft hats for him when he complained about his head always being cold. Nazee brought light exercise equipment when she noticed that his movements were declining and kept his muscles active. We played music for him, his favorite: *America the Beautiful.* And yes, we talked and talked and talked. His favorite phrase, "So…what else is new?" We all came in prepared with "something new." We always found an interesting subject to talk about—we had to.

There was a constant flow of people in his room. His colleagues, their spouses, the neighbors, his friends, our cousins Shoshana and Ilana, her husband Dr. Bander, various other family members, ex-patients, the parents and the staff from Alexa and Ava's school—all showed up on regular basis. On occasion, I had to step out and sit on a bench in Central Park for hours because his room was overcrowded.

Dr. David Spielvogel, his best friend from medical school and his proxy, was his favorite visitor. Fariborz felt safe when he was around. He loved David as a friend and respected him as a physician. When it was time for him to leave, Fariborz would say in a pleading voice, "Not yet David, please stay a bit longer."

We had a game with the visitors that he felt especially close to. We created a contest. Who could come up with the best treat or the most interesting activity for him, for when he would go back home healthy?

"Guys, think big, think unique, think special."

Dr. Spielvogel (knowing Fariborz's passion for Italian sports cars) said, "I will rent a red convertible Ferrari and we will go driving all day."

Matthew promised to throw a huge party for him on the rooftop of the new W hotel. Mitra and Nader offered to take him on their private plane to anywhere he wished to go. Fariborz had loved airplanes ever since he was a little boy. He was fascinated with them. A private jet was the ultimate luxury to him; flying on a private jet a dream come true.

"Seriously, on your private jet? To where?" he asked like a little kid.

"To wherever, whenever! Don't worry about the details, that will be arranged. Just go home soon and make it happen," Mitra said with concerned eyes.

He tried to put up a strong and positive attitude and laughed with everyone about their ideas. But he was scared. He had to talk and converse with people. Having time to think was his worst pasttime. Being alone was his worst enemy. Physicians make the worst patients; they know too much. They know the risks. They know the facts. They know it all because they've seen it all. Nothing can be sugar-coated for them. They know the truth—and his truth was dark and terrifying.

Fariborz had hand-picked each of his doctors at Mount Sinai after long research. This hospital was familiar and personal to him. He chose Mount Sinai because they didn't care so much about politics, case number, or statistics. "Just because a doctor is famous doesn't mean he's the best!" he often said. "Maybe he just has good PR, or he never takes the challenging cases, or he knows how to play politics in the world of medicine. A good doctor cares about his patients first, not how the patient makes him look!"

We loved most of his doctors and understood why Fariborz had chosen Dr. Isola; the one we didn't get was Dr. Hemorrhoids, the infectious disease doctor. Obviously, his name wasn't Hemorrhoids, but that's what we called him, because he was uncomfortable, irritating, painful looking, ugly, and the closest thing to an asshole.

Hemorrhoids was short, square, and chubby, with no neck, uneven shoulders, and buggy eyes behind thick glasses. His big face sat atop his body like a snowman's. He combed his thin hair from one side of his ear to the opposite side. When we asked him a question, he'd give us a suspicious look from the corner of his eye, while jerking his head, meaning, "Why are you asking me this nonsense?" Smiling was never one of his expressions—an unfamiliar, never-explored facial muscle, probably! He was a cold, unsympathetic, and uncompassionate being. All in all, he lacked the presence of a respectable doctor.

None of us liked him, but Fariborz had picked him so we respected his choice. He seemed exactly like one of the "best doctors" that Fariborz always warned us about. If he had a heart, it was made of scrap metal.

During Fariborz's chemotherapy, we noticed two small bruises—one on the side of his arm and another on his thigh. When the spots grew bigger and darker, Fariborz needed an infectious disease specialist, which was when we met our dear gloomy doctor, aka "Dr. Hemorrhoids" for the first time. He dragged himself in, mumbled a few dry words, and circled each spot with a marker. Before he left, he jerked his head and gave us one of his trademark sideways cold glances, as if to say, "Don't you have anything better to do than hover around a hospital bed? How many of you need to be here?" The moment he left, I asked Jennifer, "Fariborz chose this character?" "Yes," she shrugged. "But it looks like he has more issues than a newsstand!"

Nazee, Joe and a tall rabbi walked into Fariborz's room.

"Hi Fariborz, how are you feeling today?" Joe said, "This is Rabbi Metzger. Rabbi Metzger, this is Dr. Fariborz Noban, my brother-in-law."

"Hi Joe, hello Rabbi, nice to meet you," Fariborz reclined in his bed, happy to have a new visitor. His smile revealed the curled-up dimple that we loved.

"Hi Rabbi, this is my sister Soheila, aka 'The Match,'" Nazee said.

"Ah, so you are the match?" the Rabbi said with a powerful voice and a big smile.

"Yes, that's the name I go by lately. Some people change their names to Lady Gaga or Queen Latifah, but I'm 'The Match,'" I said, laughing. "But enough about me, here is Dr. McDreamy."

He turned to Fariborz. "I've heard so much about you. It seems you are loved and admired by everyone. People can't stop talking and raving about you. Tell me, what is your secret?"

Fariborz winked and tilted his head to one side. "Besides my good looks?!"

The rabbi threw up his hands in the air and said, "Yeah, that I noticed already." He was a big man with a noticeable stomach, a long beard, the customary black coat, and the biggest laugh. He looked like a Jewish Santa Claus.

"Fariborz, I told Rabbi about you and he wanted to come and meet with you personally," Joe said.

"Yes, it's true," the Rabbi interrupted Joe, "I wanted to know the man who would beat cancer."

"Of course, Rabbi, that he will definitely do," Joe said with excitement.

Joe was always involved and present in everything that was happening around him. He was at the hospital the first day he heard about Fariborz's condition. We could count on Joe when help was needed. He never left anything up to chance. He was never passive; on the contrary, he was extremely proactive. He was in control of his emotions and in charge of his life. He analyzed the situation and chose the best possibility. There was a reason for everything that he said or did. In his eyes, there were never problems, only opportunities. Joseph Moinian was a bright, hardworking, and self-made man through and through.

On that day at Mount Sinai hospital, Joe thought a respected and open-minded Rabbi from Israel could be a source of comfort to our brother, even though Fariborz was far from being religious. The Rabbi didn't talk about God, nor did he say any prayers; he just talked to Fariborz and tried to give him more courage and a few laughs. It was a brief but welcome interlude. The atmosphere and the energy of the room changed for about an hour and we were happy to see our brother light up in the rabbi's cheerful presence. Our moods, our spirits and our moments depended on the movement on Fariborz's lips and the look in his eyes. And on that day both of them were curled up.

The Perfect Match

"It's your road and yours alone. Others may walk it with you, but no one can walk it for you." —Rumi

July, 2013

I was required to be in the bone marrow transplant department by 9 am. I had been instructed to have a good, hearty breakfast and avoid coffee. "You will be attached to tubes for about five hours," I had been told by the nurse, "so walking to a bathroom is not an option. Coffee is a diuretic, and drinking it would make the situation uncomfortable for you."

I arrived on time and sat in the waiting room. The scene around me was something out of a horror movie. Everyone in that room had a sizable catheter on the side of their necks, held in with surgical tape, a plastic tube sticking out. It appeared as if the nozzle was pulled, the life would rush out of their bodies and they would fall flat on the floor like deflated balloons. They all seemed to be doing fine with an extension cord, but it looked uncomfortable and disturbing. *Thank God I had good veins on my hands and did not need to go through that procedure,* I thought.

My conversation from the day before with my brother was constantly in my head. "Soheilajon, please don't leave." I'd left. I'd left, when he was at his worst. I'd left when he was having trouble breathing. I'd left when his fever was 105. I'd left when he was scared and vulnerable.

I saw Andrea from Dr. Isola's office walking towards me. I got up and walked as fast as I could to her. "Andrea, my brother is not doing well. Will he get my stem cells in time? It's not too late, is it?"

Andrea looked into my eyes, held my hands and said, "Do you want to go to him first and have some closure, just in case?"

I took two steps back in horror. I was in shock. I couldn't believe what I was hearing. What was she saying? Closure? He was supposed to get my cells today. Today was the big battle. Those tiny but powerful little things were supposed to save him. I started sobbing and shaking. Everyone turned around and watched me as I cried out and repeated, "He is not going anywhere. My brother is not going anywhere."

"Honey, you can't go under the machine in this condition. Please calm down. Take a deep breath. You don't have to do it now. Do you want to wait?"

"No, no," I said, "Fariborz is waiting for my stem cells. We can't lose precious time. Let's get on with it." I stopped, took a small container out and asked, "I have a Xanax with me. Can I take half?" I knew time was limited. I couldn't jeopardize the transplant.

"Yes, please do. Take whatever helps you," she said.

I sat on a chair, she handed me a glass, I took the pill with a minimum amount of water and after a few minutes followed her to the room. I was no longer sobbing hysterically, but I could not keep from crying. I lay down on the recliner and the nurse started, putting a line first on my right hand and then on the left. Twenty minutes later I was attached to the machine.

Almost right away I felt the chills. The machine had become an extension of my veins. The blood was flowing through my right hand into the tube that went directly to the machine. After the stem cells were separated and collected in a plastic bag, the blood returned to my body through the line on my left hand. Since my blood was going through a process inside of the machine and not in my body, it lost its warmth. By the time it reentered my body it was colder than usual. I started to shiver. The nurse brought a heavy blanket and gently covered me with it.

I closed my eyes and started visualizing a war in Fariborz's veins. I pictured my stem cells in white outfits, holding white flags, as soldiers attacking and fighting the bacteria and the blast cells, which were in black outfits, holding black flags. It was a bloody battle. But my cells were strong and they went in for the kill. Nothing could hold them back; failure was not an option. They had two choices: either they won, or they consciously got killed for the cause. I imagined that victory and I imagined it as reality, hard and clear. I imagined my brother smiling again, walking again, working again. The normal stuff. The basic stuff. The day-to-day stuff. ·

I do not know how long I was asleep, but I heard voices next to me. I opened my eyes and saw Justin with my nephew Matthew by my side. They both smiled when I opened my eyes.

"How are you, Khaleh Soheila?" Matthew asked.

"Mom, you look very comfortable on that recliner, is there room for me? Could you move to the side a bit please?"

"Hi guys," I said. "It is a comfortable recliner. How is Fariborz?"

"Everyone is with him. How do you feel?"

"Could you please ask the nurse how many more hours I need to be here? I want to see Fariborz," I asked.

Matthew left to find the person in charge. He came back with the technician. "Mrs. Adelipour, your stem cell count is high. You did well. I think we have enough now. We will start taking off the lines soon."

"Did you hear that guys? I've got super stem cells. A whole army of them." I visualized my massive white army surrounding the defeated bad guys and mounting their white flags on top of the bloody lifeless blast cell's bodies. After a short while I was free to go. We walked towards the elevator and I pressed eleven. Justin and Matthew exchanged a glance.

"Mom, Fariborz is on the fifth floor now. He is in Medical ICU. Everyone is there with him. He is not doing well."

I looked at them in disbelief, held Justin's arms and asked, "What is a 'Medical ICU?'"

"It is for patients in critical condition. He has been intubated. He is out. The doctors agree that he is much better off if he is not conscious. They say the tube down his throat is very uncomfortable," Justin said. Matthew was just looking down. He did not say a word.

The plan was for us to be happy when the day for the bone marrow transplant arrived. It was the day we had all been waiting for. It was the day that I was supposed to help him get healthy again.

"Soheilajon, if you were not here, I would have died in less than a month." He had said this a few weeks ago.

I am here, and he is dying in about a month anyway. And I couldn't help him. What a cruel world! What a vicious game! What a...

MICU is a sad and horrible place. It is a hop, skip, and a jump from the grave; if you do not come out of that exit the next one is in six feet—under. It's next door to hell. It's truly the Twilight Zone. When I went to see Zohreh immediately after each of her brain surgeries, she was always in an ICU. After a few days, she was transferred to a regular room. MICU was a pit stop for people who needed extra care and attention, or so I had always thought!

How did this happen? He was supposed to finish his second chemo treatment and then go for the bone marrow transplant. "You are the lucky ones," Dr. Isola told us, "You are a 100% match. It doesn't happen so often!"

But then he caught pneumonia once again; the infection in his lungs returned. He got worse over the course of the week. His temperature was at its highest. "Fariborz, please take the Tylenol. You can't survive with a 105-degree temperature." I begged him.

"I can't survive without a liver either. Tylenol could kill my liver. It is as bad as alcohol. I need a healthy liver when I return home."

"Please take the damn Tylenol. Aren't we a match? I will give you my liver."

"Don't be stupid, Soheila, I wasn't talking about a kidney, you have only one liver. You can't give me your liver. I'll keep mine healthy."

I kept quiet and watched him suffer while going from extreme shivering to sweating all week. He looked horrible early that morning, the morning before he was transferred to MICU.

The doctors were surrounding his bed. Each one busy examining him for different reasons. My husband's nephew, Dr. Babak Mehrara, was there, as well as my cousin's husband and his cardiologist Dr. Jeffrey Bander. Fariborz tried to look at me from in between all those bodies fussing over him. "Hi, Soheilajoon, come in," he said, with a hard breath in between each syllable.

"I think it's better if I sit outside until your room is less crowded. I will be right here," and I walked out.

Dr. Mehrara walked out with me, sat next to me, and said, "Soheila, he is not doing well, the fever is high. He cannot breathe. He should be intubated. The pneumonia has filled up his lungs again. His body will give out. He can't continue like this for much longer."

I melted on the chair, held my face in my hands, and started crying. Crying had become my eating, my breathing, my talking. I could not believe that we had gotten to a point where I would not even be given the opportunity to give him my stem cells. What was the 100% match good for? If it is not used, it was as good as a patient with a 0% match. Where is the logic behind that?

The nurse sat next to me, held me and said, "You need to go home and relax. The last thing we want on our hands is an exhausted stem cell donor. Please go home. You will do him good if you are strong and well-rested tomorrow morning."

"She is right, Soheila. You are playing an important role tomorrow. You should not be here."

"But I can't leave him now."

"By staying you are not helping him."

My body was already aching as a result of the Neupogen shots I had been instructed to give myself. I couldn't make a sudden move or I would give out an involuntary cry. Every bone and every joint in my body was hurting. The shots helped my white cell counts; I needed those extra cells to be extra good tomorrow. I got up slowly from the chair and entered his room. "Fariborz, they are telling me that I should go home and rest," I said.

"Don't, don't go, please stay," he said, breathing short and fast.

"But everyone agrees that you will be better off if I am well rested and strong for tomorrow's transplant. I do not want to do anything that would hurt you."

He gathered his strength and begged between his breaths, "Soheila, please don't go. Stay next to me. Stay with me. Don't leave."

I looked at Dr. Mehrara. He nodded his head and looked away. "I have to go, Fariborz, I have to do the right thing," I said. He gathered his strength to say something. Maybe he was going to try to convince me to change my mind, but I didn't stay to find out. After weeks of staying next to him till late, I closed the door behind me and ran off. I did not want him to see my tears. He relied on me, I was his lifeline. Had I known that this would be the last time I would hear his warm and kind voice, I would have stayed by his side. But I left. The next day he was lying in bed, unconscious and intubated, in that miserable MICU.

To this day, those words and his pleading eyes have not left me. "Soheilajoon, do not go, please stay, stay next to me, please," my brother asked me, and I refused. It wasn't the only time that I left him alone when he asked me not to, and every time I made the wrong decision. I left him when he begged me not to. I left him when I should have stayed. I left him at the most crucial point of his life.

Things turned for the worse as soon as I left my brother's hospital room the day before. My brother's breathing had become more difficult, shorter, and heavier. His pneumonia had gotten worse. The doctors knew he couldn't last much longer; he needed to be intubated. Nazee had tried to convince him to go ahead with the doctor's plans, but he refused. With that tube down his throat he wouldn't be able to get the last radiation necessary for his treatment. If he had gone to ICU and was intubated, he would not be able to complete the last step necessary for the bone marrow transplant. There was no way he would agree.

He was breathing as if he had been running for the past two hours; his heart rate was through the roof. "You understand, if Dr. Noban was not in a good shape physically before all this, his heart would never be able to take this pressure. He would have had a heart attack by now," Dr. Bander said. The other doctors all agreed. They were amazed by his resilience and tolerance. Fariborz was a physician himself. He knew the drill. He knew he needed the radiation before the transplant. He needed to be coherent and conscious at any cost. And intubation after all that chemo would have ruined every chance for him.

Nazee decided to call Dr. David Spielvogel and ask him for help. David asked for the phone to be placed on Fariborz's ear. He talked to him with his soft voice and convinced him to go to MICU. He needed to get the critical care there. The only person Fariborz would have listened to was Dr. Spielvogel. To him, David was God. He knew the pros and cons. But our brother knew the facts as well. Fariborz knew if he went to MICU the chance of him leaving there alive was slim. He knew once you entered that zone, you have almost crossed over to the other side.

So, they transferred him here, to this miserable place, to an isolated room, and intubated him. He was in quarantine. He was in great danger; his breathing and his heart rate were alarmingly high. "He could have a heart attack any minute," I was told.

All this had happened while I was home resting. No one had said a word to me. I had gone home and right to bed, where I closed my eyes and visualized Fariborz healthy and with his family. I was sure that once they did the bone marrow transplant the following day, everything would be changed. He would have white cells to fight the infection and enough ammunition to win the match. How little I knew!

We arrived on the fifth floor. They directed me towards the MICU. I started walking faster. Time was precious now, more precious than ever. I stopped at the entrance and saw everyone there, family members, friends, colleagues. They all took a step back and opened the way for me. Nobody said a word. Nazee and Nahid walked towards the entrance with me. Nazee hit the big button on the wall with her fist and the double doors opened slowly with a dreadful sigh.

I could feel my pulse pounding in my head. I was scared. We walked in. Beeping noises and the smell of disinfecting solution had filled up the space. I had no idea which bed he was in. I noticed the nurse's station and an open area filled with hospital beds, all lined up next to the wall separated with grey curtains. Nazee stopped in front of the first room to our left, turned around, and looked at me. I froze.

He was there, flat on his back, intubated. His chest moving up and down with the help of the mechanical ventilation in a rhythmic motion. He was attached to monitors, machines, tubes, and wires. He was pale and bloated and did not look anything like our handsome brother. That guy laying in that hospital bed could have been anybody's brother. Tears started rolling down my face. I couldn't take a step forward.

"He is in a private room because he is septic from head to toe with no white cells. Bacteria has taken over his body," Nazee said. "The only things that are keeping him alive are the antibiotics and the ventilator."

"Will they do the transplant under these circumstances?" I asked.

"Yes," she said, "It is not a common practice, he is septic, but in his case, they have nothing to lose. They are giving him your stem cells so he can create white cells to fight the infection. Till then, we just have to wait and see."

"Does he have enough time to wait and see?" I asked. Nazee did not answer.

I kept on staring at him from the doorway. This was not part of the plan. Poor Fariborz, he was counting on me to save him, I was his insurance policy. I was supposed to be his savior and now it might be too late. There was nothing that I could do. I was useless now. He had to fight the cancer cells and deadly bacteria now with no ammunition.

I walked out of MICU and into the waiting area.

"Why are all these people here?"

"They are waiting for your cells to arrive, they want to say a mass prayer exactly when the doctors start the procedure," Nazee explained.

"They have been here all morning saying the prayers for you, while you were giving your stem cells," Nahid continued.

"How long do we have to wait?" I asked.

"Dr. Isola said your stem cells will be here soon," Nazee said.

"I hope 'soon' is not too late."

Everyone was either pacing around or peering into their cell phones. I was sure they were reporting to the rest of the community. They were all worried. Things had taken a turn for the worse. I sat on the floor in the hallway, head held in my hands. *This is not happening. It can't be. He has me as a 100% match. How many times have we been told how rare that was. There must be a reason behind that. He can't leave now.*

I heard a commotion in the hallway. I looked up and noticed a physician in a white uniform pushing a hospital table towards the MICU. On that table was a plastic bag filled with blood. We all stood up. Raffi, Morad, Zouzou, Jamshid, Shimon and the rest of our friends caught up with him, stopped him and started talking to him. He looked at our friends for a few seconds and nodded "yes."

The physician held the plastic bag in his hands and every person in that room gathered around him and chanted a mass prayer. They closed their eyes, begging God for a miracle. After a few minutes Raffi said, "Now we say, 'Amen,' say it loud so everyone in this hospital could hear us."

"AMEN!" everyone shouted.

The gentleman in the uniform looked at Raffi, asking for his permission to leave. Raffi patted him on his back and walked with him to the double doors of MICU.

We all waited.

First Miracle

"There are only two ways to live your life. One is as though nothing is a miracle. The other is as though everything is a miracle." —Albert Einstein

MICU, July, 2013

July 2nd was a typical sunny, hot day in New York. I sat in the backseat of a yellow cab, looking out the window. It was a normal day in Manhattan to everyone else—the usual mad rush of people, traffic, and chaos among the grey buildings—but different to me. I had not had a normal day for a long time. Suddenly the thought of running to catch an overcrowded subway, getting stuck in the office after work, commuting in freezing cold or hot and humid New York weather seemed like a privilege. Those were all part of day-to-day life. This was not!

My destination was Mount Sinai Hospital. I met the rest of my family in the chilly air-conditioned waiting room outside the Medical Intensive Care Unit, where my brother lay motionless, in quarantine, in critical condition. After four chemo treatments, he was pneumonic with a blood infection, or what the medical world called "septic shock." The MICU is for people with little chance of survival. Their hospital beds are one small step away from their graves.

We sat there in silence, waiting for the doctor to arrive. Dr. Hemorrhoids' partner, Dr. Newfart—the nickname we'd given him suited him perfectly too—walked in and looked around at the large group of people in the waiting room. He knew the drill by now. When it came to my brother, he had to answer to a tribe. Every worn-out and filthy chair was taken by a tired family member or a friend. I wondered if the germs in the upholstery were the only things that were happy to be in that dreadful room. I stared directly into his eyes.

"I just examined Dr. Noban," he said, and shook his head. Under his white coat he wore his usual polka-dot bow tie and colorful shirt. He was probably trying to belie the darkness of his profession and his personality with a cheerful wardrobe. Sadly, it wasn't helping.

Infectious disease doctors are exterminators with college degrees. They see a bug and tell you what spray will take care of it, with zero empathy, I thought. I had learned they all had some sort of distinguishing tic; it was clearly some kind of an unspoken requirement and pre-requisite for the specialty. In Newfart's case, he compulsively kept rotating his shoulder forward and pulling his chin up. He did it again as he prepared to speak.

"He has two hours to live," Newfart said abruptly, "maybe only 15 minutes. He could die by the time I reach the exit."

We stared at him, stunned.

"Is there any chance he could pull through?" My voice shook. "Any chance at all?"

He looked around the room, anywhere except at our grief-stricken faces. "None," he answered flatly, avoiding our eyes. He jerked his shoulder and pulled his chin up one last time, turned around and walked away.

No one moved, no one cried; no one said a word. It felt as though time had stopped. The only noise came from the soda machine, "Ping!" Did it feel our pain too? *Thank God, we made poor Momon stay home today,* I thought distractedly.

I lifted myself from the chair and started walking towards my brother's bed. I approached the Twilight Zone and donned a mask, hospital gown, and pair of gloves. Then I entered his private room.

My handsome, kind, accomplished brother lay unconscious, intubated, swollen from head to toe, and hairless. 36 hours into this nightmare, and there was no change. I walked over and held his heavy bloated hand. Tears rolled down my face. Everything was a blur. Nothing looked or felt real.

"Fariborz," I begged, "please hang in there. Life won't be the same without you. I love you so much. Fight! Your place is with us. Hang in there! Hang in there for your kids, your wife, your family. You have to walk down the aisle at Alexa's and Ava's weddings. You have to be there for the first dance. I love you so much. I beg you. Fight!"

Of course, there was no response—just the damn instruments beeping. The nurse walked around in her Hawaiian print scrubs, adjusting the hundred tubes sticking out of his body. She was busy pretending I was not there. I wondered how many times she'd heard someone beg a family member not to die. She was immune to such emotional entreaties; she had developed the right calluses for that. I saw a small Torah and different prayers in different religions taped to the top of his bed—Jewish, Christian, Muslim. *Please Gods, help him. He is a good person, he belongs here with us*, I yelled in my head.

I looked up and across the bed. Directly in front of me I could see Central Park from the window in his room, alive and full of people. It was a normal summer day for them. How I wished it was for us too.

The person lying in that hospital bed didn't look anything like Fariborz. The deep dimple on his chin was the only reminder that yes, this was my kind and sweet brother. The words poured out of me; I couldn't stop talking to him. I begged him to fight, to stay alive, over and over. Tears rolled down my face and landed on the blue mask covering my mouth. "Fariborz, don't leave us, it's not time for you to meet Stephen, not any time soon."

Suddenly, I felt a gentle squeeze. A chill raced up my spine. He nodded his head slowly "yes." I was in shock. I could feel every hair stand up on my body. I turned around to face the nurse, who was watching in disbelief.

"Did he just move his head?" she asked.

"I think so," I said, "did you see it too? He squeezed my hand. I swear he did!" I still could not understand what I was seeing and feeling. I looked around and saw my cousin, Houman, waving from behind the glass wall. His hands left a sweaty imprint, his eyes were wide open. He smiled and nodded at me. He was also a witness.

I kissed Fariborz's swollen hand and said, "I love you so much, I love you my handsome brother, hang in there." I ran back to the waiting room and cried out, "He responded to me! He moved his head! He moved his head! He is alive. I swear. I saw it. He squeezed my hand. He heard me. He heard me. He will be fine. He will pull through. I know he will."

The entire family stood up as one and ran to look at him from behind the glass to witness what I had seen with their own eyes. My brother was still there. His heart was still beating. He still had a chance at life. He was still in the wrestling match. It was his first miracle, but it wouldn't be his last.

Ten-Day Wait

"Without health life is not life; it is only a state of languor and suffering, an image of death." —Buddha

July, 2013

As we were all scattered around outside of MICU, some walking aimlessly, some sitting on the carpeting, some whispering and some praying, the plastic bag containing my stem cells hung on the pole next to Fariborz inside the MICU, its contents dripping slowly, drop by drop, into the tube and into his veins. The veins that were filled with deadly bacteria.

If up until now those tubes were supplying poison, today with the help of God and the universe they will give him life, I thought. There was not much anybody could do but wait. Our friends were holding their holy books, facing his room and speaking softly to God. My mother was leaning against the corner, gazing down. She was standing on her two feet, but the rest of her body parts were hanging. Jennifer and Nazee were talking to one of the doctors, trying desperately to squeeze a positive and a hopeful word out of him. I was sitting on the floor, thinking, *Everything will be fine, he is not going anywhere but home. Any other scenario would be stupid and nonsense. He got himself to this point, he finally received the stem cells, he will pull through.*

Dr. Isola stepped out of the elevator and walked towards us. Everyone stood up and gathered around him. He saw nothing but desperation and fear on those pale faces. It was obvious he was searching for the least painful approach to give us the facts. He looked at Jennifer and then my mom. "The stem cells were perfect. The white cell counts were higher than normal, which is what we wanted. From here on there is nothing we can do but to wait and see. We need ten days for the new cells to 'set up shop' in his body and 28 days to see the result. The white cell counts will not increase or change before the tenth day. If he pulls through, there will be hope."

He looked around at the mob of people listening to him and continued, "We just have to wait and see. He can't have any nutritional supplements in his IV. He is attached to strong antibiotics. We usually do not do this procedure, there is no point, without white cells and being septic from head to toe, chances of survival are slim. But we had the stem cells, we thought we should give it a try." He took a deep breath and said in a low voice, "Dr. Noban is in critical condition. He needs a miracle."

Ten days? He has to survive for ten days with zero white cells to fight the deadly bacteria? I had not been aware of that fact. I guess I failed to read the small print! I was under the impression that as soon as my stem cells entered his body, they would start fighting the damn, creepy, miserable, disgusting, monstrous, ugly little creatures.

Everyone started bombarding the doctor with questions. I tried to get up but had to move slowly. My body was still hurting from the daily injections. I left the crowd and walked towards my brother's room. There was no point listening to the rest of the conversation. "He needs to stay alive for 10 days, or else." That was his reality now; any other detail was useless. It was him against God.

I stood behind the glass wall and watched my swollen, hairless brother flat on his back. I stared at his face and his chin below the thick tube that was inserted into his mouth. With all that was going on, he was still my lovely little brother. He was still there. He was still with us.

Tehran, 1969

"Here Fariborz, climb up. You are Superman, you can fly." I went flat on my back, held his little hands, placed my feet on his stomach and lifted him high into the air with my legs. "Now open up your arms and legs. I am holding you, I won't let you fall. Pretend you are Superman."

Nazee was next to me waiting for her turn. Fariborz was only two years old. We were playing on my parents' bed. Jumping up and down, tickling each other, wrestling and acting like action figures. He was giggling and making sounds as if he was a flying superhero.

Suddenly the laughter stopped and he started screeching and screaming with pain. I brought my legs down as our baby brother rolled on the bed, holding onto his stomach and moving in pain. His cries became louder and more intense by the minute. He had difficulty breathing. His face was turning red. "Fariborz, Fariborz, what happened? Where does it hurt?" I kept on asking.

But I couldn't get a word out of him. Nazee stood there, her back against the wall, watching in horror. I ran to my mother in the kitchen, "Momon, momon, run, there is something wrong with Fariborz. He is in pain. He is crying. Run."

"What? What happened? What's wrong?" She dropped everything and raced to follow me to her bedroom. Fariborz was on the bed in fetal position; his eyes closed, his hands on his stomach, his knees to his chest. He was grunting while trying to breathe. The dimple on his chin was quavering.

My mother hit her head with her two hands and screamed, "Oh my God, look at his color. His face is blue. *Djalal, Djalal,* run. *Khoda mano bokosheh* (God, kill me). What is happening?" She grabbed Fariborz and ran towards the front door screaming, "*Djalal,* run, *Djalal* run, *Khoda mano bokosheh*" nonstop.

I was running after her pleading, "I swear to God I didn't do anything wrong. I swear I was just playing with him on your bed."

My father appeared in the living room bewildered. "What happened?"

"I don't know, we have to take Fariborz to the hospital. He can't breathe, he turned blue, and he is in pain. Run."

Nahid was standing in the doorway of her bedroom watching the chaos in shock. My father grabbed his car keys from the table and ran out of the house with my mom and my little brother. None of us said a word. We just sat there frozen. What went wrong? Just five minutes before we had been playing around like we always did.

Fariborz was such a lovable little boy. His huge dark eyes, long eye-lashes, the cleft on his chin, and the gentle smile all made him the most adorable boy. He was the love of our lives. He was the answer to my mom's prayers. He was the apple of her eye. He was the source of her happiness. What had just happened?

My sisters and I stayed in our living room and waited for our parents to return. No one spoke. We sat on the couch facing the front door and waited for some news. God, please have some mercy, don't hurt our cute little brother, keep him safe, please.

A couple of hours later the front door opened and my father walked in, the way he always walked, strong steps and with authority. My father was an impressive figure. He was tall and handsome, with high cheekbones, a strong square jaw, broad shoulders, and a head full of hair which he always oiled back, very "old Hollywood" style. "Everyone tells me I look like Errol Flynn," he boasted after parting his hair on the side and combing back every strand carefully with the use of a fine comb and paraffin. He was a very serious man and a strict disciplinarian. We all feared and respected him, but in Iran that was usually the case. Fathers ruled and the rest obeyed.

"Where is Fariborz?" I asked with wide open eyes.

"At the hospital," he said in a firm voice, "he had what they called Intussusception. Your mom called it right away. She knew the symptoms. One portion of his bowel slid into the next. Kind of like if the intestines are in a giant knot. It was life-threatening, very dangerous. The blood supply to that area was blocked, but thank God the danger is behind him. I kept my hand on the horn and went through every traffic light until we got to the hospital. They got to it very quickly. He had a procedure done. If he had not gotten to the hospital right away, Fariborz could have died."

Died? How could he put that word and my brother's name in the same phrase? I thought in horror.

"Where is he now? Where is Momon?" Nahid asked.

"Your mom stayed with him. Fariborz is out, he was put under general anesthesia. I had to come back to get my wallet and fresh clothes for him," our father answered and turned towards his bedroom, just like a general reporting and then walking back to his office.

Thank you, God. Thank you, God, for watching over our little brother and keeping him safe for us, I kept thinking.

Now I watched my brother through the glass wall and once again begged God to watch over him and to keep him safe for us. "He deserves to go home and be with his family. He is a good man. God, please save him, please help him, please."

And so the wait started. Seconds went by like minutes, minutes went by like hours, and there was nothing else for us to do but to do what we did best. We waited and prayed.

Dr. David Spielvogel visited him every day. "He's holding his own, there is no explanation for it. I have no answers. No one does."

We were all sitting in the waiting room of the MICU. It was the fourth day after the bone marrow transplant. Fariborz's white cell counts were still at zero, he was still septic and intubated, the antibiotics were still his only ammunition, and he was still not receiving any food or any nutrition. But he was alive, and that was all that mattered.

The idea of him starving for the past four days was a physical torture to him and an emotional one to us. Dr. Hemorrhoids had made his daily visits. He walked in with his dark presence, went through his chart, checked his medication, looked at us from the corner of his eyes and repeated the same gloomy phrase, "He is still septic, don't get your hopes high. I don't know how he is still alive. He could die any minute." Finally, one of those days I stood right in front of him on his way out and said, "An exterminator has more compassion than you!" He looked at me, shrugged his shoulders, and walked out.

We were counting down the hours, waiting for the tenth day to arrive, when my stem cells would kick in and "set up shop" in his body. It would then take an additional two weeks to gauge their effectiveness.

"The fact that he is still alive is a mystery," David continued. "What is keeping him alive is a puzzle to everyone. A body with all that infection and no white cells to protect it should not and does not survive. If he survives the tenth day, it would be nothing short than a miracle."

"David," I said, "Fariborz has kept himself alive for the past few days. I promise you. He is not going anywhere."

It was the Fourth of July weekend. The fifth floor had become the official hangout place for our friends and family. They could not peel themselves away from the hospital. The idea of spending the glorious long weekend in the Hamptons and escaping hot, humid and crowded Manhattan was not appealing at all.

Evening prayers were going on, not only in the hallway on the other side of the double doors of MICU but also in synagogues, churches, and mosques in Manhattan, Long Island, Los Angeles, and San Diego, just to name a few. My Muslim friends were praying the same way my Christian friends were; all were praying to the same God. They were using different vessels, different methods of communication, and different languages, but the recipient was the same.

The mood inside of the MICU was depressing and gloomy. At least once a day a lifeless body was wheeled away in a hospital bed covered with a rectangular box. The hospital staff probably thought it would be less horrific for the visitors in the hallways; better than witnessing the outline of a dead person under the white sheet. We took a step back, looked down, and opened up the way for the deceased. We had become accustomed to the wailing and screaming of family members that had been told the heartbreaking news. We had grown accustomed to the constant beeps and alarms of hospital equipment. For us it was just another day at MICU.

I had decided to stay next to Fariborz day and night until he came home. I truly believed if I left for a long period of time or went too far, something terrible would happen and we would lose him. As his 100% match, I felt that I was therefore his lifeline and connection to perfect health. I felt we were attached by an invisible cord, and that cord was not very long. I would be around him at all times. Nothing in that hospital bothered me. I did what I did best, I embraced, accepted, and adapted. I focused only on Fariborz.

I was sleeping in the old worn-out waiting room on the fifth floor. The endless noise and the heartache had become part of my life. Part of my breathing, part of my eating, part of my feeling, part of my thinking, and part of my sleeping. The constant beeps from the machines, the noise from the doors screeching and slamming, the cry and the holler from the visitors—were simply part of the hospital and its environment, therefore part of my daily life.

I decided that the continuous beeps were birds singing, the slamming and screeching were sirens from the fire trucks and the cry and the hollers were the noise from the wind. These distractions were only temporary facts of my life at that hospital.

Our only reminder of a "normal life" was the window opening towards the great lawn of Central Park. Children were busy playing, men and women were jogging, mothers were pushing strollers, vendors were selling ice-cream and tourists were taking pictures with their phones. It almost did not look real. A normal day without suffering seemed dreamlike. I watched that scene like a hungry orphan watching as a perfect family talked, laughed and ate a scrumptious dinner through a locked window, wishing I could join them and taste that appetizing food. I watched with longing and at times with envy.

Inside the waiting room, far away from the reality of most people, we had each other as support. The room was full at all times. Besides immediate family there were always friends and work associates. *Does Fariborz know how much he is loved and respected?* I thought to myself.

The routine stayed the same. We hung out in his room and on the fifth floor all day. I slept in the dingy waiting room, woke up at 6:30

and ran to MICU to check on Fariborz. Occasionally he would open his eyes, look at me and blink. I would ask for his vital signs and the numbers, text message everyone on the group text, then talk to him, even though there was no response, until I was asked to leave because the doctors had to do their rounds.

I waited outside the room for a doctor to show up and ask about the slightest improvement. But the answer was always the same, "We have no idea how he is still alive. He is holding his own." To that response I smiled. Almost a devilish smile. Thinking, *You do not know us, we are made of different weave, we do not give up that easily!* Sometimes I wondered if the doctors were there to check up on him or to feed their curiosity and see how the infection had not killed our brother yet.

My life at the hospital had become my norm. I had lost weight and I was told that I looked drained and exhausted but I was content. Days were passing by and our brother was still with us. What else could I ask for? Well, a good meal maybe? That was provided by my dear friends Ebbie and Debbie. The days that the husband and wife delivered fresh coffee and delicious sandwiches early in the morning before going to work were among my favorite days.

During the day, Nazee and I massaged Fariborz and moved his arms and legs constantly. He had retained a lot of water and his limbs were too heavy to lift. We put his legs on our shoulders and walked forward and back, or to the right and left. We pushed his knees to his stomach and pulled them back, a horizontal squat. Even his arms were heavy for us. Each day we found new ways of moving him and dealing with the weight problem. We had become very innovative and creative with our physical therapy, while working muscles in our arms we did not know existed!

We repositioned him every hour with large pillows. We pushed him almost to his right side and then almost to his left and sometimes left him flat on his back. When I was by myself and no one was looking, I kept on shaking his bed so his lungs moved. I had been told that if the body is in motion, chances of pneumonia becomes less. Later on, I found out that shaking his bed was not considered a movement! We wanted to do something to improve his condition. We tried anything and everything. *His muscles should not get stiff,* we were thinking.

The staff was efficient and caring. They were not as warm and friendly as the nurses in Oncology, but that was completely understandable; MICU was a sad and dreadful place. We knew what Fariborz would say if he could talk, "The nurses are all overworked and exhausted, take care of them. They are stuck in the hospital." And we did. We brought them lunch and dinner.

We came in with bags of bagels and cream cheese, Subway sandwiches, Dunkin donuts, shish kebab and chicken. Nazee brought them homemade food in giant pots and dishes. To celebrate the Fourth of July holiday, Matthew, Mitchie and Mahtab, Nazee's children, bought trays of food and cookies complete with American flags and Uncle Sam pointing. The smiles on their faces were our reward. They couldn't wait to go to the nurses' station and taste the food. They were helping our brother and we were helping them, the only way we knew how.

We whispered in Fariborz's ears, "We are bringing food for the nurses. The way you have always told us to do. We are taking care of them." We knew it would make him happy.

While we were feeding the staff, our brother was starving. We had been told that he had lost a lot of weight even though he looked like a samurai wrestler. The water retention made him look obese. He did not look anything like the handsome guy in the family photos. The reaction and the look on the nurses' faces were heartbreaking when they looked at the family pictures, "Is that guy Dr. No?" He was called "Dr. No," short for Nobandegani, or Noban. They were comparing a young, handsome, well-dressed guy with a warm smile to the hairless, swollen, helplessly sick person lying on the bed.

On July 7th, early in the morning, as I was sitting next to him and talking to him about anything and everything, I said, "Fariborz, you know today is July 7th, Nazee's birthday." He was still intubated, so any kind of movement was uncomfortable if not impossible. He stared at me with surprised and wide-open eyes and tried to move any muscle he could on his face. I did not understand why he was acting that way;

however, I continued talking and explaining what everyone was up to. When the round of doctors started, I left the MICU and sent our regular group text, "Guys, he is doing better, but when I told him today was Nazee's birthday, he reacted in a strange way. He was trying to tell me something."

"Today is not my birthday, it's tomorrow, July 8th," Nazee wrote.

"Oh, wow, maybe Fariborz is better off without my stupid stem cells. We don't want him to downgrade when he goes home!" I wrote.

"Soheila, your stem cells are not taking the SATs, they are fighting a battle!" Linda wrote.

And to that response we all started laughing. Later in the day I read each text to him word by word.

The next day they extubated him. He was relieved. As soon as he saw Nazee he tried to say the words "Happy Birthday." Nazee's tears rolled down her face. She held his hands and said, "You gave me the best birthday gift today by being able to breathe without that tube down your throat."

Sadly, that freedom was short-lived. He was intubated many times after that. Dr. Hemorrhoids continued on with his dark and depressing daily visits, without a sign of sympathy but with plenty of indifference.

I took a few hours of break around 2 pm. The waiting room was filled with people by the early afternoon. I had enough time to walk to Nahid's apartment, take a shower and change my clothes. That one-hour commute was the only time of the day that I was in open air. I walked and I talked to God and my son. It had become my meditation.

"God, please help Fariborz. Stephen, please help him. I know you can if you want to. Get the forces together. He is not ready to come and see you, not yet, not any time soon. He is needed here. His family wants him here. I know how sad you get when I cry for you. If you allow him to stay here, I promise you I will never again shed a tear. I will go on living and celebrate the 22 years that I had with you. I know that is what you want. Please help him."

I was told when you ask for something, be specific about what you want, and I was. I talked with him and God, I bargained with them, I negotiated with them, and I begged them. I was conversing with them throughout the walk. People looked at me from time to time, but seeing a crazy person talking to herself in Manhattan was nothing new!

Waiting Room

"The secret of change is to focus all of your energy, not on fighting the old, but on building the new." —Socrates

Mid-July, 2013

Sleeping in the MICU waiting room among the constant noise, traffic and chaos had become normal, day-to-day life for me. It was a small, filthy, crowded, and depressing place. But I had accepted the fact that the waiting room for such a gloomy and sad environment cannot be Canyon Ranch Spa! One of those dreadful days, on my way to the elevator, I noticed a room with white chairs and sofas through a glass window across the hallway. It looked like a waiting room, but none of us had ever made the right turn off the elevator to see what it actually was.

After my week-long stay in hotel hell, I decided to check it out, and my God, it was a palace compared to the room I'd been sleeping in! The room was far more spacious and much cleaner than the bomb shelter I'd gotten accustomed to. My future bedroom suite was equipped with three long sofas, a flat-screen TV, and about a dozen single sofas, cushioned and comfortable. Every piece of furniture was covered in spotless white leather. The room was clean and airy with large windows and white shades. I decided to upgrade myself right away.

I grabbed my black garbage bag of hospital sheets, blankets, and pillows and claimed my new throne. There was no going back to the old waiting room with its wooden couches, mismatched and dirty chairs, the empty cans of soda, the loud and noisy vending machine, and that tiny bathroom with a door that whined every time someone stepped inside or out.

By now I was a waiting room connoisseur. My purse was stocked with the essentials—a toothbrush and toothpaste, a contact lens case and a small bottle of solution, a hairbrush, hair pins and couple of energy bars. I had a simple routine. I'd stay in my brother's room until 11 pm, then go to the bathroom, brush my teeth, take out my contacts, fix my bed in the waiting room, and sleep in my workout clothes. I'd wake up at 6:30 in the morning and rush to my brother's room to follow the day's routine. But first I folded my sheets and blanket back into my black garbage bag and left it tucked neatly in the corner with a sign I'd written in bold letters saying, "PLEASE DO NOT REMOVE."

This newly-discovered white room was heaven. I told the night shift in charge of my brother that I'd moved on to a better life, a life of luxury, comfort and opulence, and to look for me there if they needed me. The first night, as I walked into my own personal presidential suite, a man in his 30s, with dark skin and a full head of hair, wearing a white t-shirt and a simple pair of jeans, said hello to me. He was sitting next to his wife and daughter, speaking Bengali (he told me later he was from Bangladesh) in a low voice. He had a calm presence, the complete opposite of my never-ending nervous energy. I said hello and he responded with a friendly smile. "I'm Matthew, and this is my wife Rathna and our little daughter."

I smiled at them, introduced myself, and asked, "Can I sleep on this couch?" pointing to a nearby sofa. "Of course," he said. "I'm sleeping on that one next to the window. I have water bottles, cookies, chips, soda, napkins, plates—feel free to take whatever you want. They're all stacked up next to my bed." I thanked him and dragged myself to bed, thinking how nice he was to offer me his food even though he didn't know me.

When I woke up to check on my brother, I saw Matthew praying on a small carpet in the eastern corner of the room. He seemed at peace and submerged in his prayers. It looked like he was in deep conversation and total connection with his God. He stood up, sat down, bowed forward, knelt down while whispering and murmuring words under his breath. He was physically present, but his soul was with his God. I left him alone with his prayers and rushed to see Fariborz.

After Matthew's evening prayer that night in our luxury suite, he rolled up his prayer mat and looked over at me fixing up my bed. "Why are you here?" he asked. I told him our story and he listened with a caring expression. "My younger brother is waiting for a heart transplant in the CICU next door," he said. "He just became a father a couple of months ago. Now he's fighting for his life. I quit my job to be with him here. Allah will take care of us."

Misery and heartache does not differentiate, it applies to every religion, race, color or category, I thought. I felt safe being in the same room with Matthew. Everything he and his wife did together, showed their mutual respect. They doted on their daughter together, ate together, and cleaned up the table together. He kissed his wife and daughter and escorted them out at the end of the night. He was a simple man, a good man, and I could tell he was a man of God—a God-loving man, not a God-fearing one.

The third morning, I woke up at 6:30, as usual. I saw him sitting in front of me with a cup of coffee and a chocolate donut from the Dunkin' Donuts. "Soheila," he said. "I woke up early to pray. I prayed for your brother. I asked Allah to give him his complete health back, to send your brother home to his family. I promise you, He will listen. Allah is there for us. Allah will listen to our prayers." He reached over to offer me the goodies. "I went to buy a cup of coffee and I bought one for you, too."

I couldn't believe his generous gesture. Here was a man out of work, as worried about his brother as I was about mine, but he still remembered to pray for Fariborz without knowing him. I was touched by his kindness, by his passion to help. It amazed me that he had enough love to be there for someone who had been a total stranger only days before.

That evening, I told my friends about Matthew and joked, "I've been married for almost 34 years—34 years, and I don't remember my husband ever greeting me in the morning with fresh coffee and breakfast! That was definitely a first—and to think I had to experience it in a waiting room! Maybe I've been sharing my room with the wrong man all these years! All it took was three nights with this one! I should call Jackie and tell him about my experience! He shouldn't get too comfortable in LA!" It got a big laugh in the somber hospital.

One of those nights, when I rushed to claim my bed, I saw that the room was full. My heart dropped at the thought of downgrading back to that dark, depressing room in the MICU. I stood frozen, staring at the claimed sofas covered in white sheets. Just as I finally convinced myself to turn around and walk back to Hotel Hell, Matthew stopped me.

"Wait, Soheila," he said. He was sitting in his usual spot. "I saw new people coming in so I took your sheets out of the garbage bag and spread them over your sofa. I hope you don't mind. That one is still yours." *How sweet of him*, I thought. That piece of news made me happier than an upgrade to the Presidential Suite at the Waldorf-Astoria Hotel.

Matthew started to visit us in the hallway of the MICU. He wanted to see how my brother was doing, as if he didn't have enough on his plate. He assured us that he included Fariborz in his prayers and asked Allah to send him home to his family every day, though he knew full well we were Jewish. His Allah and the Allah that I had encountered on the rooftops back in Iran could not have been the same. This one was here to help and the other was there to hinder; this one was here to heal and the other created hell.

In that hospital, there was one God, the one that everyone believed in—the God that watched over and healed the sick.

"Guys, I have to go and claim my sofa so no one else beats me to it." I had set a reminder on my phone at 6 pm, now that I knew better. I'd rush to the white waiting room, spread the sheets over the sofa, display two magazines and a piece of clothing over them (for a special touch, meaning Don't you dare touch this sofa!), and rush back to MICU.

One night I walked into the room exhausted and ready to collapse. As I stepped inside, I saw a heavyset guy sleeping on one of the couches with no sheets or pillows. He was unshaven, with messy hair and wrinkled clothes. His stomach bulged out between each shirt button and he exposed his big hairy stomach with every snore. One leg was on the sofa, the other one hanging off, one arm on his stomach, the other one hanging. He was about to roll down onto the floor.

I looked for Matthew, but he wasn't there. I tried to ignore this man's presence and sleep, but I could not. I did not feel safe. I got up and pulled the heavy sofa and the table over from the middle of the room and placed them in the opening of the door of the waiting room. The guy didn't show any reaction to the noise I was making. The waiting room was visible to people walking in and out of the cardiac intensive care unit. My plan was to block the door from locking with the help of the heavy furniture. I figured if he tried to close the door, the table and the desk would make some noise, giving me the necessary time to wake up and run out. I stayed awake for a while imagining and preparing for every possible scenario. It turned out to be a noneventful night. However, I slept with one eye open.

I did not know about the huge drawback of that luxurious waiting room. It is true when they say "every rose comes with a thorn!" One night at about 3 in the morning, a tall security guard barged in and turned all the lights on. He approached each sofa and woke the poor, tired souls up, shouting, "Wake up! Wake up, everyone. Why are you sleeping here?" Then he stood at the top of my sofa/bed and asked, "Why are you here? What is the name of your patient? How do you spell his name? How long has he been here? What is his bed number?"

My heart was beating so fast I thought I would have to go straight to CICU and check myself in. I was sure I was on the verge of a heart attack. I tried to keep my eyes open and answer his questions politely. I responded patiently and gave him the information.

"You are not allowed to be here… this waiting room is for CICU patients only," he yelled at the top of his lungs. I tried to explain to him that the other room was dirty and sleeping there was not in the cards. He was not trained to listen.

He was doing his job, of course. I was the only one in that room that did not have a patient in CICU. But that was just a small detail, I thought. The ICU part was the same, just the first letter was different. I had a patient in an ICU! The guy could have screamed till morning, I was not about to downgrade back to the old wooden sofas with the bonus sound effects. I put my head back on my pillow and pulled the sheet over my head. I was too exhausted to move.

"You can do whatever you want to do. I am not going to leave," I said. He left to check with the nurses and returned after 15 minutes. "Tonight will be your last night, this room is for CICU only," he said in a firm voice. By his third attempt at evacuation, I was completely immune to the chaos at 3 am. The same security guy kept on asking the same questions. I pulled the blanket over my head to block the light, folded my pillow over my ears, gave him the same answers, and then went back to sleep on the leather sofa. I left one nightmare to enter another one.

How dark, old, tired, worn-out and wrinkly would you become after years and years of being there, in the same corner, listening to people's heart-wrenching stories? Witnessing their sufferings day in and day out?

If I could just open that sad-looking mouth and wipe away the intricate lacework of the cobwebs, I am sure with the very first word the dust would emerge and create the sandstorm necessary to clean the cranky, tired, shaky voice. Ah, what stories one could listen to!! Stories of suffering, waiting, despair and sorrow. Stories of losing hope, losing one's belief, losing faith, losing the will to live, losing one's mind. Stories of fear, fear as one has never felt before, the worst kind of fear, the paralyzing kind. Fear of a nightmare that one cannot wake up from, one that does not end, the one that has become our reality. The stories of losing a loved one.

I just stare and wait, wait for words to emerge. I'm gasping for air. Did they close the windows or have my lungs just stopped expanding? Is it the lighting, or have I turned white and my heart just stopped beating?

So why are you just staying in that corner and not telling me something, a word, a phrase, a story, anything... anything to make sense of this horror, the horror of losing a loved one? I want to stand on my two feet and try to place one in front of the other and get closer to that corner and ask: Why aren't you saying anything? You must have seen it all, you must have heard it all, so speak. Speak! Tell me it is not so, it will not stay like this, this awful, heavy pain in my heart will be replaced with joy! Say it!

But I can't move. Did I just die, or has all the energy simply drained out of me?

Still facing me with that old, tired, worn-out, hopeless look. It's useless, there is no hope, I am losing my lovely brother. I am saying it, no need for you to tell me, I am losing my dear brother. Did you hear me? I do not want a word out of you!!

I gathered every ounce of energy left within me and turned away from that beat-up, old, tired, wrinkly sofa in the corner. I left the dreadful waiting room of the hospital and walked toward my brother's room.

Zero Blast Cells

"Life is not measured by the breaths we take, but by the moments that take our breath away." —Anonymous

End of July, 2013

"Ten! Nine! Eight! Seven!" she counted down. "Don't give up! Stay with me! One more push! Stay strong! Hang in there! Don't lose the battle!" Was she talking directly to me? It sure felt like it, though in reality such exhortations were my energetic instructor's everyday cardio-class vocabulary.

It had been 28 days since the bone marrow transplant. Time to see whether my stem cells had done their work.

The night before, for the first time after 27 days and nights, I had left my spot in the waiting room to enjoy the luxury of a normal bed and a quiet room. I finally felt secure enough about Fariborz's condition that I decided it was safe to leave the hospital to sleep at Nahid's apartment. That morning I woke up, got ready, and restarted my regular routine at the gym after a month and a half off. I knew Fariborz was not alone. Nazee had offered to go to the hospital early.

I was anxious and restless throughout the workout, unable to concentrate and be present. Something was eating me inside. I wanted to run out of the gym and get to the hospital as fast as I could. I wanted to be next to Fariborz. I wanted to hold his hands. I wanted to talk to him and check his vital signs up on the screen discreetly. Instead, I sneaked glances at the clock on the wall when the instructor wasn't looking. It appeared the hands were on strike and had decided not to move. Every minute that passed was an eternity.

I tried to concentrate on the energetic, fit young girl who wore her usual big smile. She was yelling and jumping up and down to the beat of the music, oblivious to my overly-stretched and overworked nerves. "Don't give up! Push harder," she shouted. "Time to get in shape for bikini weather."

Didn't she know today was the day we'd find out if my brother was going to live or die? Didn't she get the memo? Didn't the whole world know? The walls were closing in on me. Still, I tried my best to focus and stay in the moment.

The doctors were supposed to give us the results around 11 am. I looked at the clock for the hundredth time; it was just past 8. I had plenty of time to finish my workout and get to the hospital. But it was impossible. I was suffocating. My mind was miles away. *Done! Enough!* I thought. I stopped in the middle of the jumping jacks, grabbed my bag, and raced out of the gym. As soon as my foot touched the sidewalk, my phone rang. It was Nazee.

"Soheila, Soheila, listen to me!" she panted, crying. My knees started shaking. I leaned into the wall of the gym behind me, phone glued to my ear.

"There are no blast cells," she shouted. "None. Zero. It's all donor cells. He's cancer-free. Do you hear me? He's cancer-free! He's going to be OK!"

The city disappeared around me. I could not see the people or hear the noise. Nothing seemed real. Bodies were floating around me, cars and trucks were in liquid form, everything was moving in slow motion. "What?" I gasped. "What are you saying? Who told you? It's only 8:30. How do you know? Nazee! How do you know?"

I was hyperventilating. I kept on asking questions because I didn't know what else to do. It was what we'd all been waiting to hear, but now that I'd heard it, I couldn't believe it. We were yelling and crying at the same time. My knees buckled. I sat on the sidewalk, covered my face and started crying. *The bone marrow transplant worked,* I thought. *Another miracle. Thank you, God. Thank you.*

"The doctors were here," Nazee continued, "they were so excited about the good news they came early. It's true, he will be fine. Your cells saved him." We were both sobbing, she in the hospital room by Fariborz's side and me on the sidewalk of 63rd Street. People rushed past me, trying to get to wherever they were supposed to get to as soon as they could—a typical Manhattan morning. I wasn't nearly enough of a distraction for anyone to stop and wonder if I was all right. A grown woman in workout clothes, crying, smiling, and thanking God out loud, over and over, on the sidewalk—it was a normal scene in a not-so-normal city.

"I won't tell anyone," Nazee said. "It's your thing, your stem cells. You announce the wonderful news. I'm with Fariborz now—he is here, smiling!"

"Call Momon and tell her, please. I will text everyone else," I said.

I rested on the sidewalk for a few more minutes. Was I dreaming? Could life go back to normal again? Was Fariborz coming home soon? It was too good to be true. I didn't want to jinx it or get excited over an illusion. Even if it was an illusion, it felt good. It felt right. It felt light. I wanted this foreign feeling of happiness to stay, and I thought if I moved it might dissipate. It took an extra effort to press the numbers on my phone; my fingers were trembling. I could not see the letters on my keypad; my eyes were blurry. I kept thinking, *This is unfair to the rest of the family. They should know.* I took a deep breath, dried my tears with my workout top, and struggled to type a group text:

"Zero blast cells. Fariborz is cancer-free. He's going home!" I kept thanking God as I sent the message. I felt privileged to write those words.

"Thank you, God for letting us win the match," I whispered. "Thank you, Stephen. Thank you, my love. He will not see you, not anytime soon."

Calls kept on pouring in, "Soheila, talk to me," Jennifer said, her voice shaking. "Is it true? How do you know?"

"He's going home, Jenn," I said, "He's going home!" She started crying. We had come so close to losing him only 27 days ago. This was another miracle. Someone must have been watching over him. I kept looking up at the sky past the high-rises of New York City, picked a piece of blue that was visible through all the cement and thanked God again.

Calls continued coming in—Nahid, my sons, my nieces and nephews. News traveled fast among us. Everyone on both sides of the United States had been counting the days until they learned the outcome. Emails and texts were flying around by the hundreds.

I jumped into a cab and headed for the hospital. I wanted to see my healthy brother. I wanted to see his face free of worry, now that he knew he was going home. I rushed out of the cab, raced to the 5th floor and into his private room. *Thank God for my workout shoes!* I thought. He was still in quarantine in the same room and the same MICU. Hurriedly I donned a hospital gown and face mask.

I entered his room and yelled, "Fariborz!" I called out, fighting to catch my breath, "We did it. We did it!" I was literally jumping up and down. "You are going home. We have to write a book together! 'Miracles Do Happen.'" I raced to his side and started kissing his hands. He looked at me and tried to speak, but the trach in his neck got in the way. His lips moved, but we couldn't understand the garbled words. "Fariborz, you don't have to say anything. You are cancer-free, that's all we need to know!" He blinked, sent me a kiss and gave us a big grin. Ah, that beautiful dimple.

Nazee and I started dancing next to his bed. We hugged each other and broke into tears. The curtains were pulled to hide us from the rest of the patients and their loved ones. They had their own battles, their own struggles, their own fights. Their faces showed the same look of despair that we'd shared until this morning, but for now we were happy. Who said miracles don't happen? *They do, just have faith and believe!* I thought.

The word got around. The nurses came in one by one to congratulate us. The doctors wanted to see the medical breakthrough for themselves. Fariborz survived a bone marrow transplant while septic with ten minutes to live. He was going to be a case study—infected from head to toe with bacteria and zero white cells only 28 days ago, now he was cured. No one knew how he kept himself alive or what kept him alive for a month when normally septic shock would kill any patient in these conditions within a few hours. There was no reasonable explanation for his survival. No one had a clue. Him being alive and cancer-free was one big mystery to everyone.

I stayed next to him and told him about his past 28 days. I told him about his multiple intubations, the doctors giving up on him, the love and support of our friends and family and the evening prayers outside of his hospital room. "We have to write a book together, Fariborz. This was nothing short of a miracle," I said. He smiled and nodded, yes.

We considered celebrating with champagne and cake, but the hospital seemed like the wrong place to do it. The only happy place in that building was the maternity ward, and none of us was giving birth. We thought we'd have plenty of opportunity later on. We thought we could celebrate the day he came home, trophy in hand, the conquering hero returned. We thought the wrestling match was over. How little we knew. There were still a couple more rounds to go. God was just adjusting his mouth guard, cracking his knuckles, waiting to pin us again.

One Last Chance

"Just do it." —Nike

August, 2013

Swiftly and efficiently, nurses rolled our unconscious brother out on his bed—along with his IVs, monitor, respiratory machine, and any and every other device attached to him. The room where we'd spent so much time was suddenly empty and quiet. The constant beeps and the rhythmic breathing sound of the respirator had been reassuring proof that he was alive, a tangible sign of his existence. The sudden silence was deafening and scary.

I looked around. Only a couple of chairs and empty water bottles were left behind. The idea of my brother not being in front of me, within my sight, was terrifying. Was this something I would finally have to accept? I slumped into a chair and stared at the open space where his bed had been. I was overwhelmed by feelings of sorrow, defeat, fear, misery, despair, anger and, worst of all, helplessness.

I held my head with my arms and started sobbing. I could not stop myself; I cried the way I cried for my son. I howled and I lamented. I hit my legs with my fists. I was possessed; gone emotionally to a different zone. I never cried in front of Fariborz; I was sure he would have sensed my tears. Now he was gone and I was alone. I could cry as much as I wanted to; no one was there to see me. "God, please help me," I prayed. "Stephen, do something, please."

I noticed Dr. Florman and Dr. Kim standing in the doorway. I became as quiet and still as a lifeless person. I was drained; there was nothing left in me. I was mourning the absence of the third beloved person in my family. Would I lose my brother too? I was scared. Fariborz was slipping away again. Now I couldn't even hear him breathe.

Dr. Kim sat next to me, put her hand on my shoulder and said, "Soheila, your brother is in grave condition. His Bilirubin is in the 50s now, the liver is not functioning. The medications did not work on him. If he continues like this he will die in a week. A body cannot function without a liver."

His liver had stopped fully functioning almost from the day we celebrated his recovery from Leukemia. He'd been excited about moving out of the dark and disturbing MICU now that he was cancer-free. It had been a short-lived happiness; starting that very day his bilirubin got worse every day.

Bilirubin is a yellow-brown substance found in bile. It is a waste product that leaves the body through urine and stool, giving stool its normal brown color and urine its yellow color. It also gives bruises their yellow color. When bilirubin is high, besides yellowing the skin and the whites of the eyes, it affects the mind. Thinking straight and making sense requires great effort as the memory fails.

The Liver department replaced Oncology on daily visits. Dr. Leona Kim and Dr. Sandy Florman stopped by his room several times a day. They were as worried and concerned as we were. My brother was fighting a condition known as GVHD, graft versus host disease, a common affliction among patients who undergo bone marrow transplant. GVHD usually affects the skin, the intestines, the appetite—and, in the worst-case scenario, the liver. Of course, Fariborz got the worst-case scenario. He was jaundiced from head to toe. The doctors assured us that with enough steroids the situation could be taken care of, but nothing they did seemed to work.

Two weeks went by and his bilirubin reached impossibly high levels. His body was collecting and storing all the poison and impurities because his liver refused to do its job. After his miraculous escape from death, he was dying once again, this time from liver failure.

"There may be a way out, one possible chance of survival, and that is a definite 'maybe,'" Dr. Kim said.

I looked at her and Dr. Florman. "There is a way out?"

"Maybe, Soheila, maybe. At this moment his only chance of survival is for you to give him part of your liver," Dr. Kim said gently.

I looked at her in disbelief. How did we get here? I looked at both doctors and said exactly what my brother had told me when I pushed him to take the Tylenol for his high fever: "But I only have one liver!"

"We will take part of your liver, 60% of it," Dr. Kim said. "Your remaining 40% will grow back to almost full size in six to nine months. The liver is the only organ that regenerates itself. The 60% that we transplant into your brother's body will grow to be full-size as well. But Soheila, it is not an easy surgery, it is a dangerous and complicated one."

"He won't be able to go on a wait list for a donor liver, he has very little time left, plus his condition is too grave, he will not be considered a viable candidate. You are his only chance of survival," Dr. Florman continued. "We need two surgeons in the room at the same time. One will do the surgery on you to remove part of your liver and the other one will perform the transplant. Think about it, let us know what your decision is. We can only suggest options and give you the facts. From here on it will be your decision."

"My decision? What decision? It is not a decision, of course I will have the surgery. I am happy there is another choice besides death, I am happy we have a plan. What should I do? When do we do it?"

"It is not that simple, you have to go through a series of processes and tests. And remember, you still have young kids. Maybe you should consult with your family first. Go talk to your husband and kids," Dr. Florman added.

"It's my body, my liver, my decision. Just tell me where to go and who to see."

Dr. Kim handed me a business card. "Call this office. It is the department for living donors!" There's a department for live donors?!? I never knew!

They left. Once again I was alone in my brother's room. But I was no longer crying or sobbing, because now there was a plan. He needed new body parts and then he would be as good as new. There was a chance. There was hope again.

But how to break this news to my family, especially my boys? They wouldn't take this decision lightly. They would be scared, terrified of losing me. The idea of "death" was no longer foreign to any of us. Tragedy had touched us in the worst possible way. Life had not been so kind to us lately. What was to stop it from happening again?

Nazee walked in and stopped cold in the doorway when she saw the empty space. "Where is Fariborz?"

"They took him for an MRI," I responded.

She looked at me and said, "What's wrong? What happened?"

"A lot is going to happen."

I started explaining to her what the doctors had suggested. She looked at me with wide-open eyes, "What are you going to do? Have you decided?"

"There's no decision to be made. Life has decided for me already. I will do it. There is no doubt in my mind. My only issue is how to break the news to Jackie and the boys."

We sat there until our brother was wheeled back into the room. He looked worse but he was conscious. I stood next to his bed, put my hand on his yellow arm and said, "Fariborzjoon, guess what? You will have my liver after all! Remember you told me that I cannot give you my liver, because I have only one? Shows how much you know?! Well, I am giving you 60%. Not only do you have my blood, you will have my liver too. It's only fair to my poor blood to go to a familiar liver, don't you think?!"

He stared at me in disbelief and shook his head back and forth, trying to tell me he was not okay with this decision, probably as a physician knowing that it was a dangerous and risky operation for both of us.

"You can't change my mind. It is what it is, we will go ahead with it. It will be just another chapter to our book."

Nazee turned around in frustration and said, "I think your book has enough chapters already, we could have done without this one!"

My brother looked at me with his sad eyes. I held his hand in my hands. His yellow eyes were pleading, begging. I noticed a tear rolling down—even that small drop was yellow. Damn the bilirubin, damn the infection, damn the leukemia. Damn this unfair world!

I touched his face with my hands and said, "Listen to me, you would do the same if I was laying in that bed. You know that and I know that, so no more tears."

I left the room, called Dr. Kim, and asked her for an appointment to begin the necessary testing as soon as possible. There was not a minute to waste.

"Make sure you come here alone, you cannot be influenced by anyone. It should be your decision only," the doctor cautioned.

Nazee wanted to accompany me to Dr. Kim's appointment. "Thank you," I told her, "I would rather be alone." I couldn't bear to look at another worried face, my own was enough.

"The liver consists of two parts, one bigger than the other," Dr. Kim said, holding a sculpture of a human liver in her hands. The sun shone brightly through the big windows of her little office, illuminating many happy pictures and giving them life. Pictures of her smiling and hugging her family covered her desk, shelves and bookcases. I could see how loving and close her family was from looking at the photos, and I envied how carefree they seemed. It had been six years since I took a picture like that, six years since my son passed away, six years since I had known happiness.

Dr. Kim was as warm with me as she looked in her pictures. She was the only doctor as convinced as I was that my brother would survive. As

I sat clutching my hands in my lap, she started explaining the transplant procedure. "The gallbladder is attached to the bigger part, which is 60% of the liver, and that's the part we're using," she continued. "After the operation, your gallbladder will be useless. We're going to cut it out and throw it away. We have to make sure your liver is in a position that we can have access to. We work around the organs to get to it without harming anything else in your body. It's a complicated surgery, so you'd better think about it very seriously. You need a complete physical, a chest x-ray, an MRI, several blood tests, and a CAT scan to make sure we can access your liver. Oh and by the way, you have to see and talk to a therapist and a social worker."

I sat there without showing any reaction or saying a word. I wasn't afraid of the surgery, I just wanted to get it over and done with. I wanted to see my brother, happy and healthy, home with his family, just like Dr. Kim in her pictures. I wanted… I wanted our lives back.

"I understand the tests, but why do I have to see a therapist and a social worker?" I asked.

Dr. Kim leaned over towards me, looking at me with her kind eyes, like a friend, not a doctor. She said, "We have to make sure you're of sound mind, that you understand the consequences of this decision, and that you don't make it hastily. You have young children, they still rely on you. You should know exactly what's involved. Plus, it's required by law," she pressed her lips together and narrowed her eyes. She looked worried. She took a deep breath and didn't speak for a few seconds, which to me felt like an eternity. *What else is wrong? Why isn't she talking?*

"Soheila," she asked, "How old are you?"

I was surprised by the question. "54," I said. "Why?" A look of relief spread across her face, along with a soft smile. "Lucky," she said. "The cutoff age is 55. It is the law. After that, the liver is not good for a TP."

I thought this was a sign from God. If I had been just seven months older, or younger but sick or pregnant, if I wasn't a 100% match, there would be no hope for my brother. There must've been a reason for this, my brother was destined to live.

"When do I start?" I said. I got up to go. I couldn't bear to waste another minute. "Who do I see?"

"You'll have to see Nancy at the Living Donor Transplant Department." She got up and held me in her arms. I felt safe with her.

"After the transplant, your brother's bilirubin should start going down gradually. He's going to be fine," she assured me. "I have never seen a family so loving and so caring. With all that love, I'm sure your brother will be home soon. You can't be in touch with me anymore," Dr. Kim warned me with a look of apology. "Whatever questions or concerns you have, you'll have to contact the Living Donor Transplant Unit. I can't advise you if you should or shouldn't go ahead with the surgery. I gave you the facts. From here on out, it's your decision. Remember, you can change your mind anytime, even on the day of the surgery."

"It is an easy decision, doctor. Nothing will change my mind."

I entered my brother's hospital room and said, "Guess what, Fariborz? We're going to share a liver soon! Sharing is caring! Just call me Soheila 'Chopped Liver' Adelipour!"

Fariborz was asleep most of the time, but he still managed a shocked expression when he heard the news for the second time. He shook his head "no" as I explained the situation. His yellow eyes were wide open, and he struggled to speak. I was having the surgery no matter what anyone said, even him.

The evening prayers continued as usual, but I could hardly go to any of them. I had one test or doctor's appointment after another and right after I'd rush to Fariborz's room. Nahid would come after work and massage his head. "I would rather stay with my brother, he needs me more than God." He loved her head massages. Nazee joined the group every evening and, at the end of the prayers, begged God for mercy.

People came from everywhere to join in, show their support and love. The only thing anyone could do was to pray and beg God for help. They prayed he would decide to intervene; maybe he would be a kinder, more compassionate God. Maybe a bigger crowd would get his attention.

I sat in the doctor's office, staring at pages and pages of questionnaires. The room was basic: no windows, a shelf, and three chairs. The assistant handed me the papers and a pen and asked me to fill them out. I was going through every appointment, test, and meeting like a programmed device. I filled out the stack of paperwork and left, happy to get one step closer to the surgery. There was just one problem. None of the surgeons had agreed to perform the surgery.

I looked at my schedule and headed to the next appointment. It was time for the necessary blood tests. I was seated in a small cubicle and a nurse walked in with a tray filled with vials marked in different colors and categories. I looked at those tiny little bottles, more than 20 of them, then looked at the nurse and asked, "Are you kidding me? I have to fill all these?"

"Yes, it's part of the process!"

"Will there be any blood left in me for the surgery?" I asked with a smirk.

"Each color is for a different test. Now make a fist."

None of the nurses had a problem finding a good vein in my arm or on the back of my hand. "Ummm, you have good veins!" was the compliment trending that week. I'd never imagined that one day my weight lifting and daily exercise would get people's attention this way. There was never any talk about my abs of steel or my muscly shoulders. But my veins—impressive, wow, they looked great! Just because they were popping out under my skin, it was easy to stick a needle in!

"Wait, I want to take a picture, my sisters will never believe me!"

I took a picture of that colorful ensemble, sat back, closed my eyes and tried to visualize happier days. I had about an hour between my next two appointments. I was standing in the street wondering what I should do to kill time. Right in front of me was the answer. A manicure and a pedicure! Who knew when I would be able to sit up for an hour and get a service like that? I crossed the street and entered the nail salon. "Can I have a mani/pedi at the same time please?"

"Yes, yes, peek a cala! Peek a cala?" one of the women said with a heavy Korean accent.

"Peek a what?"

"Peek a cala," pointing at the racks of nail polish bottles.

"Oh, I should pick a color!"

"Yes, yes." I picked out a turquoise blue, sat in a seat, placed my feet in the lukewarm water, and they got busy. I rested my head on the leather chair, closed my eyes, and tried to make sense of the series of unfortunate events, which had turned fortunate and then unfortunate again. My brother's face was constantly in front of me. He beat pneumonia, recovered from septic shock, survived leukemia, he was cancer-free... and now he was dying because of liver failure?

I begged God to spare his life. *He is a good boy. A great human being. A kind person. What happened to karma? Are you asleep? Are you paying attention to what you are doing? Are you telling us it doesn't pay to be good? Are you teaching our kids that this world is cruel, and the good die young?!?*

Tears started rolling silently down my face. After a few minutes I was sobbing. I could not stop. I had found a spot where I could cry as long and as hard as I wanted to without worrying that a family member, a friend, or a doctor would see me. The manicurists watched me from the corner of their eyes and whispered to each other with their heads down.

One of them walked over and started massaging my back and shoulders gently. Another one offered a glass of water and asked if she could help. One handed me a box of tissues. I was just a few blocks away from the hospital; I am sure they had a good idea why I was crying. I thanked them for their kindness, paid them, and walked out with my freshly painted nails a happy turquoise color.

There were just a few more appointments and procedures left. By 4:30 I was done. I decided to walk back to the apartment because again, I had no idea when I would be healthy enough to walk freely. I stopped on 77th Street and Madison Avenue, made a left turn and entered my favorite bakery, Lady M, where they served the most delicious Mille Foglie cake. Ah, it smelled heavenly. I walked inside, thinking, *Go for it, enjoy it, while you have a gallbladder you might as well have something with fat and cream.* I knew that after the surgery I would have to avoid both until my body got accustomed to breaking down fat with the gallbladder missing in action.

The Mille Foglie at Lady M is the most famous, the most expensive, and the most delicious in the entire city of New York. I eyed a couple of different flavors behind the glass and chose one. The young girl brought a beautifully cut slice and placed it in front of me. I looked at that divine delicacy, at the layers and layers of crepe and the soft cream, put my fork in it, bent the corner of the triangle, where deliciousness meets perfection, took a piece and placed it in my mouth, anticipating that scrumptious taste that would make me happy! I was waiting for my taste buds to celebrate the experience and for me to enjoy the not-such-a-cheap thrill. But I could not taste a thing, there was no flavor, the familiar delicious treat was almost bitter!

I spat it out in my napkin, thinking, *Even my taste buds have given up, even they are disappointed, even they can't feel anymore.* I couldn't savor my most favorite cake, the one that I could never resist. The creamy, moist, soft pastry was staring at me, like always trying to seduce the poor helpless, sweet lover. But that gaze wasn't tempting anymore. Why bother? I pushed the plate back. "Not today, not tomorrow, maybe never. My dear, lovely Mille Foglie, you have just lost all your appeal. Our love affair is over," I murmured. Disappointed, I got up, left that cute bakery and continued walking towards the apartment.

I was in my own world, talking to God. At times, I spoke so loud that innocent bystanders heard me, turned around, and stared at me. I did not care, I wanted to get his attention. Maybe he would hear me, maybe he would turn around... and listen. Maybe he would reconsider, thinking he could do without this one trophy!

The Decision

"Being deeply loved by someone gives you strength, while loving someone deeply gives you courage." —Lao Tzu

August 15, 2013

I got a phone call from the transplant department Thursday morning. The receptionist sounded worried. "Mrs. Adelipour?"

"Yes!" I said. "Anything wrong?"

"By any chance, have you had a mammogram and a colonoscopy recently?" she asked. "It is part of the procedure needed for the surgery."

"As a matter of fact," I responded, "I did both back in LA just recently." I called the two doctors and asked them to send the records directly to Mount Sinai, emphasizing that it was a matter of life and death.

My next appointment was at 11:00 in the morning. Besides the series of MRIs, CT scans, the x-rays, angiogram, and blood tests, I had to see a social worker as well, which I didn't think was necessary. I had already told the therapist, "I am more than willing and very much able to donate my liver. A stranger should not have the right to decide for me. If I want to give a piece of myself to my brother, it should be my right. After all, it's my body, my liver, my decision." But rules were rules and I didn't want to piss anyone off.

I looked at the first page of paperwork and sighed. Here we go again with the same questions. Was I sexually active? How many people had I slept with? Did I use drugs? Had I been to Africa? Did I ever share a needle? Did I have a tattoo? Did I accept money for sex? Was I an alcoholic? Did I smoke? Did I have hepatitis? This must have been the fifth time that I had been handed a questionnaire asking the same things. The answer was 'NO' all the way down. Once again I checked every box, the whole time thinking, *My life must sound extremely boring to these people!*

Stepping into the social worker's cluttered and dim cubicle from the spacious, open, and sunny waiting room where no one waited, was a shock to my senses. It felt like the giant waiting room had slowly swallowed up all the space and pushed the therapist to the corner of his tiny room. Most likely one day, little by little, without him noticing it, the walls would push his face against the water cooler in the corner of his office. He greeted me and pointed to the small couch to my right. I sat down facing the wall three feet away from my face.

The therapist sat with his hands steepled in front of his desk. The back of his chair was touching the only window in his claustrophobic room. He was a young man, tall and skinny, in a conservative grey suit. His kind face was framed by thick dark eyebrows.

"I've been told that you want to donate your liver to your brother," he said. "Why do you want to do it? Are you familiar with the complications?"

I stared into his eyes. "Of course I am. I am also familiar with the fact that he needs a liver to survive, and I'm the only one who can give it to him."

He nodded. "You realize you have three other children you have to be there for, and they want you alive and healthy." I could tell he was choosing his words carefully. "Do you carry any guilt about losing your second son?" he asked.

I was shocked by his blunt question. "I couldn't have done anything to save him. No one could. It was five in the morning, a fire accident. I don't carry any guilt about my son. I did my best when he was with us, I gave him wings to fly, I gave him as much love as was humanly possible, I was there for him. The fire was out of my control. This one isn't. If I can save the precious life of someone I love, I certainly will. With or without my second son." I could hardly speak. My words came between sobs. He handed me tissues with the same placid expression of concern.

"I'm his only chance," I continued, "you can't expect me to go through life knowing I could have saved my brother but didn't do anything about it. How could I live with myself? If my brother was in my place, and I was in that hospital bed, he'd do the same thing." I looked up and added, "To me the one that does not consider the surgery and refuses to do it should see the therapist, not me. I am in a position to save a life. Give me one reason why I shouldn't do this?"

"How does your husband feel about this? Is he OK with it?" he asked. "Your children?"

"My husband? What century are we living in? It is my liver and my body, why should I base my decision on how someone else feels about it?! My husband and my kids are worried, they are against the operation, of course, but everything will be fine. It will be just a temporary inconvenience for me, but hopefully life changing for my brother."

I cried the whole way through the next hour as we went over my history, repeating over and over, "My brother deserves to live, he deserves to see his children grow up." As the interview drew to a close, I added, "Sir, if my brother is saved, hundreds of lives will be saved as a result. He is a physician and a damn good one!"

He got up and shook my hand. "I'm very sorry for everything you've been through, and everything you're going through now. We'll have a meeting with all the doctors involved at 6:00 this afternoon. You will be informed if we agree with the surgery."

"Just remember," I said, "we can save his life tomorrow. By Monday it will be too late." I walked out of his office exhausted.

Justin had left work early and joined me at Nahid's apartment. I knew what our conversation would be about. He would beg me not to have the surgery, even though deep down he knew no one could change my mind. We decided to talk about happier days, and that brought a smile to our faces. In the middle of our conversation my phone rang. It was Diane from the Liver Transplant department. "Mrs. Adelipour, I apologize, but your last CT scan wasn't clear enough. You have to come in and have another one done ASAP."

I didn't want Justin to come with me, but he was worried. To him these were our last few hours together.

"Mom, please, if it's OK with you I want to come with you."

"Of course it is."

The wait at the hospital wasn't long; I got the CT scan done and we decided to walk back to the apartment. It was a beautiful evening with a nice breeze. Even though August could be hell in Manhattan, that evening was comfortable. To our right was the one and only Central Park and on the opposite side, rows and rows of massive limestone pre-war residential buildings complete with uniformed doormen standing by each entrance, waiting for one of their tenants to get close so they could open the door, smile, greet them, and help with their bags.

It is a privilege to live on Fifth Avenue. It is an exclusive club, and membership to that club is not easy to obtain. Every building makes sure that the flowers, the shrubs, and the trees outside of the building or in tenants' balconies are perfect and the building is always looking its best. If the leaves have turned yellow but are still attached to the poor plant, it would be considered a Fifth Avenue disaster. Walking down and passing by the most exclusive club in Manhattan on a beautiful summer day is a treat! But not tonight.

How I wish this was just another August night for us, too, I thought, *I just want what I had and nothing more.* Justin and I started talking about life and how nothing made sense anymore. He was crying as we were walking.

"Mom, I can't lose you, too. I always imagined us sitting around a dinner table with my children, happy like before. I want my children to know their grandmother. Like a normal family. I want us to laugh and have light dinner conversations. Like the days before losing Stephen." He took a deep breath, wiped his tears and said: "I miss him so much."

He had been closer to his brother than I was with Fariborz. They traveled together, they partied together, they were each other's sidekick. Death is unfamiliar to most families; he knocks on the grandparents' doors and they "pass away." Stephen didn't pass away. Death took him.

Death snatched him away young, and Justin was still suffering. Death had been knocking at our door too often, as if it had an open invitation.

"Justin, I'm not going anywhere," I said. "I promise you, but you can't expect me not to do this. I'm his only chance. I'm his lifeline. We're at Mount Sinai hospital, with the best liver transplant department in the world, and here I am, a 100% match."

Justin shook his head. "I know why you're doing this," he said. "You can't fool me. You have found a way to go see Stephen."

My breath caught in my throat. Did my son think I was committing suicide, so I could depart this world and join my son? I stopped walking, held his arm and said, "Why would I go see Stephen now when I have three Stephens right here with me?"

He stared at me with an uncomfortable smile, then nodded and hugged me tight. We continued walking. He seemed relieved that he had put his worst fear into words. He turned to me with a real smile and said, "Mom, what do you think people are thinking when they see me, a grown man, crying next to you? Could they even imagine the subject of our conversation?"

The thought made me laugh. "Yeah, how many bonus guesses should we give them? Do you think after the 2000th they would get it?"

We got back to the apartment. My husband and my son Cameron were on the flight from Los Angeles. Jordan was in Alaska with his best friend Evan. Nadia, one of my good friends, knowing how worried I was about Jordan being home without me in LA, had invited him to join them on their family trip. My sisters arrived a few minutes later, followed by my nieces and nephews. Every member of my family was there except for my mother; she couldn't face any of us. She was sobbing at home.

I tried to keep the ambience and the conversation light. We ordered in and chowed down on falafel and hummus. It was 9 pm Thursday night and no one had called to tell me if they were going ahead with the surgery the next day or not. I didn't know what the verdict was. I kept thinking of Dr. Kim's words, "By Monday, it might be too late."

I decided to call the number I had been given and find out myself.

"Hi Serina, I know it's too late to call you, but I have not heard from anybody. As you can imagine we are very anxious."

"Sorry Soheila, they are still at the meeting, Dr. Myron Schwartz will call you as soon as they are done."

"Who is that? I was seen by a Dr. Marcelo Facciuto for the possible surgery."

"He will be your surgeon if they decide to go ahead with the surgery. Dr. Facciuto is not available tomorrow."

I hung up the phone and started laughing, "If you want a fun boyfriend, go with an Italian name like Dr. Marcelo Facciuto, but if you need surgery, look for a Cohen, a Schwartz or a Goldstein. I feel much safer now."

When my phone rang around 10, we all got quiet. It was Dr. Myron Schwartz. He had a calm, quiet voice. I pressed the phone to my ear and shushed the crowd.

"Hello Mrs. Adelipour, this is Dr. Schwartz."

"Hello Dr. Schwartz, I have been waiting for your call. So, are we going ahead with the surgery?"

"You don't waste time, do you?" he asked.

"We don't have much time to waste, Dr. Schwartz."

"No, we don't. Your brother's condition is critical," he said. "Actually his condition is grave, and such a complicated surgery is risky. To be honest with you, chances are he won't survive."

My breath caught in my chest. "But if we don't go ahead with the surgery, he will definitely die."

"That's true," he replied, "but we're putting you in danger, too. You have kids and a family. You're healthy, so I don't think it's the right decision for you to try and save his life when he's in such a critical condition."

This was not what I wanted to hear. "I've made up my mind, Dr. Schwartz. My brother's mantra is that there's always hope as long as the patient is alive. I want to believe as he believes. He's still alive, but next week we can't be sure. How can we turn our back and pretend he is dead when he is still breathing? Right now, there's still something to be done. Right now, we have hope, even if it's not much."

There was silence; I was sure I had made him reconsider his decision. I looked around the room. Everyone was looking at me, holding their breath, waiting to hear the verdict. I was willing to say whatever it took to convince him.

"Tell me," he said. "Why do you want to do this?"

I gave him the same answer I'd been giving everyone for the past two days. "If I was fighting for my life in that hospital bed, my brother would be on the phone with you right now, begging you to change your mind. He is a neurosurgeon. He turns over every stone for his patients. He deserves the same from you." I took a deep breath and said, "Please go ahead with the surgery, please."

Neither of us spoke. There was a long pause. I closed my eyes and pressed the phone to my ear. "I know where you're coming from, Soheila, I know your culture, I know your family ties, and I know your community. I know what you've been through. I have never done this in all the years of my practice, but I will give your brother another chance." He paused again as if he wasn't sure of what he was going to say next. "The surgery will be at noon tomorrow. My secretary will call you. Let's hope for the best, and I'll see you then. Oh, one more thing."

"What?"

"No food or drinks after midnight tonight."

"Don't worry Doc. I just ate enough falafel to last me for two days."

"Good, I will see you tomorrow."

"Thank you, thank you so much. I will see you tomorrow."

I hung up the phone. Justin's face was white. Nobody said a word. "We're going ahead with the surgery tomorrow, around noon," I announced. They were too stunned to react. They didn't know what to say. They didn't know whether to feel happy or sad. I knew Justin had been hoping the doctor would not agree to proceed. He was looking down at his hands. It was only a small victory, but I hoped it would prove another miracle. After struggling for so long, it finally felt like I had the right moves in my wrestling match with God.

A five-star general would not have received the attention I commanded the next morning when I reported to the gastro-intestinal floor of Mt. Sinai at 10 am. When my husband, Justin, Camy, and I entered the waiting room, Nahid, Nazee, and our friends Sima and Azita all leaped to their feet. They rushed over and hugged us. We all settled into seats close together but did not speak much. We were deep in our private thoughts. The nurse approached us. "Dr. Schwartz is still in the operating room, I suggest you go out, walk around and get some fresh air. I will call you on your cell phone as soon as he is out."

"How long do we have?" I asked.

"Not long, but enough for a quick stroll."

We left the office and started walking around Central Park. We settled on a huge rock under a tree on the lush green lawn.

I watched people walking, playing, laughing. Baby-sitters pushing strollers, kids running after their balls, Manhattanites jogging on the paths. It was a beautiful setting. But the huge building looming in front of us was not just another massive high-rise. It was Mount Sinai hospital, where my brother lay in a bed in one of the rooms, yellow from head to toe, unconscious and fighting for his life. Fariborz was fine only two weeks ago! How did we end up here?

"I will give you my liver if anything happens, please take the pills."

"Soheila, don't be stupid, you have only one liver!" Those words, meant to be sarcastic, had, incredibly, become our absolute reality. Only two months after that exchange I was doing exactly that: giving him my liver. *What were the chances?* I thought. *If Stephen was here he would say "apparently plenty!"* To my surprise I wasn't worried or scared, not even a bit. I was anxious. I wanted the surgery to be over so I could see the result, to know that my brother pulled through and had made it out of surgery alive. I remembered a quote I had read, "Everything that you do in life is either out of fear or love." In this case it was both, fear of losing Fariborz and the true love that I had for him.

I turned around and looked at my two boys. Justin was pacing back and forth, looking tired and pale. Camy was talking to whoever was close to him. I jumped at the sound of my phone ringing. It was the nurse, "Mrs. Adelipour?"

"Yes."

"Please come back to the office. Dr. Schwartz is waiting for you."

"Be there soon." I hung up. "Guys, time to go back."

We all got up and walked back towards his office. We took our seats once again and waited in the waiting room. A few minutes later, a gentleman walked in with the nurse by his side. We all stood at once. He looked at the large group of people and said, "Good morning, I am Dr. Myron Schwartz."

I took a step towards him and introduced myself.

"Hello, Dr. Schwartz, I am Soheila Adelipour, your next patient." He was a fit, skinny man, with glasses, thinning hair, concerned eyes, and a warm smile. He looked calm and kind.

He shook my hand, looked around, smiled at everyone and said, "Can I see you in my office?"

Justin walked forward, "Good morning Dr. Schwartz, I am Justin Adelipour, her son. Do you mind if I join you, too?"

"If it is okay with your mother, of course," he answered.

"I have no problem with that, Doctor," I said.

Dr. Schwartz led the way to his office and we followed. We entered a small room. He pulled up a chair, sat across from me, and started talking while holding my hand. I couldn't help but think that he was a doctor that my brother would have loved to meet and know. It was obvious that I was not just another "surgery" to him. He gave me, and I am sure every patient of his, special care and attention, as if I was the most special case he had ever had. His specialty was "Surgical Oncology, Liver Transplant." He started explaining what the procedure involved (something that I already knew).

He went over every small detail. The only new piece of information he added was the location of the incision on my stomach. "I need a good opening so I can have access to your liver. You will have three lines, starting from between your breasts down to your belly button and then to either side—kind of in the shape of the Mercedes Benz sign."

"Dr. Schwartz, I don't care if it's in the shape of a stop sign, really! Can we 'just do it,' as Nike says?"

"But you have to know what is ahead of you."

"OK, fair enough," I said with a smile. "Can you at least give me a tummy tuck while you are at it? I always wanted one!"

"The last thing you want is for a Liver T.P. surgeon to perform tummy tuck surgery on you, or for a plastic surgeon to perform a liver transplant," he answered, laughing. He squeezed my hand, looked directly into my eyes and said, "You can still change your mind and leave, no questions asked."

"Thank you, but I won't."

"You know your brother is in critical condition? He might not survive the surgery."

"Yes, I know, all the more reason why we shouldn't waste any time."

Tears were rolling down Justin's face as he listened to every word but was unable to speak. I took my gaze away from Justin and turned towards Dr. Schwartz. "Dr. Schwartz, could you please tell my son that I will not die on the surgical bed?"

He let go of my hand, put his hands on my son's shoulders and said, "My first liver TP surgery was in 1988. Your mom is in good hands. I will take good care of her. I promise you."

Justin's tears rolled down even faster. He was now crying like a baby. "Thank you, Dr. Schwartz, thank you."

"Your mom will be fine." He took a deep breath and added, "Okay, I have to go for a jog now. I will see you on the O.R. floor at 12 noon."

What? Jogging? Seriously? I thought.

As if he had read my mind he said, "I am a much better surgeon after a good jog, it clears my mind." He kissed my forehead and told Justin again, "I will take good care of your mom."

We walked out of his office together. As soon as we stepped into the waiting room, everyone got up again and walked towards him. He said, "The nurse will take you for pre-op, I will jog for half an hour only."

Everyone showed the same reaction—they looked at him in disbelief. "We have a star athlete for a surgeon," I explained to the crowd.

He patted my kids on their backs, winked at them, and left.

We left the building and started walking up Fifth Avenue towards Mount Sinai Hospital. I walked into the waiting room of the OR floor with my "entourage." The whole family, our friends, my sons' friends and their moms—all were already waiting there for us to arrive. They got up and hugged me. I asked the nurse to wait for a few minutes.

My mother was seated, wiping her tears. Our eyes locked, then she turned her head to avoid my gaze. My poor mom, so much sorrow, so much pain, so much heartache. She had lost a daughter in April, her son was fighting for his life, and now I was going in for a major surgery. She couldn't bear to look at me. I knew why—she felt guilty for not stopping me. If she had stopped me, her son would certainly die in couple of days. If she asked me to do it, she would be putting another one of her children in danger. It was all too much for her; she just sat there and cried.

I hugged her and said, "Momon, he will be fine. He would have done the same for me. I will be uncomfortable for a short while, that's all. So what? This too shall pass. It is just a big bump in his way to recovery. He will go home soon. I am sure of that."

She did not say a word. Her shoulders were slouching as if the weight of the whole world was on them. She looked at me with an apologetic face. I could see it in her eyes, she was apologizing for not stopping me for going under the knife. She had surrendered.

"No one can change my mind, not even him—that is, if he could speak." Camy and Justin were standing right behind me with tears in their eyes. They couldn't let go.

I laughed and said, "After this you can call me chopped liver, officially." They did not laugh in return. "Don't ask me not to do this. I could not do anything to save Stephen, but now I have a chance to save my brother. I will do whatever it takes."

I looked for Serina, the nurse, signaled her, and followed her to the OR. As I was leaving the waiting room, I saw Dr. Schwartz walking in wearing sweats and sneakers. I stopped and introduced him to the crowd. "Everyone, this is the guy that is performing the surgery on me." They all got up and started talking to him at once, my mom edging close to hold his hand. He looked at the mob of people with astonishment.

Nazee asked, "Dr. Schwartz, just tell me, when can Soheila start belly dancing again?"

He looked at me with a smile and asked, "Soheila, you belly dance?"

I answered, "Yes, yours truly is pretty good at it too—though I don't dance professionally, of course. I can dance to any music, even if I don't know the steps, I improvise. But I assure you, I will dance the dance."

He turned to Nazee, "This girl? I assure you, she will be on her feet, dancing again very soon."

We continued walking towards the OR. Justin ran up behind me and said, "Mom, I love you, just come back home, please."

I hugged him and said, "I will, I promise."

The nurse took my hand and escorted me to a small room. More questions, more reminders that I could walk away any minute from the surgery. This time I asked, "Has anybody ever actually walked away at this point?'

"Yes, just recently, a 20-year-old boy. His mother needed part of his liver."

I asked, "So what happened to the mother?"

"She is still suffering from the same problem. The son thought he was too young to put his life in jeopardy for his mom."

I put on a hospital gown and followed her to the O.R. We walked into an open room with beds lined next to the walls. Each bed had a curtain that pulled around for privacy. She told me to lie down on one and wait. I did. I started doing what I did best. Recently, I had become the Steven Spielberg of my visualizations. I wrote, directed, and produced each one. I closed my eyes and imagined my brother healthy and happy at home with his kids. I imagined him at his beautiful office again, with a full head of grayish hair. I tried to imagine these scenes as strongly as I possibly could. I thought the more often and vividly I imagined, the better the chances of these scenes becoming a reality.

It also kept my attention away from the cold hospital room with the constant beeping sounds.

I jumped as I heard a thick voice with a heavy accent, "Hello, I am Dr. Edmond Cohen, I am the anesthesiologist. How are you?"

I opened my eyes and saw a jolly face at the top of my bed. He looked just like Doc, one of Disney's seven dwarfs. He had a chubby face with an adorable smile. His cheeks stuck out on both sides of his face and a puffy nose held up a pair of circular wire-rim glasses over twinkly eyes. The resemblance to the cartoon character was unreal, right down to his perfect round body. I was charmed.

"I am fine, thank you, how are you?"

"I'm okay," he answered, "So tell me, what did you have for breakfast this morning?"

I looked at him with a surprised face, glanced at his sizable stomach and said, "An order of nothing with a side order of double nothing. It was good. Better than usual, maybe you should try it."

Shocked, he said, "Are you telling me that I am fat?"

"I am not telling you anything, just saying that every now and then you should have what I had, which was nothing!" I shrugged my shoulders and rolled my eyes towards his stomach.

He turned around to the two nurses (both holding their hands to their mouths in disbelief) and said, "I am going to put her under anesthesia and she is insulting me?" He pointed at me and continued, "Young lady, I'll have you know I swim every morning!"

"You mean, you float every morning," I responded.

A few nurses were listening to our conversation and giggling. Dr. Cohen was trying to hold his own laughter back. "Listen—" he craned his neck, trying to read my name from the chart—"Sooheyela, what you see is layer over layer over layer of muscle," pointing to his oversized stomach.

I said, "I am actually very familiar with those layers. My husband has the same layer over layer over layer of muscle, as well. I am a seasoned 'muscle layer' connoisseur."

He turned to the nurses and said, "That's it, I'm out of here!"

To which I said, "Dr. Cohen, you are going to have lunch, right?"

He laughed and said, "Yeah, how did you know?"

"Told you, I have one at home, I know the drill."

He turned to one of the nurses while stroking my hair. "Get this cutie ready for me, I'll be back soon." He smiled and said, "You're all right. I'll see you soon," and walked away.

I yelled at his retreating back, "Hey, enjoy your lunch while I lie hungry here!"

He yelled back, "Oh, I will!"

After I was done with the preparations I was pushed into the cold, sterile OR. As we entered, I swiveled my head, looking for Fariborz, but there was only one bed in the middle of the room. I panicked, "Where is my brother? Is he OK?"

One of the nurses answered, "He is in the OR next door. Dr. Schwartz will hand your liver to Dr. Florman, who will continue with the transplant there." She pointed through the double doors to my right. I put my head down and thanked God for keeping Fariborz alive. I was transferred to the bed in the middle of the room and, after a short while, Dr. Cohen walked in. By now every nurse present knew about our earlier conversation. They were repeating it to the ones who had not been present at the time.

I asked, "How was lunch?"

He answered, "Very good, you should have tasted it. Oh too bad, you can't! By the way, do you cook Gondi?"—a customary Persian Jewish Shabbat dish.

"Yes, of course," I said. "How do you know what Gondi is?"

He explained that he was Israeli and, after serving in the Army, had gone to live in Italy for a couple of years. He'd befriended a couple of Persian Jewish families there, who invited him to dinner on Friday nights. He added that though he had been living in the US for a long time with his wife and children, he would never forget those delicious Persian dishes. He was also Shomer Shabbat, like Dr. Schwartz (observing Saturday Jewish rules—part of which is not working).

As soon as I heard that he had lived in Italy, given my great love for that country, I switched to Italian, *"Allora, Parli Italiano?"* (You speak Italian?)

He responded, *"Certo, per che tu parli Italiano?"* (Sure, why do you speak Italian?)

"Perche mi piace parlare Italiano. Mi piacciono tute le cose Italiane." (Because I love to speak Italian and I love everything Italian.)

A nurse with big black eyes joined us in our conversation. She had been born and raised in Italy. A couple of nurses were still repeating my conversation with Dr. Cohen before entering the O.R. The rest were talking about their favorite Italian dishes. Everybody was smiling and talking in the room. There was so much happiness and good will in that OR that for a few minutes we all forgot about the transplant. It felt like we were at a social gathering and had all found new friends. The only thing missing were a couple of cappuccinos and biscotti, though a marble water fountain by Bernini would have helped the decor! We carried on for a few more minutes, talking about the delicious food and the friendly culture in Italy.

The Italian nurse looked at me with those large dark eyes framing the top of her surgical mask and said, "Sit up and hold me tight, bella, do not move. The doctor is about to put a needle in your spine."

Serina walked towards me. "Soheila...."

I did not let her speak. I said, "Nope, I will not change my mind." She stepped back.

I almost wanted to ask her, "Can you video this surgery so when Fariborz goes home we can have a good laugh over it?" But I kept quiet. I sat up, took a deep breath, and put my arms around my Italian nurse.

She put my head on her shoulder and stroked my hair, repeating in my ears, *"Tutto andra' bene, hai le spalle grande."* Everything will be fine, you are strong.

Dr. Cohen smiled at me, kissed my forehead and said, *"Ciao,* Soheila. See you when you wake up." I smiled at all those beautiful, kind and caring masked faces, said, "Please God" and fell into a deep sleep.

Hope

"May your choices reflect your hopes, not your fears." —Nelson Mandela

August 16, 2013

I tried to open my eyes. It wasn't easy. I didn't know if I was awake or dreaming. I had no idea where I was. I noticed a couple of blurry lights around me. While I was fighting to keep my eyelids open, I saw Dr. Schwartz and Dr. Cohen through the haze, smiling on either side of my bed. I moved my head slightly to see who else was there. All I saw was hospital equipment, grey walls and grey curtains pulled over the glass dividers. It felt like midnight.

I looked at them, gathered all my energy together and said, "So what happened to you guys being Shomer Shabbat?" I saw huge teeth and thick lips floating on top of my bed. Their faces were changing shapes and positions. *I am either hallucinating or dreaming,* I thought. I couldn't remember why I was there. When I remembered, I wanted to know how the surgery went. How my brother was, but I didn't have the power for another question—or I thought that I didn't. I felt one of the doctors squeezing my hand and heard him say in an echoing voice, "Everything is OK Soheila." I think I fell asleep again.

I have no idea how long it took me to open my eyes again, but this time I saw Justin leaning over my bed with Camy and Matthew close by. I was confused, not sure if what I was looking at was real. I tried raising

279

my hand to touch their faces, to feel their skin. Something was attached to the tip of my forefinger. I brought it close to my face to have a better look. It was a pulse monitor with a red light shining through the tip.

I leveled my finger at the kids and said, "ET PHONE HOME! ET PHONE HOME!" All three of them laughed with relief and started kissing me. "Go home, guys, seriously," I said. "You must be exhausted."

They were happy that they had me back and that I was well enough to kid around with them. They didn't know what to do next. They wanted to be helpful, they wanted to do something, so they started massaging my hands and feet. "Guys, I appreciate it. But it's late," I said. "Please go home!" I suddenly remembered.

"Did Fariborz make it?" I asked with fear in my voice.

"Yes mom, he is alive," Justin said.

"Thank God," I whispered. "Thank you, God."

All I saw were a multitude of hands and faces over my bed and nothing else. I must have fallen asleep after that.

I remember waking up to a voice calling, "Dr. Florman, Dr. Florman." I opened my eyes. I was in the same dark room with the same lights shining in front of me. I lifted my head as much as I could and noticed a nurse's station in front of my bed. It was around 2 o'clock. A tall gentleman in a doctor's uniform was leaning against the counter, reading a chart.

I mustered whatever energy I had left and called out, "Dr. Florman, are you there?"

He walked towards me and said, "Yes Soheila, I'm here."

I always thought he had a kind face, but at that moment he looked exactly like a guardian angel. His white coat was a suit of shining armor, his chart a flaming sword, the fluorescent light a halo around his head. *Fentanyl can turn a liver transplant surgeon into a winged warrior!* I thought. "How is my brother? Did he pull through?" I wasn't sure I wanted to know the answer.

"Yes, he's in the room next to you." He pointed to my right.

I tried to turn my head to see my brother, but a grey curtain was pulled over the glass divider. I looked back at Dr. Florman with a big smile. I wanted to jump out of the hospital bed and kiss him, but I could hardly move. I was attached to wires, tubes, and monitors.

"Thank you Dr. Florman, thank you!" I gushed. "Did I tell you I love you? Please let your wife know, tell her I said I love you. I'm sure she understands!"

Dr. Florman laughed and rested his hand on my arm. "I want your brother to go home for selfish reasons. I want to get to know the man everyone loves and admires so much. I want him to live. Last night, more than 50 people were in the waiting room praying for him. I want to know this man. I want to be his friend. I want him to dance at his daughters' wedding. For now, just try and get well, Soheila. We'll do our best for your brother, I promise."

"You call this 'selfish reasons?' You and Dr. Schwartz change destinies. I have always said, 'After God, if there is one, there are doctors.' I don't want anything more than my brother going home and getting to know you caring doctors as well. Thank you."

"Not sure about God and destiny; however, I think you are one of the strongest people I have ever met. In the face of so many things you found the strength to do what many think they might be willing to do but few actually do."

I wanted to kiss his hands, but I couldn't even find my own hands! I thanked him again and he left.

I had ended up right next to my brother in the Surgical ICU, sharing the same bone marrow, the same liver, and now the same glass divider. We were both flat on our backs, unable to move, just a few feet from each other, him unconscious, me thanking God for another miracle. I was overcome with happiness. I lay in my bed, looked at the depressing grey ceiling and smiled. *He pulled through, he is alive. The doctors were wrong. They don't know Fariborz. They don't get it. He wants to go home.*

I realized what the purpose of my life was. I had saved a precious life. My existence helped another human being. I lost my son six years ago, and I couldn't do anything about it, but we would not lose Fariborz. I felt a newfound inner strength, an unfamiliar joy. I had hope again. We had hope again. We'd pulled off the impossible. There is no logic to life, but there is plenty of magic! He had a new liver, a new beginning and an exciting new chapter in his life. Thank you, God! We had both won in this round.

I opened my eyes and looked at the clock directly in front of me. It read 6 o'clock. *Am or pm?* I once again wondered. No matter what time of day or night, the lighting in ICU was always the same. It was somber and sad. The computers and the monitors improve with the times, but the atmosphere of an ICU always remains the same. I called for a nurse. A woman with short red hair, pale skin, and a serious face walked to my room and stopped at the door.

I asked, "Could you please tell me how my brother is? I believe he is in the room to my right."

She left and returned after a few minutes. "He is okay, but he is not awake yet. He has a private nurse because of his critical condition."

Mission accomplished, I thought. *Thank you, God.* We were both alive, and that's all that mattered. I was filled with joy, I was happy, I was at peace. It felt right to feel light after 6 long heavy years. We had pulled off the impossible. It was a miracle. He was a miracle. Life was a miracle!

I wanted to run out of that room and hug my brother. But that was not in the cards. I was uncomfortable and unable to move. I had a funny and strange feeling in my abdominal area, an unfamiliar burning sensation. My shoulders were aching. I felt a sharp pain behind my neck and chest. *Funny, why do I have pain there?* My feet were itchy and uncomfortable. My throat was dry. I called for the nurse and the same woman walked in.

"Can I have some ice chips please?" I asked. She left the room, came back after a few minutes, and left a cup filled with ice chips on the table in the far corner of the room. I looked at the cup with longing. I certainly wanted to taste those refreshing and cold ice chips. *But it might as well be in China,* I thought. I called again. She came back with a surprised face, wondering why I called her back.

"Am I supposed to get the cup myself?" I asked.

"At some point you have to get up, don't you think?" she said with an accent.

"Well, it's not happening now, so please hand me the cup."

She rolled her eyes, stared at me for a few seconds, grabbed the cup, and held it in front of me. She was about to leave when I said, "Could you please bring the bed up a little?" She looked at me with a shocked face. (How dare she be so demanding?) She pressed the button, brought the bed up and left.

Had I gotten the nurse from hell? After all the wonderful, caring staff I had met at Mount Sinai hospital, now I was stuck with her? Every nurse I'd known so far had been warm, kind, and attentive. Now, a few hours after my surgery, this one wanted me to get up and get my own ice chips? I tried not to let her annoy me. I sucked on those small, refreshing, thirst-quenching pieces of ice as if they were the most delicious sorbet. The ice soothed my dry throat. It was invigorating. I finished the cup to the last piece.

I felt happy. I was grateful to have my brother back. I was overwhelmed with emotion. I thought about Stephen. I knew he was there, watching. I knew he was my guardian angel. I knew he was next to me. Tears of gratitude rolled down my face, disappearing into my hair. "Thank you Stephenjoon, thank you for saving Fariborz. I know you are watching over us." I called for the nurse again.

"Yes? How can I help you?" she asked.

"Can I have tissues, please?" I said.

She came back a few minutes later carrying a small box of tissues, left it on the same table, and walked out. I was shocked! One has to realize, I had stitches not only on my stomach, but inside as well. I was attached to IVs, tubes, and all sorts of wires. The idea of moving even half a foot was impossible. I ignored her behavior and wiped my face with my sheet. *Don't let her bother you, not now!*

Dr. Schwartz came to visit. He examined the scars on my stomach, "Your incision was not in the shape of a peace sign, but one straight line from between your breasts down to your belly button."

He pulled the cover over me and continued, "You were skinny enough, we were able to get to where we needed to go," he said. "There was no layer of fat covering the area."

"All those years of eating right and exercise came in handy. Who knew I was getting my body ready for a liver transplant surgery?" I said. "Dr. Schwartz, why do I have this shooting pain in my shoulders and on the top part of my chest? It makes it difficult for me to breathe."

"In order for us to get to your liver, we had to position you in a way that your mid-section popped out, so we rolled your shoulders back and tied them down under you. If you want to imagine, almost the same position as dissecting a frog. You were held in that posture for a long time. That is why your chest and shoulders are hurting."

"Honestly, I don't care what hurts. I was just curious why here," I said. "All I want is for my brother to get well."

He looked at me with concerned eyes. "Your brother has a long way to go."

The light and wonderful feeling of happiness escaped me like air escaping a popped balloon. I'd thought he had made it through the surgery and that's what mattered. I'd thought from now on the difficult days were behind us. The liver transplant was the magic spell, the answer to our prayers, the solution to his problems. Obviously not. He still had a long way to go and many battles to overcome.

Instead of panicking, being the ultimate optimist that I was, I answered, "One step at a time, Dr. Schwartz. One step at a time."

He smiled and left. *No negative thoughts*, I told myself. *He is still here. He is still with us. That is all that matters*. I did not want to let go of the rare and wonderful sensation of feeling light and joyful.

Dr. Florman and Dr. Kim also came to visit. They looked content with the results of the operation and my brother's condition. They told me that he was the first leukemia patient to have liver transplant surgery from a live donor in the history of Mount Sinai hospital, maybe even the medical world. "What happened was a miracle, a medical breakthrough."

They will study his case for years to come. We should definitely write a book together. I imagined sitting with him, Fariborz in his favorite brown leather armchair with a cup of coffee in his hand, talking about his hospital stay and how the doctors gave up on him so many times yet he still pulled through. Now we could share his story and thousands of people would benefit from his suffering. Nazee thought we could have done without another chapter, but we needed it so that people who had completely given up could find hope again. Yes! Miracles do happen.

The flow of visitors was constant. Liza had flown in from Miami the night before. She was the first one through the door with Linda, Justin, and Camy. They were all in good spirits. Camy started massaging my feet again. The sequential pressure boots (used as preventive measures for blood clots) were itchy and uncomfortable. His massage felt heavenly.

Justin said, "Mom, there are so many people outside waiting to see you. Everyone is happy that you two are fine." Then he continued on, telling me that our friends had asked everybody in our community on both coasts to participate in a mass prayer on the day of the surgery. Everyone had to stop doing whatever they were doing and pray for us at 1 pm. People stopped working, driving, walking, eating, talking... and prayed.

The love and kindness that we were receiving from everyone, everywhere was overwhelming. I felt lucky to have so many people genuinely worrying and caring for my family. Their love felt like a warm and soft blanket. Our pain and suffering had become everybody's pain and suffering. They all knew about the smallest problem or improvement. Emails, texts, and phone calls flew between East and West coasts. It had become a "reality soap opera," but the screenwriters were all on acid.

Nurse Feelgood walked in, looked at everyone in the room with indifference, and said, "I have to put a new line on the back of your hand." She turned to my visitors, "You are more than welcome to leave." No one moved. She shrugged her shoulders and got busy poking me. I had been told countless times that I had good veins, but she had a problem finding a vein suitable enough for her, I guess. To make matters worse, she was poking me without wearing surgical gloves! Liza, Linda, and I kept on exchanging glances.

Finally, she stuck a needle in. I gave out a loud cry and yelled, "Take it out. Take it out. It is hurting me."

She said, "What's wrong? I know what I am doing."

"Obviously not!" I said, "Look at my hand. I said take the needle out!"

My hand had immediately swollen up like a balloon. She looked at it and took the needle out. Pain started shooting up my hand. At this point, I had had enough.

"I am sure you know what you are doing, but please, get me another nurse."

She looked at me with a mixture of disgust, disbelief, and anger, and walked out. My hand had blown up to twice its regular size. I had tried to keep my cool with her but I had reached my limit. I could not look at her cold, indifferent, and lifeless face for another minute. A robot had more compassion than this woman.

I asked Liza to go to the nurse's station and ask for a new nurse. When they asked why, she explained the reason. They were all in shock. For the remainder of my stay, Nurse Feelgood ignored and snubbed me every time she saw me. My hand hurt for a few months after the surgery.

To change the mood of the room, Justin started telling me funny stories about our friends and family in the waiting room while we were undergoing surgery. "Mom, we had been waiting for a couple of hours with no news about your surgery. Suddenly the double doors to the OR opened and a doctor in scrubs walked out. He was holding a white box in front of him with his two hands. Dad jumped up and ran to the doctor and asked, 'Is that my wife's liver? Are you holding the cut piece of my wife's liver?' The doctor looked at him in shock, then looked at the box in his hands and said, 'No sir, this is my lunch, Chinese food, if that is okay with you?' We all started laughing."

Camy said, "Momon was crying. Jacklyn (our friend) was trying to feed her because she wanted to fast (a strong Jewish belief, by fasting and being in agony, God would listen to your prayers). Every time she opened her mouth to say something, Jacklyn and Hilda shoved food in her mouth. It became funny because after couple of attempts, Momon was too scared to say a word."

Linda said, "The kids were playing ball across the waiting room. People joined in, no matter what their age. It was a fun distraction for everyone. But Justin was crying the whole time. He sat in a corner by himself or paced the room. He did not want to talk to anyone."

Justin chimed in. "It was past midnight by the time the surgery was over. When Dr. Florman walked out it was as if the prophet himself had shown up. He said, 'They are both fine. The surgery went well.' He looked at everyone and almost with a laugh continued, 'However, I have a question. Can someone please tell me what kind of a diet is Soheila on? I really want to know.' No one could imagine why he was asking that question. Everyone stayed quiet and stared at Dr. Florman. 'She had one of the healthiest livers I've ever seen,' he continued, 'and believe me, I have seen a lot. Is she a vegetarian?'"

The truth is, I never smoked, never did drugs, only drank wine occasionally, never ate junk food, always exercised, and ate a lot of fruits and vegetables. I just thought, what is the point of smoking or doing drugs? Why should I get drunk and make a fool of myself? The idea of not having control over my own body scared me. Why put drugs, chemicals, or garbage in it? We have only this one body, and spare parts are difficult to come by! All these good habits and healthy lifestyle choices had come in handy for such a bizarre reason. Life plays stupid games. There was no dress rehearsal once the game started, you had to be ready to rise to the occasion.

Justin concluded the story, "With that liver, Fariborz's recovery should be faster."

After that everyone had gotten up and started kissing Dr. Florman. They gave each other high fives and hugged each other. Some cried, some laughed. It became a real celebration, a celebration of life, a celebration of a new beginning.

Now it was well past midnight, but everyone was still in my room. I listened to these stories with joy and gratitude. I wanted to know about every second of it, every last detail, every single word. My brother had spare parts. He was "new and improved!" We just had to wait for his bilirubin to go down. With a functioning liver, that should be easy.

We were all hoping for the best result. Hope: a feeling of expectation and desire for a certain thing to happen. Such a small word, but so powerful. My brother was still in ICU in critical condition, but we all had hope. It was a new beginning, and that made a world of difference. Thank you, Stephen. Thank you, Universe. Thank you, God, for giving us our hope and our Fariborz back. "You know God, by keeping him alive we both win."

Dead For Eight Minutes

"Life and death are one thread, the same line viewed from different sides." —Lao Tzu

October, 2013

It was late October, and Jordan was back in Los Angeles in school. This meant I had to travel back and forth more often. It bothered me that my youngest was home with his mom missing in action. I told Rabbi Tokeyar in one of our conversations, "I feel guilty, my son hasn't had a normal evening at home since January when Zohreh lost her hearing." My dear Rabbi responded, "The lesson that he gets out of your commitment to your family is more valuable than any normal evening. Do not worry about him. He will be a better person as a result." Those few sentences gave me the much-needed reassurance I needed to stay at my brother's side. However, I decided to fly to Los Angeles more often to be with Jordan for couple of days in between.

My last night in town for that week was just like any other night. As always, my brother's hospital room was full of people. Family members came and left, friends came and left, doctors and nurses came and left. Nahid, Nazee, and I took turns massaging Fariborz's head, legs, and feet. We helped the nurses reposition him on the bed as often as possible so he would not get bedsores. They kept cleaning out his trach, which was too uncomfortable for us to watch. I gagged every time I witnessed that long tube going down his breathing pipe. Momon kept on talking to him, telling him how much he was loved by so many people, begging him for a smile. If and when he smiled, he briefly became our brother again. That smile, with the dimple on his chin, represented the man we loved. My mom had always bragged about the cleft on his curled chin.

"He takes after my father. They both look like movie stars, just like Cary Grant," she boasted. He did look like a movie star. His female patients wrote numerous love letters to him after they were treated by him and were sent home. He read them to Jennifer and blushed. It was not only his good looks; his kind and warm personality shined through. Now the only thing left of that man was his smile and the beautiful deep dimple. We lived for those few seconds and those brief reminders.

Fariborz was more responsive and alert now. His new liver was a functioning one, he was weak and his recovery was slow but promising. The bacteria showed up once in awhile in his system. But altogether he was in much better shape. He watched a Bond movie and nodded yes or no to our questions. Just another night at SICU, but a better one. Around 8 pm his friend Phil walked in. He visited Fariborz after work and stayed by his bed regularly. He held his hands and talked to him or just stood there and stared at his friend for hours. You could have touched the sadness on his face. "Fariborz helped my mother and father when every other doctor had refused to perform surgery on them." Phil told that story to everyone that came to visit.

"How is he?" he asked. The answer, of course, was "the same." We were happy with "the same" as long as he was holding on and not getting worse.

"Why don't you leave, Soheila? Go relax, I am here," he suggested. "No need for two of us to be here this late." I was tempted.

"If you don't mind," I told Phil, "if it is not a problem for you to stay here by yourself. I usually leave at 11."

"Not at all. I will stay with him until he falls asleep."

I welcomed the idea, thanked him, picked up my bright green iPhone—my only connection to the outside world—and called Justin and his wife Setareh. "Can we have dinner together?"

"Sure, where would you like to go?"

I kissed Fariborz's forehead, repeated numerous times that I loved him, said goodbye (he smiled, sent a kiss and nodded), and left. I was in good spirits; there hadn't been any horrible news or setbacks. We just had to wait for him to recover little by little. It was a long process, but it was going in the right direction. As I rushed to cross the huge, open lobby to leave the hospital, I came face to face with Dr. Fab, Fariborz's respiratory doctor.

"Hello Doc. You are here late," I said.

He turned his body first and then his head in slow motion, looked at me from behind his glasses, and asked, "I had to see a patient, how is Dr. Noban?"

"He is the same, which is good. I'll take that."

"You know, Soheila, I was thinking, with everything that he has been through since April, all the pain, suffering and complications, the Almighty should send him home, to his family. Don't you think? He has survived so many impossibles! I think he has paid his dues," he sighed. "He deserves to go home."

Go home to his family? I thought. The idea of Fariborz being home, reading the newspaper on his favorite low, brown leather sofa while eyeing Ava from the corner of his eyes doing flips on the floor and answering Alexa's questions did not seem possible. At least not for a while. Not for a long while.

"Who knows what the Almighty thinks? Who decides who deserves what? All I know is that if he really wanted my brother with him, he had the chance to take him—more than once, didn't he? And he is still here, isn't he?" And I walked away. "Good night, doc." I hailed a cab and joined my son and his wife at a Thai restaurant. We talked about everything but the hospital. The time for our annual trip to the Bahamas for Thanksgiving was coming up.

"Do you think we can go this year?" Justin asked.

"Why not? Fariborz is getting better, he is on the road to recovery," I answered. "I will look into it."

He talked about his work, his challenges, his problems. But every once in awhile he punctuated his remarks with, "I know, mom, these are not problems compared to what Fariborz is going through!" Justin was too good for his own sake. I looked at him and said, "If my headache is worse than your headache, it does not mean that you are not in pain. Everyone has their share of problems, some more than the rest."

We were all in a good mood. We ate and talked. I reached my hotel around 10:00 and started packing for my early flight the next day. I was in bed at 11:00. I was almost asleep when my phone rang. I jumped. It was Nazee. "Where are you?" she asked.

"In my bed," I answered. "What's the matter? What's wrong?"

"I am at the hospital with Joe," she said with a somber voice. "They called us to come in. Fariborz's heart stopped. He went into cardiac arrest."

My hands started to shake. Was this a cruel joke? Was I having a nightmare?

"He is not dead," she continued. "They revived him after eight minutes, it happened at 10:15. He is completely unconscious. He shows no reaction. They do not know if there was any damage done to his brain. He is breathing with the machine. Fariborz looks dead, but he is not."

"But how is this possible? When I left him, he was fine. Phil took my place and stayed with him. I did not notice anything different," I said.

"No one knows," she answered. "The nurses said that Phil left when he was sound asleep. It must have happened right after, when he was alone."

I was numb, unable to move. My hands continued to shake. My heart seized; I was sure it had stopped beating. I felt cold, freezing cold. I felt heavy. I had become one giant piece of ice; a frozen volcano ready to erupt. I wanted to throw up. I could feel my heart beating so hard that it was pushing with every beat to come out. I was suspended between what was real and what was not. What was reality and what was a nightmare. I tried to put my hand on my heart. I wanted to push it back into my chest. But it wanted to be free. My heart was tired of feeling sad and disappointed too. It did not want any part of this. It was quitting on me. I was in agony; I could not breathe.

I heard someone calling me from a distance, "Soheila, Soheila, are you there? Answer me."

The faraway voice came from that green rectangular-shaped device. I picked up my phone and pressed it to my ear and said, "Sorry Nazee, I will stay in my bed, I cannot come to the hospital now, I cannot think, I cannot do anything for him now anyway. This is a cruel joke. When I left, he was fine. He nodded and smiled at me when I told him I was leaving for L.A. I don't understand."

"I don't know what to tell you. It hurts to look at him, there is no sign of life in him. We will leave soon too." She added, "Do not come, he is completely out, but let's not tell Momon. It would destroy her."

I hung up the phone, lay flat on my back and stared at the ceiling. *The Almighty should send him home, to his family. Don't you think?* Who was I to think? Who am I to wish? Who am I to want? Obviously, there is a force out there greater than all of our thoughts, prayers or wants.

He died? My brother died!? That was not part of the deal. He was supposed to go home. He was getting better. They all said so. He nodded and smiled at me before I left. Phil was there. We watched a movie together. I should not have left. If I had stayed, I would have noticed if anything had gone wrong. This was the first evening that I had left before 11 pm. I should have stayed next to him. I should have stayed in his room. It was my fault. I could have prevented it. I could have done something about it. Why did his heart stop?

Tears were rolling down my face. I could not stop them. I was lying there flat on my back as teardrops raced each other down my face. Why did this world have to be so sad? My beautiful and kind brother *died?*

Finally, it came to me. *Of course,* I told myself, *if he was supposed to die, he would have been dead.* But he is not dead, is he? That is still more proof that he is going home to his family. Another round of wrestling with God. Who won this one? I am not so sure! No one knows the result yet. But we will find out soon.

I woke up the next day with my stomach in a knot, not knowing what to expect. For a few seconds, I hoped my conversation with Nazee had been a bad dream, but recently, reality had proven to be worse than any nightmare. It was a nightmare that we could not escape. A perpetual, living nightmare. I called Nahid and told her about Fariborz's situation. I was disgusted repeating what Nazee had told me; I did not want to hear the words that were coming out of my mouth. She kept on repeating, "What?" and "How?" as she started to cry. "I will not go to work. I will be in the hospital soon."

I froze at the entrance to the room, holding onto the frame of the door so I would not fall at the terrible sight that greeted me. Fariborz looked dead. His head was tilted to one side, motionless, his arms by his side, his hands open. His color was changed; he was pale. His chest was moving up and down with the help of the respiratory device. Nazee walked in. Not a word was exchanged. We looked at each other and then looked at our brother.

"The doctors said he could be brain-damaged," she said. "No one can tell for sure, but there is a big possibility. This is what Fariborz was afraid of all his life, isn't it? He was afraid of being dependent. He asked us not to keep him alive if he is not coherent. He was the first one in the family that had a living will. Look at him now. What are we going to do?" Tears were rolling down her face.

I looked at what was left of the brother we used to know, the almost dead man in front of us, the bald head, the puffy face, the grey complexion and said, "Fariborz will be fine, he is not going anywhere. There is nothing wrong with his brain. This too shall pass. He is still here. His heart is beating. We cannot tell if any damage was done or not, no one can, so why worry about it? We have to concentrate on bringing him back. He is still here. I'm telling you, Fariborz is not going anywhere. The only place he is going, is home." I refused to hear anything negative.

The doctors came in one by one, all puzzled and sad.

"Whatever could go wrong has gone wrong with his case, even things that we did not anticipate."

"I have never seen or heard of a case like this."

"He was getting better; yesterday he was fine."

No one had an answer for us. Why did he have a cardiac arrest? His heart was never part of the problem! Nahid and Jennifer arrived. Now we were worried about how to explain his condition to our mother. She was relentless... 82 years old and she commuted more than an hour each way to come and sit next to her only son. Today she would see him unconscious. How could we justify that? She was a smart woman, and sometimes that could be a serious problem. My father, suffering from Alzheimer's, was the lucky one!

Momon arrived, took one look at our faces and dug her fingernails into her face. "What's wrong? What happened?" She rushed to the room and saw her son's seemingly lifeless body. She gave out a loud cry, melted to the floor next to his bed, and repeated, "What happened? Talk to me? Why does he look like this?"

Nazee answered, "Something happened last night, we do not know what, they cannot figure it out either. He is asleep."

"This is not sleeping, he is not sleeping," she said in a pleading voice.

She got up slowly with our help, walked towards Fariborz, and tried very carefully to open his eyelid. We reminded her that she should wash her hands; she ignored our comment. She bent over Fariborz again and gently tried to open his eyes. She gave out a loud cry, turned towards us and said, "His pupil is all the way up, that is not a good sign, all you see is the white of his eye. Something has happened and you are not telling me." She collapsed on the chair and started crying, mumbling, "He was fine yesterday, he smiled at me, remember?"

Dr. Fab walked in and looked at me with sad eyes. "The Almighty should send him home, you suggested last night!" I said with a bitter smile. He turned his body, then his sad eyes, and stared at the monitor.

Dr. Spielvogel came to visit after work. He was shocked and beside himself. It was difficult for him to see his best friend in that condition. "I bet mucus was the cause of this. It got stuck in his trach and blocked the airway. I have seen it happen before."

"If that was the cause then I will never forgive myself for leaving him before 11 at night. I was with him till late every other night. If I had been next to his bed I would have noticed it as soon as he had shown signs of difficulty breathing. Why then? Why the only night that I was not with him? He must have suffered so much," I said. I couldn't even cry anymore. Maybe I was in shock, maybe in disbelief, maybe disgusted, I don't know, but I could only stand there and stare at the shadow of death on his face.

We stayed in his room, but there was nothing for us to do. We just moved his legs and arms around and kept on repositioning him. An act of desperation. Now the conversation centered on the possibility of him being brain-damaged, Nazee's first fear. There was no way of knowing. He was unconscious.

"He is not going anywhere, he is going home. He is fine," I kept on repeating. "If God wanted him dead, he's had many chances by now to kill him. His brain is fine."

Fariborz remained in that situation for about a week. We kept on talking to him and moving his body as much as we could. One morning I came in and did what I did every morning. I opened his eyelid, but this time his pupil was in the right place, right in the center. *That must be a good sign,* I thought, *an improvement for sure.* I ran to the doctors at SICU and told them about the possible improvement.

They examined him. "He still has a long way to go."

Our dear, dark, dorky Dr. Hemorrhoids walked in, examined him, jerked his face, and looked at me from the corner of his glasses. "What do you think?" I asked.

"I told you before, he never had a good chance of survival. The liver transplant was a mistake."

"I did not ask you about the transplant, your opinion is worthless to me. Plus, it's done. Tell me about his condition now."

"You are wasting your time."

To that response I started yelling, "Get the hell out of here. You are not a doctor. You are not human. You are worthless. Get out!" He looked at me and without showing any feeling stepped out.

Little by little Fariborz started moving his head to the left and to the right. First slowly, but after a few days, he started shaking his head vigorously, almost violently, as if he had seen a beast, a monster, a ghost, and was trying to escape. His eyes were rolling up in his head and he was trying very hard to say a word repeatedly. He kept on opening his mouth and bringing his tongue out as much as he could to mouth a word that looked like HELP!

We tried to calm him down, but we couldn't. His behavior was so alarming that when he fell asleep we were relieved. It was altogether a disturbing scene and an exhausting situation. When he started moving his arms around, shaking them in the air, he looked possessed and frightened. His body gestures were almost those of a creature, not a human being. He wanted to get away from something or someone. He looked scared. More than scared—it was horror.

Having been in a hospital bed for 7 months, he had very little control over his limbs. His arms were creating serious problems, flailing about in the air with extreme force. He had tubes, catheters, and wires coming out of different parts of his body and he pulled them out involuntarily with his hands and fingers.

We stood guard at the top of his head and when he opened his eyes, we held his arms down and kept on repeating, "It's fine, Fariborz, we are here, we will not leave you, we are here to help." But that did not stop him. He was scared. His eyes were popping out of their sockets in fear. He was begging for help. A couple of times he pulled out his breathing tube with his fingers, but by now, we had all learned how to attach it back.

I had to think of some way that his fingers would not get tangled up in the wires and tubes. I looked around the room and saw the two hats that Liza had knitted for him. I put each of his hands into a soft hat and used the hospital tape to secure the bottom of the hat to his wrists. This way his fingers were safely covered.

After couple of hours, Felice, our kind nurse, came in and stared at my ingenious creation. "Why did you do that?" she asked, staring at what looked like two muffins.

"So his fingers would not get stuck in anything accidentally," I answered.

"Why didn't you tell me? We have special mittens for that," she said as she left the room.

She came back with two soft white mittens. Ah, they thought of everything. A small part of the problem was solved.

Morning till night, it was the same story. He woke up, moved his arms around, and begged for help. By now, we were sure that he was reliving the night that he was suffocating, but of course no one heard him until the alarms went off, when he had a cardiac arrest. The idea of our brother suffocating to death and, worst of all, remembering and reliving it, was like a dagger in our hearts. I could not stop imagining the horror of that night. My lovely brother, he felt helpless and scared. It was no different than someone putting a pillow over his face.

We had hardly ever left him alone throughout the long months of his hospital stay. Then, on the one night that no one was there, the Angel of Death seized the opportunity and crept out from behind the curtains. He walked towards him in that dark room and stared at my brother from under his black hood, looked around to be sure he was alone, showed his yellow and crooked teeth, gave an ugly smile, exposed his filthy hand, put his ugly black finger with its filthy dark nail in the hole of his trach, and closed his airway while my brother was trying to cry for help.

The dark creature had waited patiently for the perfect moment and he found it, with no one to shoo him away. He brought his face lower and whispered, "See you on the other side. The match is over," and smiled a victorious smile. He stayed until my brother's heart stopped beating. Only when alarms went off everywhere and nurses and doctors rushed into the room, only then did he pick up his black robe with bony fingers, look back at the lifeless body of my brother, smile his creepy smile, and slink back to his hiding spot.

The room was full of doctors and nurses doing whatever they could do to bring him back to life. They revived my brother after eight long minutes. The Angel of Death looked through the curtains, cursed under his breath, spat his thick black spit and murmured, "There will be another chance! It is not over yet."

My brother's face, especially his eyes, told me that story over and over again. He had seen the Angel of Death face-to-face.

Dancing in the Dark

"Sometimes you find yourself in the middle of nowhere and sometimes in the middle of nowhere you find yourself." —Unknown

November, 2013

Since the liver transplant I was not allowed to sleep in my luxurious waiting room of the hospital. The week of Thanksgiving, I'd decided to stay at Nazee's apartment in the city. On Tuesday morning, I woke up with a strange pain in my side. I looked at my alarm clock. It was 5 am. The pain was dull at first, but when I got up to use the bathroom, it quickly spread across my lower abdomen and into my side. I had to take my time walking carefully back to my bed. I lay there thinking of my trip. Today was the day I had been waiting for. I was supposed to fly to the Bahamas to spend the Thanksgiving weekend with my family and friends, the same as every other Thanksgiving for the past 10 years. I didn't want anything to ruin those few precious days for me. Not even this pain.

It had been more than a month since the cardiac arrest. His recovery had been slow and daunting. With all those horrible incidents that he had to overcome, the deadly bacteria in his lungs never left him alone. They were hiding somewhere deep waiting to strike back again. A well-trained army of small but efficient devotees to the dark side with one mission in life only, "to attack and kill at any cost." Antibiotics were part of his daily diet. His "go-to drug." His "savior." But for now, my brother was himself again, the "himself" that we had gotten used to during his hospital stay. He was not brain-damaged, which was another miracle. He watched TV, smiled, and responded to us when we asked him a question. I felt comfortable enough to leave him for a few days.

I inched my way to the bathroom, got the Advil bottle, took two tablets, and went back to bed. I lay down and tried to sleep, but the pain just kept on getting worse. It was too early to call anyone or to wake Nazee up, so I stayed in bed for another hour.

Around 6:30, I heard a noise outside my room. I managed to get out of bed, but standing up straight was not an option. I was hunched over and could only take small steps towards the bedroom door. With one hand on my side and the other leaning against the wall, I made it to the door and opened it. Morgan, Nazee's daughter, was in the hallway onto which every bedroom opened. She was getting ready for school. I caught her the moment she left her room. She looked at me and said, "Khaleh Soheila, what's wrong? Are you OK?"

Morgan was 15 years old. She had been involved in everything that had been going on with my brother. She'd come to the hospital to visit Fariborz with her twin sister Michaela whenever they had some free time. They came to the prayer sessions, they invited Alexa and Ava to spend time with their friends. The girls were 15 but going on 25.

I took a deep breath, "No, Morgan," I said, "I'm not. Please call your mom and tell her I don't feel well. I'm in a lot of pain." I leaned against the wall, closed my eyes, and waited. I heard Nazee and Morgan coming towards me.

"What's wrong?" Nazee asked.

"I have a horrible pain in my right side. I can't breathe. It hurts more every minute. Please call Dr. Schwartz. His number is in my cell phone."

She took my phone and searched for his number. I writhed with pain, clutching my side. Nazee's face was white with fear. She had never seen me complaining of pain before.

"Good morning, Dr. Schwartz, I'm sorry to call you so early. This is Nazee, Soheila Adelipour's sister. Soheila woke up this morning in a lot of pain. It's her right side," Nazee stopped talking and looked at me. "I don't know," she said, "Let me ask her. One minute please... Soheila," she said, "Dr. Schwartz wants to know if the pain is constant, and where it is exactly."

"It's my right side, towards the back," I said, "and it's been constant since five o'clock. Tell him it's getting worse. It hurts here." I put the palm of my hand on my back, above my right hip. Dr. Schwartz stayed on the phone with Nazee for a few more minutes. When she got off the phone she said, "He's pretty sure it has nothing to do with your liver transplant; he thinks you probably have a kidney stone. He said we should go to the emergency room at Mount Sinai as soon as possible."

"Kidney stone?" I said. "Oh, no. I'm going to the Bahamas today!"

"I don't know what to tell you," she said, "but for now, we are going to the hospital." She looked at me in my pajamas and said, "Do you need help changing?"

I looked at my luggage in the corner of my bedroom. Tears started rolling down my face. "No, thank you, I can manage."

My phone rang. It was Dr. Schwartz. "Soheila," he said, "don't go to the ER. Go directly to Dr. Kim and Dr. Florman's office. I'm scheduled for surgery, but they'll be waiting for you." I told Nazee about the change of plans as we left the apartment.

Dr. Kim and Dr. Florman rushed out when they saw us through the glass office doors. As always, Dr. Florman's kind smile greeted us. "Soheila, what is going on? It's never a dull moment with you." He held my hand and walked us towards the sofas.

We sat down at a corner sectional. I explained to him where the pain was and what it felt like. "I'm pretty sure you have a kidney stone," he said. "We have to check you in."

I looked at him in disbelief. What was he saying? "I'm supposed to fly to the Bahamas today. My husband and my children are already there waiting for me!" I hadn't been with my kids on a normal family outing in nearly a year. I had been looking forward to this vacation. I missed being with my family. I missed sitting around a table and talking about everything and nothing. I missed normal days.

"But, Soheila," he said, "you know very well you're not going to the Bahamas. You have a kidney stone. You should be happy that this happened now. Imagine if you got this while you were there."

I was crying, half because of the pain, half because of the disappointment. Nazee was quiet.

"I'll take you, Soheila," Dr. Kim said. "Are you able to walk with me to the hospital? I want you in a room right now. You can't sit in the ER with this pain."

I felt defeated, there was no sense arguing, I didn't say another word. It was decided. I had to surrender. I just nodded yes.

We stood up, ready to leave. Dr. Florman said, "I'll see you on the ninth floor." Ninth floor? Where Fariborz and I were after the liver surgery? My brother was now on the fifth floor and I'd be back on the ninth floor again. *How,* I wondered, *can this universe play such cruel tricks on us?*

Dr. Kim asked for a private room as soon as we stepped out of the elevator. She got a number and we went directly towards that room. A nurse helped me climb onto the bed and I lay there in my own clothes. By now I was begging for something, anything, to help me. Another nurse walked into the room with an IV. She looked for a vein on the back of my hand and inserted the needle in. Almost immediately I started feeling light-headed and relaxed. I saw Nazee watching from the doorway. This was not reality, it was another scene from the Twilight Zone.

We were supposed to be by my brother's bedside; he was well on his way to recovery. Instead, we were on the 9th floor worrying about me. Who plans these unfortunate events? Who thinks of these incidents and thinks it would make sense? Who takes responsibility for this scenario? The narcotics were working. I loved it. It felt good not to have that physical pain anymore. Pain made every minute drag for an eternity. Finally, I was relaxed.

After only about an hour of relief, the horror was back. And it came back strong. I cried out for the nurse and was given more morphine. I was relaxed for a short while, but my happiness was short-lived. I felt utterly nauseous. I couldn't hold anything down. I started gagging and throwing up without a break. Nazee ran to the bathroom and got me a bucket. I kept my face inside of it and kept on gagging. The pressure was non-stop and strong. I was sure my organs were going to detach and come up with the liquid. In the middle of all that I had to go for a CT scan.

The pain returned full force. I kept calling for a nurse, but there wasn't much they could do. My adverse reaction to the narcotic meant taking more of it wasn't an option. Finally, the urologist walked in, introduced himself and said, "Mrs. Adelipour, we've seen the CT scan results. You do have a kidney stone. We'll have to wait and see if you can pass the stone. If not, we have to put in a tube which requires surgery, but it can't be done till tomorrow morning."

To say I was disappointed didn't even come close. There was no point fighting, the universe had plans for me and going to the Bahamas as scheduled was not part of them. It was out of my control. I picked up my phone and called Jack and the kids. I had to tell them why I could not join them today. None of them believed me; they all thought I was making up a story to cover for some other unfortunate event. Sadly, that had been our story for past few years, expecting the worst in every situation.

"Nazee," I asked, "who is with Fariborz?"

"Shoshana, Linda, and Jen."

"Please go back to Fariborz. Tell him what happened and tell him that I'm fine. He'll wonder what has happened to us all, we have been missing in action today," I said.

Meanwhile, word got around the hospital that I'd been admitted, and every doctor that we knew came to visit. Around noon the always caring, positive, smiling, and kind Dr. Kim returned to see how I was doing. She held my hand and said, "Soheila, you have to get rid of that stone and get on your feet again."

"Oh Dr. Kim, I was supposed to leave for the Bahamas today," I said, "you have no idea how much I want to get rid of this damn stone and leave this hospital, to get away, to sit with my kids and laugh, to have a normal day. The plane leaves at 4 pm, and if I don't leave here by two, I'll miss it," I said.

"Let's be realistic," she said, "it's around noon now. You are not going to get to that plane. But think about your brother. Dr. Noban is getting better. He is going home. His infection is finally under control. He'll be out of this place soon. Please be happy about that," she said.

My eyes filled with tears. Could it be true? Could Fariborz return home and resume a normal life? Could he look like his old self again? He'd been in the hospital since early April. Since his first round of chemo, the dangerous, disgusting, dreadful and destructive bacteria had never fully left his body. It was now two days before Thanksgiving, his favorite holiday. He always had the family over. He always gave a toast with his wife and his two beautiful daughters by his side. It was always the same toast. I could hear it now.

"I consider myself a very lucky person. I am an American and I am proud of it. We are who we are because we are in this beautiful place, the land of opportunity, the land of freedom. Here is to the greatest country... the United States of America."

Fariborz cherished Thanksgiving, he cherished being an American, he cherished his life, and now with his family by his side, with his infection under control, he'd get to say it again. Not this year, but next year for sure. "You're right Dr. Kim," I said, "You're absolutely right. I have to look at the big picture. Nothing else is important but his health. Thank you. You made me happy with your news, thank you."

My poor mom was commuting between the fifth and the ninth floors. She just sat in front of me and watched me gag. The urologist had told me that walking would help my situation, so I decided to walk, even if it was just a few steps towards the bathroom. I held onto my IV stand with both hands, shaking from pain, and started taking small steps. The nurse had left a container on top of the toilet seat. It looked like an upside-down cowboy hat with measurement markings on one side. I did not think much of it. I used the bathroom, walked back towards my bed and lay on top of it.

Something strange happened. Even though I was exhausted, I felt light and free of pain. As a matter of fact, I felt fine. I felt so good that I was afraid to make even the smallest move for fear I would irritate something and the pain would return. I stayed in that same reclining position for about an hour, too scared to move. I felt like myself again. Was it possible that I had passed the stone when I used the bathroom?

I called the nurse and it was confirmed. I was free of the damn stone. I wanted to fly out of there and go see my brother. But flying with a huge needle attached to my arm was not in the cards. "Can you please take this IV out?" I asked.

"Hospital regulations do not allow us to do that. That will come out when you are discharged," she said. "But it won't be long."

I was beside myself. I texted everyone, "I gave birth to a big, beautiful, black, bouncy stone. LOL!" My intense reaction to morphine had helped the situation. Throwing up and spending hours continuously gagging had helped pushed the stone out! Who said drugs are bad for you? I had overdosed on drugs, but it turned out to be the cure! I stayed in bed, waiting for the doctor to arrive. I answered everyone's texts and called my family in the Bahamas with the good news.

But getting released turned out to be the difficult part. No one was available to sign me out. I just sat and waited. I called the nurses every half-hour begging them to find the doctor.

"We are sorry, you can't leave now, the doctor is in the OR. You just have to wait," I was told. Many times. I closed my eyes and tried to relax, thinking, *This is not the end of the world. I will wait a bit longer. Tomorrow will be a better day. I just have to wait...*

Iran, March, 1979

In March of 1979 the revolution in Iran was going full force. Living a normal life was becoming more and more difficult. The Islamic extremists controlled everybody and everything. Life as we knew it was gone, replaced by fear. Reminders were displayed everywhere. People were killed and hanged in plain sight every day for no reason. Not only were these images printed on the front page of the daily newspapers, but the bodies were left hanging from cranes for days for people to witness.

Our beautiful and peaceful country had been taken over by bearded angry men trying to get back at everything and anything that they thought was the cause of their misery. The law was "There was no law." The law was "We will barge into anyone's home and arrest everyone, just because we can." The law was "What is mine is mine and what is yours is mine, too." It was the best of times for them and the worst of times for us.

My mother, Nazee, and my brother were among the lucky ones that had received their visas. They had left on December 14th, 1978. I was the only one of my siblings left behind in Iran. I was a student at Pahlavi University in Shiraz, but I was home in Tehran because every university, college, or institution was closed.

My father got his passport and his visa the same time as the rest of the family, but he decided to stay in Tehran with me. He kept in touch with the latest news by going to the synagogue every week, even though he was not a religious man. He wanted to know every detail. At one of the Saturday morning sermons in a local synagogue, he met a Rabbi from the Lubavitchers community in Brooklyn, a missionary Hasidic group founded in the 1700s. The congregation had surrounded the Rabbi, and were asking him tons of questions.

"Does the CIA know what will happen next?"

"Are our lives in danger?"

"What is Carter's plan?"

"I really don't know. Gentlemen, please listen to me, I do not have an answer to your political questions, but I have an answer and a solution for the future of the younger generation. If you want to save your children and send them to America, I can help you. I will take them to Rome, stay there for a short while, and apply for an American visa from the consulate there. If anyone is interested, please do not hesitate to contact me. Your kids will be in good hands."

He assured the community that arrangements had been made with the American Embassy in Rome "to issue visas for your children." We all wanted to be in America, and "the rabbi connection" seemed like the only way to get a visa to enter the promised land.

The Lubavitcher Rabbi, Rabbi Herschel, was a tall and skinny man in his early 20s. He wore a long black beard and a kippah. The words came out of his mouth like an auctioneer, fast and with excitement. He was Iranian but had been raised in Italy. He spoke with enthusiasm in the animated Italian style, with his hands, his face, and his head.

My father saw an opportunity and did not question it. He came home from the services, opened my bedroom door, and said, "Soheila, in couple of weeks, you are going to Rome and then New York. I found a way through the synagogue." He sat with me and explained what he had learned.

My father contacted Rabbi Herschel the next day through the synagogue and gave him my name and the necessary information. I started calling every one of my friends about the new opportunity to flee the country. I was excited. The word about "the rabbi connection" had spread, quickly.

Things were moving fast. A month later, my friends Shahriar, Vahid, and I, along with about 50 of our mutual friends, were in Tehran's International airport, excited and happy waiting for our flight to Rome. The laws had changed during the revolution. Upon applying for a passport, after numerous background checks and making sure the applicant was not among the Shah's entourage, the office sent the passports directly to the recipients at the airport. Travelers were only allowed to pick up their documents right before boarding a flight.

"Yes, can I help you?" I heard someone say. It was the Pan Am agent.

I walked to the counter and said, "Good evening, I'm here for my passport. I'm on the next flight to Rome. My name is Soheila Nobandegani."

Nineteen years old, standing at the window of Pan American Airlines at the international airport in Tehran, I was anxious and eager to leave Iran and put the revolution behind me. The American Embassy in Tehran was swamped with applicants. The line was around the block by 6 am every morning. It was a time of confusion, chaos and uncertainty. No one knew what would happen next. Anything was possible.

"With the end of uncertainty, came the uncertainty of the end." People were scared. They could not trust anyone. Their best friends, their neighbors, even their spouses changed overnight, turned against them, and became a revolutionary. If you were not pro-Khomeini and you had the means to leave the country, you would pack your luggage and leave the country. We had made that choice, and it made those devoted to Khomeini angry. To them every single person standing on those long lines at the airport was "a pro-Shah" and not supportive of the new leadership. They all needed to be taught a lesson before they left.

I was anxious to go. After weeks of waiting, the day that I had been looking for had arrived. *Tomorrow*, I thought to myself, *I will be in beautiful Rome, free and safe from danger and harassment.*

"One moment please, Miss Nobandegani," the Pan Am agent said, and got busy looking through the large stack of passports. He seemed genuinely nice. He was not one of those unkempt, pro-Khomeini people who were constantly roaming around the airport and terrorizing the poor passengers. He was clean-shaven and dressed in a Pan Am uniform.

This is it. The minute I have my passport in my hand, I am free to leave. I will head straight for the gate. Next stop, Rome, I thought. I looked around, trying to locate the direction for my gate number. I noticed two young guys with thick, dark beards holding machine guns, walking around the airport area, bullying and interrogating people. I turned back towards the counter right away. I did not want to be noticed. They were nothing but trouble. The agent looked up and said, "Please wait here for a moment?" and walked away.

The scene at the airport was chaotic. People had their luggage and their passports and were ready to leave but looked tense, scared, and worried. The hostile crew of Khomeini devotees kept watchful eyes on the lines of trembling souls and their hands on their guns. Their angry faces were intimidating and terrifying. They had the right to pull anyone out of those long lines and question them. No one was safe. One wrong answer and someone could end up in a hot seat at the local police station instead of in a window seat on their flight out of the country.

Wearing a chador and covering our hair was not mandatory yet. We had dressed as we normally did, in jeans and shirts. As my friends and I waited for the agent to return, we talked to each other excitedly. Suddenly I noticed Vahid staring at something or someone behind me. Everyone got very quiet. I turned around and saw a man with a full beard wearing a dusty black windbreaker holding a G3 machine gun. He was listening to our conversation.

Looking back, I still don't know how I kept my cool and didn't faint. I looked at him directly in the eye and said, "Can I help you?"

"Where are you going?" he asked in a commanding and intimidating voice.

He stared at me with angry eyes. His teeth were black and crooked. His breath smelled like sewage.

"Rome," I said.

"Why? Are you running away?" He shouted, "You don't like the new regime? Why isn't your head covered? Button up your shirt, sister!"

Everyone turned around and watched us in horror. Thank God my father had stepped away to talk to a friend, otherwise he would have created a scene we all would have regretted.

I looked him straight in the eye as I buttoned the top button on my shirt and said, "I am not running away, I am going to school abroad because my classes were cancelled here. As soon as my studies are finished, I will return to my country, brother." I said, trying to sound sweet and friendly.

"Where are you flying to?" he asked. His tone was much calmer.

"I told you," I answered. "Rome."

"As long as you aren't going," he said, pointing directly at my face, "to that Satanic land, America." His voice was filled with hatred. He spat on the floor, turned and walked away.

I could feel I was red from head to toe. It was a close call. He had been gone for a good minute and still no one dared to speak. Suddenly, we heard a loud scream, "Let him go, let him go. He has done nothing wrong."

We turned towards the noise and chaos and saw the same guy holding a young guy by the collar of his shirt and yanking him out of the line. The woman next to him, probably his mother, was trying to stop him by holding onto her son and positioning herself between the two of them, screaming.

"Please let go of him. I beg of you. *Khoda mano bokosheh* (God, kill me first). Oh God, do something."

"Don't stare, don't stare. Look the other way." Everyone was whispering to the person next to them. We all lived in fear. Fear was part of our daily diet. We walked in fear, talked in fear, watched in fear, and lived in fear.

I turned away to avoid the depressing and heartbreaking scene and faced the runway. I concentrated on the activities through the giant glass wall. And there it was, the majestic sun, the source of life, in all its glory, in different shades of orange and yellow, like a skillful artist, coloring everything in sight. The beautiful sun was setting graciously behind a Pan Am airplane. The heat halo around the huge ball of fire made every plane, every truck, every person, and every tree move and dance to a hypnotic rhythm. I was mesmerized by the beauty and the colors. I was in a trance. There is life, peace and warmth out there, somewhere, after all. The sun is setting here but after a short darkness, there, in another place, there will be a glorious sunrise. A new beginning, a new birth, a new day will start off between the dark and the morning sun. This death is followed by a beautiful birth in another land.

"I beg of you, let go of him," the woman screamed again, breaking my reverie. I turned towards the noise and saw the bearded guy, with the help of one of his friends, dragging the young man across the floor. They took him into a small room and slammed the door on his hysterical mother. The helpless woman melted to the floor, held her head between her knees, and cried. No one got involved. No one said a word. No one moved. They all stood there and watched the injustice. They didn't want to jeopardize their own departure from hell. They wanted to leave.

The Pan Am agent walked back towards the counter, went through the stack of passports in front of him again, and looked at me.

"I'm sorry," he said, "Your passport is not among the ones delivered today."

"What do you mean? This can't be. I have a flight soon. I was told my passport would be here today!" I said. I started pleading. "Please look again. Please."

The poor agent went through the stack one by one again. He looked at me with apologetic eyes.

"So sorry, miss," he said, "your passport hasn't arrived yet. I even went to the back room and checked the rest of the deliveries. I looked through each box. There's nothing we can do. It is not here. The passport office is closed now. You just have to wait till tomorrow."

My friends and I had been standing at the airport untouched by the intense environment—we were excited, laughing and talking—until the moment I was approached and questioned by the extremist. Now everyone was quiet and I was crying. I became inconsolable. My friends were about to board the Pan Am flight. I wanted to leave with them. I wanted to join my family. I wanted to be with my brother and sisters again. I wanted to walk in the street and not be scared of my own shadow. I wanted to sleep and not wake up to gunshots. I wanted a normal life.

I was crying and begging the agent. "I am sorry," he said again, "but you can't leave now. You just have to wait until the passport office opens in the morning."

"Wait?" I said, "How? How can I wait till tomorrow? My flight is tonight."

I turned around and looked at Shahriar. "I am so sorry Soheila," he said, "don't cry please."

I stepped aside and opened the way for my friend to approach the agent. I was taking too long and people were getting restless. I waited next to my joyful friends, crying. I waited till every one of them left for their gate. I waited and hoped for a miracle. Maybe it was misplaced, maybe there was a late delivery, maybe...but my passport did not appear. I would have to wait just a bit longer...

I got tired of waiting. I continued to call the nurses' station every half-hour begging someone to find the doctor to release me. By now it was around 6:30 pm. Enough waiting! I called Dr. Kim directly and explained the situation to her. She was at my bedside in fifteen minutes. She took the line out of my arm and got me signed out. At last I was free to go. I thanked her, gathered my phone and purse, and ran towards the elevators. I couldn't wait to get to my brother and tell him what Dr. Kim had told me a couple of hours ago. I wasn't sure if he knew. I wanted to jump up and down with joy in his room and hug and kiss him.

I got to SICU and saw him through the glass door. I had to stop myself from bursting in; I still had to wash my hands and put the yellow hospital gown and cobalt blue gloves on. I did that in record-breaking time and stepped into his room.

Shoshana, Nazee, Nahid, and Momon were in the room. Nahid was massaging his head as always. He still had the damn trach on so he was unable to speak. He looked at me with wondering eyes, asking, "Where've you been all day?"

I was beside myself, I was speaking mile a minute. "Fariborz, you won't believe it. I just passed a kidney stone. I was on the ninth floor the whole day." I bent down and kissed his hand. "But that is not important, guess what? You're getting better, you're going home. Did you know that? It's true, Dr. Kim just told me. You'll be fine."

He just stared at me with indifference, didn't smile, didn't move, didn't show any reaction. I looked at my family members for an explanation. They just looked back. None was given.

"Fariborz, your infection is under control. Everything is looking good. I'm not making it up," I continued. "Now I can leave for the Bahamas happy. Yes, I'm leaving for the Bahamas tomorrow, just for a few days. I'll see you when I come back. Fariborz, you are going home. *Ghorboonet beram.* You are going home. Do you believe this?"

He looked into my eyes and kept them locked. He did not show any reaction for a few seconds, just stared. "What is the matter, Fariborz?" I asked. "I will be back soon." He shook his head back and forth. NO! I walked closer to him and said, "Fariborzjoon, my love, I haven't been with my children for a long time. They're all there waiting for me. I'll be back Sunday. It's Tuesday night now. I'll be back before you know it. I need to be with my kids. Please understand." But he kept on shaking his head left and right, staring and begging me with his sad eyes not to leave.

In hindsight, I shouldn't have left. Each time Fariborz asked me to stay and I left, I realized afterward that it was the wrong decision. His eyes were trying to communicate something to me, but I didn't comprehend it. Maybe I didn't pay enough attention because I was happy about the positive news and giddy from being free of that damn kidney stone. Maybe I was selfish and didn't want to miss the opportunity to be with my kids and ignored his pleading. Whatever the reason, I didn't want to see what he was trying to tell me. All I could think of was Dr. Kim's words: "He is getting better. Your brother is going home soon."

I kissed him goodbye while he watched me with sad and pleading eyes. "You know I love you as much as I love my kids. I will see you soon, in a couple of days. Stay strong and fight. You have my bone marrow and my liver. That should be enough ammunition for now. You have more bone marrow stored somewhere as a backup. I did the same procedure again a few weeks ago based on Dr. Isola's suggestion. God forbid you need a kidney—I have one reserved for you too, but we won't talk about it now. How about a pair of balls? I've been told mine are bigger than yours! Fariborzjoon, just hang in there. Remember, we have a book to write and I can't do it by myself. I don't know any of the medical mumbo-jumbo. I'll be back before you know it. Be strong, I'll see you soon."

He shook his head again but he was calmer. He tried to say something, whatever it was, I would never know. He just followed me with his sad eyes until I left the room. I stopped, turned around in the doorway, and shouted out, "I love you Fariborz," and ran out of the ICU and left the hospital, as if I was running away from a force that was trying to keep me there. I ran as fast as I could so nothing would hold me back. I reached the sidewalk, took a deep breath, and hailed a cab. I wanted to move forward. I wanted the past behind me. I wanted to have a normal day with normal problems again!

"Your brother is going home." That was all I could think of... that one phrase. I was holding onto those five words. The future looked great and promising. Thank you, God, for those beautiful five words. Thank you for letting him go home. Thank you for realizing that this world will be a better place with him in it. Thank you for finally throwing in the towel. We won the trophy and we will take it home with us. Miracles do happen. He is living proof.

"Excuse me, miss, can I talk to you for a second?"

I turned around and faced a tall young guy, in his late twenties, with a head full of black hair and a thick mustache.

"Can I help you?" I asked.

"Yes," he said hesitantly, "can I please ask... do you mind giving me your phone number?"

My father and I were still at the airport. My friends had all left for Rome. I was still standing next to the airline counter, waiting and crying. Waiting for what? I didn't know! I could not leave the airport and return to my house. I already had said my farewells to every wall, every corner, every sofa, and every doorknob. I was supposed to move forward, not walk back into that dark past. I just stood there and watched my father. He was a few yards away speaking to an older gentleman in a Pan Am uniform.

"Why do you want my number? Do I know you?" I asked the guy.

"No, but I was watching you. Your friends left for Rome, right? My younger sister was on the same flight. Why didn't you go?"

"My passport did not arrive on time. I can't leave tonight. I have to stay in Tehran for now," I said, checking for my father from the corner of my eyes.

"Do you believe in destiny?" he asked. I turned my eyes away from my father and looked at him with a puzzled face. "Your destiny was for you to miss your flight and stay in Tehran so I can date you. It is nothing but destiny. It's our fate."

I was shocked. What was he saying? I wanted to leave that place along with everyone else. Now some stranger was telling me that I was going to remain in Iran?

"Excuse me sir, but I am not staying here, there is no 'our fate' here. My destiny is very clear, the fortune teller behind that counter just told me, I am leaving tomorrow on the next flight out," I said.

"See, you are fighting your destiny," he said. "If you were supposed to leave, your passport would have been here like everyone else's. Please go out with me tonight. You are here anyway. You never know. Maybe you'll change your mind when you get to know me. Maybe you'll decide you want to stay. Maybe your future is here with me."

"Sir, I will not and do not want to stay. I will not and do not want to go out with you. I will not and do not want my future with you. You are wasting your energy. I want to go to Rome. Now if you do not mind I want to take care of my problem," I said with teary eyes.

I saw my father approaching me with a middle-aged gentleman in a Pan Am uniform. "Hello," he said. "I am the director of Pan American Airlines here. I heard you have missed your flight because your passport did not arrive. I am so sorry," he said in a gentle voice.

"Yes sir, all my friends are on that flight. Everyone had their documents but me. My passport was the only one missing," I said.

"Please do not cry," he said in a kind voice, "I promise you, you will leave on the same flight tomorrow. I'll tell you what I will do for you. You can take as much luggage as you want, no questions asked. I will even arrange for a better seat for you. Please, don't cry anymore."

"Are you sure I can leave with tomorrow's flight?"

"I promise you. I will inquire about your passport myself. Do we have a deal? Are you happy now?"

"I am, of course I am. Thank you, sir. Yes, I am happy. You are so nice." I hugged him and kissed his face, turned to the tall guy next to me, wiped away my tears with my fingers, and said with a smile, "I am not so sure about destiny, but 'our fate' for tonight is, I will go out with you, here is my number." And walked away. "See you," I yelled. "There is a pizza shop at the corner of the street where I live. Are you brave enough to come out of your house late at night with all that's happening?"

"I will figure it out. See you!" he called back.

As soon as we returned home, my father got busy packing two more suitcases full of valuables. Our antique silverware was rolled in old embroidered fabrics. He folded our valuable silk Persian rugs and placed silver frames, vases and trays in between them. I was busy getting ready to meet my date! Why not? I had nothing else to do. It would make the time go faster!

The next day I was in my window seat with extra leg room, ready to take off for Rome. I had the address for where I was supposed to meet everyone written down in three different places, just in case. I was beside myself with joy. It felt like I had grown wings. I was free of that damn place with its depressing environment and the constant noise from the *"Allah Akbar"* chanting or the machine guns. The future looked promising and beautiful.

"I'm Going Home"

*"This place is a dream. Only a sleeper considers it real.
Then death comes like dawn, and you wake up laughing
at what you thought was your grief." —Rumi*

Thanksgiving, 2013

I arrived in the Bahamas in the early afternoon. My kids had already texted the name of the restaurant where they were all gathered, waiting for me to arrive. It was a beautiful day. The green was greener, the blue was deeper, and the sun even brighter than usual. The ocean was sparkling on the horizon in different shades, changing colors from sapphire to turquoise and ten different shades of blue in between. The white sand had the shine and softness of velvet. The palm trees were greener and more graceful than ever. I reached the hotel, dropped off my luggage, and went directly towards the restaurant.

My vacation has started, I thought, *I should feel happy. So why am I not?* I was worried and anxious. My friends were talking to me, but I was distraught and distracted. I couldn't stay calm. I kept texting Nazee and Jennifer to see how Fariborz was doing. "The same," they replied.

I kept repeating Dr. Kim's five words in my head to calm myself down. *Your brother is going home.* But I still couldn't relax. My brother's face was in front of me, shaking his head, looking at me with his sad, pleading eyes. *I am here now physically, so I should be here now mentally, too,* I told myself.

Everyone was in a good mood, so I decided to join in. I had learned how to be a great actress, an Oscar-winning one! If I can't be it, then I act it. Hopefully I will become it. As crazy as it might sound, somehow it works. It becomes a cycle: you pretend to be happy, as a result people around you are relaxed and act normal. They do not walk on eggshells or become concerned if they laugh or crack a joke. The environment is carefree and light. There is not a constant reminder of sorrow and long faces around you. The absence of sadness and the presence of laughter changes the color of your mood. That's what I wanted and that's what I needed, even if it was for only a short period of time.

The next day, Thursday, was spent at the villa playing cards. I had never been a big fan of cards, but it started raining and we could not do anything else. I kept on joking with my friends, "If you are nice to me I will mention your names in my book."

They started joking around, "Soheila, would you like more wine?"

"Take this seat, it's more comfortable."

"You know guys, it will be a bestseller. Fariborz and I will start writing as soon as he goes home," I said. "God willing, as soon as he is healthy enough," I added.

"Of course he will be," they replied in unison.

The day went by slowly. I was not receiving any texts from New York. *Are they avoiding me?* It was an uncomfortable feeling, but I tried to ignore it and think, "No news is good news." I was in a beautiful villa with my friends and my kids and daughter-in-law. *I should seize the moment and take it in. I am not in depressing hospital surroundings,* I thought. *I am in the beautiful Bahamas.*

But somehow I wished I was back in that sad hospital environment, looking at the monitors and watching my brother's vital signs instead of that magnificent view. Somehow, being there did not feel right. Somehow, all that love and attention was not doing me any good. I looked at my kids and smiled; they smiled back. Happy to have me around.

The next day I got up earlier than usual. I felt light and in good spirits. I remembered my dream early in the morning about my brother. He was standing in the hospital room next to his bed in a grey suit, dressed up Fariborz-style. He was very thin, skin and bones. He was leaning on the handle of his bed with one arm, and he had placed his other hand in his pants pocket. I looked at him with disbelief. I asked, "Fariborz, how are you standing up? You should be in bed." He smiled and said, "Why can't I stand up? You can see very well that I can."

"But it's impossible, you have no muscles left. You have been in bed for eight months," I said.

"Well, I am not in that bed anymore. I am leaving this room, finally," he said in a calm voice with a beautiful smile.

"But it can't be! Where are you going?"

"I am going home," he said, and started walking towards the door.

"Wait, you can't go," I screamed, "the doctors have not discharged you."

"I am going home, Soheila, love you." He turned, looked at me, blew me a kiss, smiled and walked out. At that point, I woke up.

I could not stop thinking about my dream. *It must be a positive sign*, I thought. *The universe is giving me a message, he is going home.* I put my bathing suit on and went to the pool. I needed to be by myself. I asked for a coffee and texted Nazee, "How is Fariborz? I had a dream early this morning. He was all dressed up in his room ready to leave the hospital." There was no answer. It was an uncomfortable and frightening feeling.

Half an hour later I sent another text. "Please give me some news." Again, no answer. An hour later my phone rang. It was Dr. Iris Sherman, family friend and doctor. As soon as I saw her name on my phone my heart dropped. I picked up the phone, my hands trembling, my heart pounding, my voice shaking. "Good morning, Iris."

"Good morning Soheila, I apologize for calling, but Fariborz is not doing well. His pneumonia is back. He is in critical condition. You better fly back as soon as you can. I know he wants you next to him. He has only a few hours left," and then she added, "I am so, so sorry."

My whole body felt cold. I started shivering. Tears were rolling down my face. I grabbed my phone and started running towards the hotel. When I reached the lobby, I saw my friends Nader and Mitra. "What is wrong, Soheila? What happened?"

"Fariborz is dying, my brother is dying. His doctor just called me. I have to fly back to New York now. I have to see him before he dies. I shouldn't have left him, he knew, he knew," and I started crying out loud and shaking. It did not matter where I was or who was around me. It felt as if I was in complete darkness, chaos, turmoil.

Nader said, "The doctors make mistakes all the time. Don't do this to yourself. They could be wrong. Do you want me to arrange a flight for you?"

"No, thank you, I will ask Justin to find the first flight out for me. Fariborz has just a few hours left," I said and ran out of the lobby. Their faces were as pale and scared as mine. What could anybody do or say at these horrible and terrifying moments, besides being supportive and caring? They were exactly that, supportive and caring.

I called Justin, "Justinjoon, Fariborz is not doing well, I am coming upstairs, please get the first flight out for me."

He did not ask any questions, just said, "Sure thing mom," and hung up the phone. I raced towards the elevators. I think everyone there waiting saw the fear in my face. The hotel guests took a step aside and opened the way for me. I got to my room and told Jack with broken words, crying, "I am flying back to New York. We are losing Fariborz. I have to go back now, I have to go back this second." I got a change of clothes and ran to the bathroom to change.

"Mom, please be careful, I am sorry, I am so sorry. You have a flight in an hour and half. I just emailed you the flight information. Do not forget your passport." Justin was standing in the doorway, next to Camy, Jordan and Jackie, crying. They knew firsthand how it felt to lose a brother. They had experienced and witnessed a lot, my boys.

I picked up my purse and left the room.

"Mom, be careful, please. Be in touch," they yelled after me.

The drive between the hotel in Paradise Island and the airport is about half an hour with no traffic, and I cried all the way. After all that, after eight long months in the hospital, we were losing him to pneumonia. He had survived pneumonia, septic shock, leukemia, a long and difficult liver transplant surgery, cardiac arrest... he survived all those to die from *this?* The first thing that almost killed him at the very beginning of his hospital stay?

"Guys, tell them I have pneumonia, I can't breathe well. Ask them to bring an X-ray machine to the room. Insist, do not take no for an answer. I know I have pneumonia," he had told us when he started with his first chemotherapy, that damn Cytoxan. Exactly then his series of unfortunate events started and never stopped. Now here we were. He is dying, he is dying from pneumonia. The angel of death had never left his bedside. He was just waiting for the right moment to get him again. Very soon he would raise his flag of victory.

The airport was filled with people; it was Friday morning, the day after Thanksgiving. I did not see any reason to call or text anyone in New York. I knew what I had to know, that he had only a few hours to live, or did he have only a few hours to die? How strange that the outcome for both was the same, death. I knew that everyone was next to his bed, crying. My poor mom. At least my father was spared.

The flight was on time. The three-hour flight felt like an eternity. I got off the plane and ran to the taxi stand. The line was long. I went to the front and begged the tired passengers to let me take the next one. I arrived at the hospital around 3 pm. I got out of the car, stepped onto the sidewalk, looked up, and stared at the familiar huge building in front of me. I was too scared to walk inside.

If I entered that building, then I had to go up the same elevator and walk through the same hallway to the same SICU, but this time I would watch my brother die. "Soheila, make sure you tell Stephen, I do not want to see him, not anytime soon." He had said that to me so many times, and every time I smiled a bitter smile. Hearing that sentence from him pained me in different ways. It reminded me that my son was gone, gone somewhere that no one wanted to be, and that there was a huge possibility that Fariborz might join him there. He was scared. He knew his odds of survival. He knew every detail about his condition.

But not me, I just stayed positive and optimistic. As Nazee was googling her head off and trying to understand the smallest details about this horrible disease, I was thinking, *Why waste time? He will be fine. He is not going anywhere.* I had been wrong. He was leaving us. As he told me in my dream, he was leaving the hospital. He was leaving the hospital, but from the wrong exit.

I walked to his room. My handsome brother was flat on his back, swollen, his head tilted to one side, his eyes closed. He was still alive, according to the monitors, but dead otherwise. It was strange that we had seen him close to death, or almost dead, or even actually dead before, but this time it felt different. We all knew this time it was final. None of us had any hope left. What was hope? A tease, a lie? I had had so much hope, but at the end "hope" made the fall greater and steeper. Had I seen the reality all along, I would have been better off.

I looked at my family standing around the room. Everyone turned around to see me walk in, but did not say a word. I walked up to his side and touched his fingers. I said, "Fariborz, *Ghorboonet beram,* I am here, I am back from the Bahamas. I told you I will be back soon. I am standing next to you, do you hear me? I am back. I love you so much." Of course, there was no reaction.

"I was sure he would not leave us until you got here. He was waiting for you," Nazee said.

"Where is Momon?" I asked.

"In the waiting room, with Uncle Parviz."

I kissed Fariborz, left the room and walked towards the waiting room. Two mothers who had lost their sons. As of this night, my mother and I would carry the same pain. I stopped at the doorway. She was hunched over, covering her face with her hands, crying. My uncle was trying to calm her down. I touched her head, she looked up and as soon as she saw me she cried out loud, "Why? Why? He was getting better. What happened? Let me die too. Please let me go with him. Please, I beg of you. I do not want to live anymore."

I could not say anything. No one had anything to say. Our kind and caring Uncle Parviz said in a calm voice, "Please do not say that. Your family needs you. They look up to you."

I held her for a few minutes and walked back to Fariborz's room. "I am here Fariborz, right next to you." The vital signs onscreen were declining. His blood pressure was getting lower and lower. No one called anyone, or tried to do anything. There was nothing more to be done. We were just standing there. Jennifer had left to be with the kids; Nahid called her and told her to hurry back.

Soheila, please tell Stephen I do not want to see him, not anytime soon. His voice echoed in my head. I wanted to whisper in his ears, "When you see Stephen, tell him that I miss him, that I love him, that his brothers are suffering. Tell him we missed him at Justin's wedding." But I didn't. By saying those words to him, I would confirm the fact that he was dying. That he was going to see Stephen "anytime soon." That I had finally lost hope.

I whispered in his ears, "I am sorry I could not save you, you relied on me, I was your only hope and I failed you." The numbers, those damn numbers on the monitors, kept on declining. There were no doctors in sight, only the nurse on duty. The staff was heartbroken too. My brother's case had become personal for everyone. Even the janitor and the cleaning crew were involved with his day-to-day progress or decline. Every morning they stopped by to see how he was doing. Such kind hearts. "Fariborz, Alexa and Ava are fine, we will be there for them. We will be on top of everything, until you are home."

Who was I kidding? This time we all knew there was no returning home. These were words of desperation, of hopelessness, of extreme disappointment. I did not know if I should stay with my mother or my brother. Deep down I knew Fariborz could hear and feel us. It was important to him to have people around him. He didn't want to be alone, ever. I was sure he knew exactly who was standing there, even now.

I had lost Stephen in a second; he was mine one day and gone the next. I did not get a chance to touch him, hug him, or even help him. Now Fariborz was in front of me and I was touching him, hugging him… but he was slipping away. I was still unable to help him, unable to do anything. The one he relied on was useless now.

None of us spoke. Each person was holding their own. We had created a steel facade, hard and cold. We looked like flat copies of ourselves. Just standing. Tears rolling down our faces and dropping one after another, not even the smallest attempt to wipe them away as they fell.

We were just there, waiting for the angel of death to show his ugly face again. He was somewhere close, hiding, waiting impatiently. I could feel his darkness around us. My brother was still breathing with the help of the ventilator, but the numbers started declining faster and faster. Nazee just sighed, "Oh God no, please no. No. No. Please, please, God have mercy, Fariborz don't. Please."

And then our brother was gone. At 9:20 pm, the Friday night after Thanksgiving, his most cherished holiday weekend, the beeping stopped. Fariborz was gone forever. I just stood there and stared at the monitor. I had seen it in the movies many times. The line goes flat and then the continuous beeping sound. This time it wasn't a movie, this time it was real. This time I lived it. *Soheila, please tell Stephen I do not want to see him, not anytime soon...*

"Fariborz, send my love to Stephen, you will see him soon. Please tell him I miss him," I whispered in his ear, "I am sure he is waiting for you to hold your hand." I kissed his cold hand and left his room and dragged myself towards the waiting room. I did not think there was another person there that could give my mom the tragic news but me. As soon as she saw my face, she started crying out loud and hitting herself in the head, scratching her face and pulling her hair out.

I tried to stop her. "Please Momon, do not do this to yourself. He is free now. He suffered enough. We did whatever was possible and more. Some force wanted him on the other side. Please do not do this to yourself. He loved you more than any son could ever love his mother."

"But, why? Why?"

There was no answer, no rhyme or reason. It simply was. With every miracle that happened during his hospital stay, an invisible force cast a dark opposing spell and made the situation worse. We were in constant struggle. The frustrating part was we could not see our opponent. Whoever or whatever it was, they had won the match, the battle... and the war.

We tried everything. We turned over every stone. We did the unheard and the impossible. He survived the unheard and the impossible, but in the end, he lost, and we lost. I walked back to his room. Everything was exactly as always. Fariborz was in bed, his head tilted to one side, his eyes closed, his blanket covering his body. The nurse was busy preparing him for transfer. The only thing that was different were the monitors. They were silent. Even they were quiet and speechless. Even they were mourning. Even they were heartbroken. After months of reporting every little change in his vitals like loyal subjects, they were grieving too. Not the smallest sound from any of them.

For months, I had hated those annoying noises. They came in every tone and every length, every second and every minute of every day. But now that there was only silence, complete and utter silence, how I wished for those annoying beeping sounds to come back. They were his vital signs and a reminder that he was still with us, a reminder that his heart was beating, his lungs were breathing, and his blood was flowing. They were signs of hope and life. Now, they were gone too. Total silence.

Our kind and lovely cousin Shoshana, after months of being present and doing research on all the latest medications, just stood there and observed everything with a watchful eye. She wanted to make sure everything was done correctly and according to the Jewish law.

"Please make sure that whatever holds his blood leaves with him," she said to the nurse.

"Yes, of course," the nurse said, avoiding eye contact with us while picking up every tube that held even a few drops of Fariborz's blood.

I could not believe the conversation was about my brother. He was supposed to leave on his own two feet to "go home soon" with warm blood running in his veins, not on a cold stretcher.

Shoshana walked towards me and said, "Soheila, please leave, you do not need to be here. I will take care of everything. Go home. There is nothing anybody can do anymore."

I did not want to let go of him. If I left it would be the last time. After that moment, he would be gone forever. I just stood there and stared at my brother. My sweet and wonderful brother. There was no point talking to him anymore. I closed my eyes and imagined him the way he was and said, "I love you Fariborz, send my love to Stephen. I am sure he is there with you."

I walked over and touched his hand. It was cold. His voice was echoing in my head, "I am leaving this room, finally." Standing next to his bed in his grey suit.

He knew he was leaving us. When I came to his room after I passed my kidney stone and told him I was leaving for the Bahamas, he knew he had just a few days left. He knew he was losing the battle. He knew he was dying soon. He always knew before anyone else. He tried to stop me from leaving, but I left anyway.

Now we just stood there, Jennifer, Nazee, Nahid, Shoshana, and I, all crying in silence. Joe was watching us from the doorway.

Jennifer said, "I have to go to my kids and be with them."

"Please go home," Shoshana said, "all of you. I will take care of everything. There is no need for any of you here anymore. He is in a better place. He is free now." But leaving meant letting go, and I was not ready to let go of him. Why is God taking the young and the good people? Is there a truth to what my mother used to say, "God is scared of bad people himself, that's why he leaves them here and takes the good ones." Fariborz was a good and kind person. He paid for it dearly. He would have been much better off being cruel.

I kissed Fariborz's hand one last time and went to be with my mom. "Momon, let's go to Fariborz's apartment. We have to be with his kids. They need us. He would want us to be with his family."

My mom looked at me with pleading eyes. She looked like a helpless and lost orphan. I had never seen eyes so sad. My heart went out to her. I knew her pain firsthand. She was 82 years old, she could have done without experiencing such a huge loss. I remember thinking, "Wouldn't she be better off dead than alive?" The idea of wishing death for my mom was an escape from the hell she was living in that very moment and every moment from then on. How else could she ever find peace and happiness again? I had not. There was not a day that I did not think of my son and his untimely death.

I held her arms and with the help of my uncle walked her slowly to the elevator. Her body was moving but the soul was missing. I don't think she knew where she was or what had happened. She stared at people's faces—strangers, doctors, nurses—begging for an explanation for what she'd just been told. Her only son—the apple of her eye, the source of her pride and joy—was gone forever. She was an empty shell, just a body moving forward, as people moved around her.

Nahid walked towards us and said, "Wait, I want to come with you too. I need to be with his family." Joe held Nazee and said, "I will take her home." I left my mom with Nahid for a second by the elevator and ran back to Fariborz's room. I just stood there. I wanted to say my farewells. Shoshana was still there. I hugged and kissed her and as I left the room, I turned around for the last time and looked at him. I said, "I am so sorry Fariborz, I couldn't save you. You relied on me from day one and I failed you. *Bemeeram barat*," and left for the very last time.

When we entered Fariborz's apartment, Alexa and Ava walked towards us. We hugged each other tight and long. I thought how much Fariborz wished he could be here and hug them too. How much we had all been wishing and hoping for the day that he would return home.

It felt uncomfortable standing in the living room and seeing the brown leather chair, my brother's favorite, with his groove chiseled in the seat, empty. I hugged Jennifer and her parents and went straight to that chair. I touched and stared at the wrinkles in the cushion. I was scared to ruin what was left of his existence by sitting on it.

No one was crying. There were no tears left. I remembered asking Fariborz two days after I had lost Stephen, "Could your tear glands dry up? I can't cry anymore." He just looked at me with sad eyes and shook his head, *No.* But it had happened again, our tear glands had dried up. Everyone was trying to deal with their own pain and suffering. Poor Alexa and Ava. They'd had a taste of a wonderful dad and lost him so young. They could never call anyone "Daddy" anymore. The day-to-day word that most everyone uses so often would be out of their vocabulary forever, unless used in the past tense.

My mom was sitting on the couch, Nahid next to her, staring at the wall. Their color was no different than Fariborz's. The color of death is almost the same on the person that died and on the remaining loved ones who are mourning. There is a variety of colors in nature that we see and enjoy every day, and there is the sad and heavy color of death.

Ava said, "At least we will not hear sad news any more, it is the end of his suffering."

Jennifer said, "He is here, he is with us, he will always be with us. You know your dad, he will be on top of everything guiding you."

My mom did not even look up. She just stared. It was Friday night, Shabbat, the day after Thanksgiving, the first night of Hanukkah. If life was normal, we should have been celebrating all of those. But we were all sitting wearing the color of death.

I kept on touching the armrest of the leather seat, desperately trying to feel my brother. I was sure he was around us. I wanted to tell him again and again, "We are here for your family, we will take care of them." Suddenly I looked up, turned to Alexa and Ava and said, "Girls, where do you want to go for Christmas? Anywhere you want, just name it, we will go. Do you want to go to Europe? How about Italy or France? Let's go to Paris. I hear it's beautiful during the holidays. Jennifer, is it OK with you? Can I arrange a trip for all of us? We will all go, Justin and Setareh, Camy and Jordan. Let's all get out of New York, let's fly somewhere, anywhere."

Jennifer looked at the kids and said, "Girls, you want to go? I do not see why not. Do you want to go to Paris?"

Nahid said, "I wish I could come, but I have to work. I wish I could be with you guys."

My mom did not look up.

"Momon, you will fly back with me to Los Angeles next week. You can't stay here. Girls, I will arrange for the tickets and hotel reservations," I said, "just give me the dates and I will take care of everything. When is the last day of school?"

We sat there for another half an hour talking about everything and nothing with the kids. We were all exhausted and drained physically and emotionally. It was time to leave, everyone was tired. I held my mom's arm. She looked at me with pleading eyes. I understood her pain, but I still could not say anything that would comfort her. Fariborz is gone forever, we will never see his handsome face again. We will never hear his deep voice again. We will never be able to hug and kiss him again.

"Soheila, please tell Stephen I do not want to see him, not any-time soon."

Are you with my son now, Fariborz? How is he? Please kiss him for me and tell him we miss him. We miss you. I am so sorry for you guys. Tears started rolling down my face. I did not want my mother to see, but it was too late. I hugged her and said, "He is with Stephen and Zohreh, there is nothing to be done. He is free now, he has no more pain. We did whatever we could do. We tried everything. It was time for him to go. He couldn't fight anymore." She looked at me with her sad eyes, wanting to say something, but kept silent, dropped her head, and walked out with us without a word.

The wrestling match was over. We all lost. His family lost, his friends lost, our community lost, the medical world lost, his patients lost. It was done. The result was out. God, who should I hand the trophy to? Not us! Had we won, he would have been our trophy. His smile, his kindness, his presence, would have been our trophy, but we all lost and we lost big.

Dancing with Life

*"Life isn't about waiting for the storm to pass;
it's about learning to dance in the rain."* —Vivian Greene

The Reverend Billy Graham was asked, after his wife of fifty-four years passed on, "Aren't you scared of death?" He answered in a calm voice, "I am not afraid of death. I am afraid of the process of dying."

His words echoed in my mind throughout the long, devastating illnesses of my sister Zohreh and brother Fariborz. Why did they have to endure such a long, painful process of dying? Why the torture? If it truly was "their time," could they not simply have died, without the months and years of suffering along the way? No, they went through the process step by agonizing step. They experienced death many times before actually dying. This was the reality that was eating me up and causing much of my anguish and heartbreak.

The look on Zohreh's face and in Fariborz's eyes had spoken of pain and fear. After years of fighting, Zohreh eventually surrendered to the angel of death—indeed, welcomed him—while Fariborz fought tooth and nail till the very last day. In the case of my son Stephen, I will never know (and prefer not to know) what he experienced during the last minutes of his all-too-brief existence on this earth. However, in Stephen's case any suffering was, compared to that of my siblings, mercifully brief.

My family lost 3 people in a matter of 6 years (not counting my father who died less than a year after our brother). Three kind, well-loved people. Three productive, contributing members of society. It didn't make sense. It was the ultimate cruelty. I was angry, hurt, depressed, and disappointed at the whole world. I kept questioning. Why couldn't my brother and sister have gone quickly and been spared so much suffering? Why all the pain and torture? Why had I lost my young, kind son in a terrible accident? Ultimately, I had to wonder, what is the purpose of this life? Why so much darkness?

The answer is not easy to accept, but it is simple. There is no answer— at least not one that is evident to us. As long as we inhabit this physical body, we are earthbound; our eyes cannot see and our minds cannot comprehend what lies beyond our immediate senses. This world consists of the known, the unknown and the unknowable. The known is what we see and understand, the unknown is what could be discovered and understood, the unknowable is a mystery and will stay a mystery forever. Our "senses" cannot comprehend nor understand it and that is why to most people it is all "nonsense." There is no rhyme or reason, there is no explanation for the tragedies that ensue. There is no true answer. There is no dress rehearsal for tragedy. There are no guarantees for "Happily Ever After." Each day is different than the one before, and no two moments are ever exactly alike. Life is not on a written schedule. Life doesn't come with an unlimited warranty, a road map, or a built-in navigation system; on the contrary, it comes with a lot of curveballs. Life is like a wave, constantly changing as it moves along. It rolls on, the only way it can: forward.

Imagine an ocean, in all its grandness and splendor. The ocean waves never cease to move, always forward, one wave after the other, through the light of day and the pure dark of night. In the heat of the summer and in the cold of the winter, the ocean keeps on creating endless waves, in every form and size. Oblivious to their conditions, environment, or the circumstances; they move forward one by one, until they hit the shore and disappear.

Imagine how beautiful and soothing the ocean appears when the sun's rays reflect themselves on the blue water; yet in the same turn, how horrifying and intimidating it can be when the skies are stormy and the water is rough and choppy. Life is that ocean: constantly fluid and in motion. It moves forward every second without fail. It never stays the same. Beautiful and soothing one day; horrifying and intimidating the next. That is the nature of an ocean and that is the theater of life.

As one grows older, one is bound to experience pain, anxiety, discomfort, sadness, anger, disappointment, failure, loss, worry, stress, sickness—and, ultimately, death. No one is exempt from the inevitable. We all enter into this world and we all leave it in the same way. Some suffer more than others, but the pain and agony are universal. It is the truth of life. It is the nature of this existence. We are constantly taught and told in Western culture that we can control and manage our lives against undesirable changes and circumstances. News alert! No one—not the strongest, not the wealthiest, not the smartest, not even the most powerful person on the face of the earth—is immune to suffering. Everyone has heartbreaks, everyone feels pain, everyone gets sick, and everyone will eventually die.

Nothing stays the same forever; in fact, change is the only constant in life.

Harold Kushner expressed it best, when he said, "Pain is the price we pay for being alive." But he also urged us to further explore our pain; "What do we do with our pain so that it becomes meaningful and not just pointless empty suffering?" Yes, indeed. Pain is inevitable; suffering is optional. And yet, one should not be defined by his or her suffering, anguish, or stress. One shouldn't take his misfortunes personally, because nothing in this world is. It is only human to be affected by those feelings, but it should not define us or change us forever.

The past and all its hardships are not present in your current physical reality; they exist in your mind only, and your thoughts give them more life and more strength than they deserve. Nietzsche said, "Thoughts are the shadows of our feelings, always darker, emptier and simpler." Any feelings or emotion that you carry around are created by your own mind. The source is always in your thoughts. It's on you to choose your thoughts wisely. With practice, one learns to *respond* mindfully to hard times rather than *react* emotionally.

To lessen suffering, become more aware and careful of what you busy your mind with. You have the choice of thinking happy, peaceful, loving, and joyful thoughts. Don't get sucked down the whirlpool of "What is wrong?" Or "What went wrong?" These will pull you down quicker than you think. It's really true: "Change your thoughts and you will change your world."

Our lives are like the ocean, or a river: smooth and calm in some areas, and wild and angry in others. Water goes where the river takes it: through deserts, forests, cities, and countries. It goes wherever the path leads, strong over the rocks, through every opening and down the falls with force and passion, without slowing down or stopping.

When one falls in the current of life, one has to become liquid, fluid and free of any form, following the heart and the flow of the river. Swimming against the current, holding on to a piece of rock or a branch of a tree, or curling up on the riverbank leaves you exhausted, angry, and frustrated. You have to become one with the water and submit to the ups and downs. You have to give in and try to enjoy the ride and dance through it while constantly moving forward.

The key is to be one with the nature of life; to be fluid but not hard; to be in motion but not stuck in your rigid ways as you make your way through life's adversities. Throw a rock in water, no matter what size, watch it sink instantly. Throw a ton of water into the ocean, watch it blend in and become one body.

Life is full of ups and downs, happiness and heartbreaks, miracles and disappointments. While we welcome the joyous and pleasant times with open arms and do not question our good fortune, we become distraught and depressed when we are beset by sad and tragic events. Life is full of surprises of all kinds. We don't mind a surprise when it suits our lives, but what about the painful variety? "Expect nothing and be ready for everything." Expectations and disappointments come hand in hand. Nothing is guaranteed in this world. One has to become fluid and able to float, adjust and adapt. One must learn to move and go with the flow, to ride the waves and accept all of what life has to offer.

"It is not the strongest of the species that survive, nor the most intelligent, but the one most responsive to change." —Charles Darwin

We can't press the undo button when heartbreak and tragedy happen. We can't rewind our lives and relive them differently, but we can change ourselves and our outlook towards the situation. We have a couple of choices. The easiest one is to give up: withdraw from the unfair world, go to a dark room, shut the door, pull the blanket over our heads, and sob. When tragedy strikes and each and every cell in our body is injured and hurting the thought of gradually dying instead of continuously living sounds like a reasonable option. The last thing we want, when our world has changed, when we are miserable and life as we knew it does not exist anymore, is to be in the outside world with happy people enjoying normal day-to-day life.

It's normal to think, *Why me? What have I done to deserve this? I hate this cruel world and my miserable life.*

The second day after my son passed away was more difficult than the first. I was in a state of utter shock, disbelief, and sorrow. I wanted to throw everyone out of the house so I could go to a corner, curl up, lick my wounds, feel my misery, and cry for days. One look at my kids' devastated faces was enough to give me the necessary courage to carry on. *They need me to be their rock. I cannot fall apart in front of them,* I thought. *They are too young and innocent to experience such a tragic loss.*

Staying under the covers is nothing but a slow death. By trying to help my boys, I helped myself. I did not hide in my room, I did not dive under the covers and stay there. I put on Stephen's shirt, left my room and joined my family in the living room. They looked up at once, not knowing what to expect. I walked forward, hugged them, and said, "Stephen wants us to live through this. He is watching us."

Our friends and family started arriving in groups for morning prayers. They were there for us, to support us and protect us during those first devastating days. I accepted their love and kindness with an open heart and wrapped myself in its comfort. I embraced and welcomed their good intentions and their compassion. My faint smiles gave my friends an extra boost and my kids the courage to stay strong.

Carrying on was not easy. At times, it felt impossible. Waking up in the morning was the most difficult part. I had to face the reality of our lives, and the reality was unbearable. But I thought of my kids and I got the necessary determination and encouragement to leave my beloved bed and get dressed. One look at their faces and I decided to change my focus. In the words of Nietzsche, "He who has a why to live for can bear with almost any how." I had three "whys" in my life to live for, and those three whys were watching my every move and my every mood. I couldn't disappoint and hurt them any more than they had already been disappointed and hurt. I had to rise above the horrible circumstances.

I tried to put on a happy expression. With even the faintest smile their faces would immediately brighten up. When I started wearing make-up, they hugged and kissed my face repeatedly. I stopped wearing Stephen's shirts, and they took a sigh of relief and gave me compliments. My behavior influenced them in a way that no words could. I had decided to make an essential and necessary change in my attitude towards life. I could not change what had happened, but I could change myself and my approach for the remaining part of my life and the unavoidable suffering. I realized even the freest of the free man is restricted to the circumstances and conditions of this life.

It dawned on me how the minute we accept the new reality of our lives, the easier we can pick up the pieces, positive and negative, and continue with our lives.

Part of picking up the pieces requires our reexamining how we see and experience death. Is death final? Is death the end? Or is the journey ongoing, and death just a new beginning? As dark and tragic as it may look to us, we will not know the exact answer until we join the one that has departed and arrive at the new destination.

One evening I got home, mentally and emotionally drained and exhausted. It was one of those days that I could not stop thinking about the series of the unfortunate events that had befallen my family. I kept on dragging myself around, asking, Why? I walked into my bedroom, took off my clothes, and let them fall to the floor. I brushed my teeth, washed my face and walked back to my bedroom. As I walked past my clothes left on the carpeting, I stopped and stared at the pants, shirt and jacket. It looked like a crime scene from a movie, a deflated person. The legs of the pants were folded in different directions on the floor. The shirt lay flat with one sleeve up and the other down next to my jacket.

Think about it: the sleeves of my jacket and shirt and the legs of my pants had been moving and in motion all day, right up to the moment I stepped out of them. Every time I raised my arms, the sleeves followed. Every step that I took, the pants shifted with my legs. Now the clothes and the physical body had separated; one left behind as the other moved on. It struck me that our physical body does for the soul, what clothes do for our bodies. Bodies move because the soul is "wearing" it. And when the day comes that it has served its purpose, the body is left lifeless on the floor and the soul moves on.

"Soheila, imagine a glass of water," my mentor Mr. Shahparaki told me. "If I pour it over your hand you would know it's water, right?"

I nodded "yes." I couldn't figure out what he was getting at.

"Now, if I put the glass of water in the freezer, by touching the ice and looking at the frozen piece, you would know it's the same water but transformed into something completely different?"

"Yes, of course," I said.

"Now, imagine I put the same water, the same ice, into a kettle and let it boil. Just because it starts evaporating into thin air, does it mean it's completely gone? Just because you can't see it, just because you can't touch it, just because you can't feel it, does it mean it has ceased to exist? You know it is still around you. Once again it has changed its shape and form, but it still exists. It is present, but in a different form."

He held my hand and said, "Your son is around you, he just changed his form."

Nothing anyone had shared with me before had resonated the way that explanation did. From that moment on, I tried to look at the bigger picture. I was still depressed and traumatized, but I was open to his idea. Why? Because I knew I couldn't go on living with a broken heart. I knew I couldn't hang onto that bark of the tree or the slippery rock and hold myself against the current forever. I knew I couldn't walk around with a smile and pretend everything was fine for much longer. I was drowning, and I was drowning fast. I had to be flexible and willing to leave my old beliefs behind. I had to become fluid and go with the flow of life. It was time to move beyond logic and follow what I felt with my heart.

My logical mind was confined to the limited boundaries of my own reasoning. But I knew there was more—not because I had read it anywhere or I acquired that knowledge, but because I have authentically felt and known the experience. I sensed it deep inside. I shifted from thinking with my head to feeling with my heart. I started listening to my inner gut and let that guide me, without thinking what is wrong or what is right, or what makes sense and what doesn't.

I started talking to Stephen out loud. I started reading books on a variety of related subjects. I joined classes on spirituality and listened to any related lecture possible. I started going to mediums in different cities. I wanted to believe my son was still around, still with me, in any shape or form—even if I couldn't see him, even if I couldn't touch him, even if I couldn't feel him. We had all received signs from him, but at the beginning, I didn't give it much thought.

Don't be a fool, he is gone forever, I used to tell myself. But the signs were so obvious that little by little they made me wonder, *If I stay a "nonbeliever" do I ignore my son?*

But then, the most incredible thing happened in the Bahamas. We were there with our friends as always for Thanksgiving. I was walking around the casino and talking to him in my head, "Stephenjoon, remember we were here together two years ago? Remember how much we laughed? Remember dinner at the sushi place? We are going there tonight, but you will not be there. I miss you so much, *Ghorboonet beram.* I love you."

Since Stephen's passing my kids and I have used his birth date, November 19th, as a tool to include him in our daily lives. Number 19 represents Stephen. It is our way of connecting with him. We reserved our seats on row 19. We got hotel rooms either on the 19th floor or ones that had the number 19 in it. We added the tip in a restaurant in a way so it ended in 19 cents. We bought lottery tickets with number 19. And yes, if we played roulette, we bet on number 19.

After I spoke with Stephen in my head, I found myself standing in the middle of the casino with Justin. We were staring at four roulette tables across from each other, on all four corners of the walkway. We didn't need to speak; we knew we were both thinking about Stephen.

"Justin, we should put $5 on number 19," I said.

"I don't feel like playing, mom." He was as sad as I was.

I looked at the first table in front of us. The dealer flicked the small white ball in the opposite direction of the spinning wheel. The tiny ball started rotating, circulating and turning until it made a couple of jumps, at the beginning long and then slow, switching into short and fast ones, landing on different numbers until it fell for the last time and settled into a slot.

"Justin, it's number 19, look!"

"Yeah, I see," he answered.

"We would have won."

He gave me a faint smile.

The electronic stand on the corner of the roulette table flashed number 19!

I know you are here, Stephenjoon. I love you, I thought to myself.

From the corner of my eyes I noticed the second roulette table. I just glanced at it and that one started flashing number 19 as well. I turned to Justin and said, "Do you see what I see?"

"Yes, mom, he is here," he said.

"Two 19s at the same time, Justin!"

Just then I turned towards the third roulette table. I grabbed Justin's arm. It, too, was flashing 19! And a few seconds later the fourth one followed! Four roulette tables. Four winning numbers 19 at the exact same time. I looked over at Justin.

"Mom, four 19s at the same time! Do you know what the odds are for that?" he exclaimed.

"If you weren't here to witness it, I would think I am imagining this," I said.

"No, mom, you are not imagining anything. It is unbelievable. My hands are shaking. Mom, he is here."

"Is it even possible?" I asked, "There are 38 numbers on each table and for all four of them to show the same number at the same time! There is no rational explanation."

The electronic stands on top of each table were flashing 19 at us. Bright lights blinked on and off, on and off. It felt like a scream, or a cry for attention in the busy casino. "Mom I'm here, look at me. Do you see me? I'm right here. I'm with you guys." It felt like a whisper and a secret message in my ears at the same time. "Mom, I love you. I'm next to you. Can't you feel me?"

We both stood there and stared at the numbers until they were replaced by the next roll. Thank you, Stephenjoon, I love you too, *Ghorboonet beram.*

What had just happened defied all laws and logic. We knew in our hearts that Stephen was there and that he was trying to communicate with us the only way he could—using his number. Our logical minds at that moment were of no use. Our loving hearts were. We took in the miracle, this gift, and embraced it.

The following Thanksgiving, I was seated next to my friend Sylvie, watching her play roulette at one of the same tables. I told her the story of the consecutive 19s at the four tables in that very casino.

She looked at me with a sad smile and passionate eyes and did not say a word. We both turned towards the table and watched the ball spin. Eventually it slowed and made a couple of hops on different numbers, finally settling into a slot. It was 19. The electronic stand on the table started flashing number 19. Sylvie looked at me with amazement and disbelief.

I stood up from the chair and looked at the three other electronic stands on other tables.

"Look Sylvie, look at the table next to you," I said. "It is flashing 19 as well."

Sylvie grabbed my hand and squeezed it.

"Now do you believe me?" I asked her.

"Soheila, no, I can't believe it. I have goose bumps all over my body. How is this possible?"

"I don't know how, but if Stephen were here and I were to ask him, 'What are the chances?' He would reply with a calm smile, 'Apparently plenty, mom!'"

How could I ignore this? How could I pretend it wasn't a sign? There were clues and cries of "I am here, mom," around everywhere. There always had been. I was just more open to them than before. I had finally let my heart lead me to see what my mind couldn't.

At another incident, my friend suggested meeting a medium named Tim Braun in Los Angeles. He was a soft-spoken young gentleman dressed in a white shirt and khaki pants. We entered a small room with a few pieces of furniture and posters. He offered me a seat and took his chair in front of me. As soon as I sat down, without hesitation he began to talk. "There is a young man, about 22 years old, with a big smile in the room. He is hugging you and kissing you," he continued, "he is kissing your face. He was waiting for you to come here."

I was shocked. Tim didn't have any information on me; he didn't even know my first name. I tried not to show any reaction; I just sat there and stared at him. He spoke nonstop. Everything he shared with me rang true. Near the end of our session, Tim said, "Your son wants you to know, on your next trip, he will be right there next to you, sitting beside you on the plane." He looked at me and said, "You know how much he loved to travel?"

Stephen was passionate about traveling. He used to say, "One day when I am financially set, I will go to the airport, close my eyes, and put my finger on the screen. I will go wherever that choice takes me."

A few weeks after my meeting with the medium, I was on a plane to New York to see Camy and Justin. I asked for a window seat on row 19. I placed my carryon in the overhead compartment and took my seat. I was deep in my thoughts, looking out the window, when I heard someone talking. I turned around and saw a gentleman sitting on the aisle seat. He leaned over and asked, "Are you going to New York too?"

"Yes, I am. I guess we are all flying to the same destination." (I was, of course, thinking to myself, *What a stupid question! Obviously! This is a nonstop flight that is taking off from Los Angeles and landing in New York!*)

"Where is your accent from?" he asked.

"I was born in Iran," I replied.

"Oh, we are kind of neighbors, I am Lebanese."

"Beautiful country, Lebanese are such wonderful people. I am Soheila, what is your name?" thinking he must have a familiar Middle Eastern name.

"Thank you, you are kind. My name is spelled, S-T-E-P-H-E-N," he replied, pronouncing each letter.

I froze. My hands started to shake. I could feel my heart beat in my head.

"I am sorry, but what is your name again? Could you repeat that?" I asked.

"My name is Steven, but it's spelled, S-T-E-P-H-E-N, I wish they would call me Stefen," he repeated.

I just stared at him, not knowing how to react or what to say. I took a deep breath and said, "Nice name." I turned towards the window. I didn't want S-T-E-P-H-E-N to see my tears. He didn't just say, "My name is Steven"—in that case I would have never known that he shared the same spelling as my son's name. He went out of his way to spell his name out for me. Yes, my son wanted to make sure I knew that he was there, sitting right next to me. How could I stay a nonbeliever?

"Life after death" is a subject that can't be analyzed, evaluated, or investigated by logic or calculation. It is a subject that can only be figured out by one's heart and not the mind.

Let's compare it to love, another subject that is a matter of heart and not the mind. Let's talk about the connection or the philosophy behind "falling in love." Can anyone find a logic or a reason of why when two people meet, they have this strong mutual feeling of passion and affection? What is "love at first sight?" How does one explain "infatuation?" In Greek mythology love is called *theia mania* ("madness from the gods"). This love passion was described through an elaborate metaphoric and mythological psychological schema involving "love's arrows" or "love darts," the source of which was often given as the mythological Eros or Cupid. In truth, no one has ever seen "madness from the gods" or an actual "love's arrow" hitting anyone when they feel an extreme romantic attraction. But it is there, millions of people have felt and experienced it. They felt it deep in their hearts and never in their minds.

You cannot study love, you cannot measure love, you cannot philosophize love. You have to just love and feel its strong force. If you leave it up to your intellect only, you can never fall in love and enjoy that unique and special feeling. Even the most rational, logical, and reasonable people have fallen deeply in love. As Einstein said, "You can't blame falling in love on gravity." Love is a fact of life. You cannot touch it or measure it, it is not an effort, it has always been there; it is a feeling available to everybody, but unless you allow your heart to take over you will never feel it deep within.

Try to follow your heart and trust where your intuition takes you. Throw away the old beliefs and throw yourself into the new ones, no matter how unlikely or unfamiliar they sound or feel. Jump into uncharted territory. Lose yourself in the current of the unknown. Accept it all with open arms and welcome it with willingness, peace, and love.

Imagine a beautiful harbor with rows of boats in all different sizes and colors. They sit calmly and bob gently in the water in peace and harmony while attached to the wooden dock. The sunset behind their colorful sails, the golden rays on the shimmering water, the boats' reflection on the ripples—all create a breathtaking sight. Until the day... the day that wild winds pick up, dark clouds gather, and a massive and vicious storm approaches. The peaceful, quiet harbor is engulfed in violent chaos. The boats slam fiercely, each colliding with its neighbors and slamming against the dock. They are on the verge of destruction. One huge wave, and they are destroyed and ruined.

If they stay where they are, and they are not able to move and dance with the strong waves, chances are when the storm is finished and the blue skies are back, very little will be left of those beautiful boats. The wise thing to do is to move them into the heart of the storm, in the middle of the water away from the wooden docks, away from their limited and familiar world and surroundings. By relocating them and changing the way they have been positioned, you give them a chance of floating free over the massive waves. They are free to move, free of their once restricted environment. They approach the chaos head-on and naturally adapt and adjust to the flow.

In the midst of adversities, we, too, must change our positioning, our direction, and our point of view to free ourselves of old constraining beliefs in order to float through the stormy unknown.

Let's discuss life after death a bit more... or, as I like to call it, "life after the previous life." I'll use Y.M. Tuckachinsky's story about a pair of twins inside their mother's womb as a starting point. Let's call one twin the Believer and the other the Skeptic and imagine a dialogue between the two:

B: Have you ever thought what will happen to us when we leave this place?

S: It's simple, that's the end of us, we will fall into an abyss and disappear.

B: Maybe there is another world, a vast world full of colors and sounds. Instead of living in this dark place, we could see the bright, warm sun, beautiful blue oceans, birds flying high in the sky, and taste our food through our mouth instead of this tube attached to our belly.

S: Who has gone to the other side and returned with this information? Don't be a fool. Nothing exists past this life of warmth and comfort. We started here as a single cell and look at us now, we are complete. This is reality, everything else is a myth.

B: But we will enter another world that is not limiting. In our new world we can walk around with these curled-up feet, we can explore and see!

S: Fool! That would be the end of us. Life is what we know, here and now. There is no proof for any of these other notions.

Now imagine the mother goes through labor, and the Believer exits his mother's womb first. The Skeptic is scared and watches his brother's parting in a panic. Their calm world is now chaos. He hears screams and loud shouts from the distance. The horror of his brother's cries confirms the fact that he is gone forever. He has joined the dark and scary side. As the Skeptic predicted, his brother has fallen into an abyss and is indeed gone forever.

The Skeptic is scared, scared of the unknown and the unseen. Until the moment that he, too, is pushed out of his familiar surroundings he would never have believed that he would be joining his brother in a completely different existence for a completely different life.

Let's use these twins as example again, this time during the 9 months of pregnancy. All this while they are protected and taken care of by their mother. The muscles and the skin surrounding them not only create a safety shield, it also limits their world, their perspective, and their existence. From the moment the fetus is conceived until the day it is born, the moist, dark, warm, and comfortable environment is the only one he or she knows.

B: You know, there is a supreme being around us, or on top of us, but we can't see it, we can't comprehend it or talk to it. However, this supreme being is the cause of our existence and creation. She is feeding us, breathing for us and protecting us. We are here because of her, we are alive because of her, but for a limited amount of time only. We can't see it or feel it because our senses don't allow it. But we are all "one."

No matter how much the Skeptic looks up, down, and around himself and tries to figure out who this "supreme being" is and how they are "one," he can never recognize or realize that he is being surrounded and protected by it. Occasionally he might feel a sense of unease, wondering, *Yet, how can I end up here if there isn't anyone in charge of my existence?*

Still, the idea sounds absurd to him. He simply cannot hear anyone or see anything, no matter how much he tries or searches. He can see his creator and the supreme being, the one who has been fussing over him for 9 months—which to him is a lifetime—only on the day he exits one world and enters the other. When he can step out of the previous existence and look out at the whole picture.

Exits and entrances are differentiated by a fine line. One never leaves a place without arriving in another. Any door that opens up, opens up to an exterior area, unless there is a wall behind it; in which case, it is not considered an exit. In the case of our twin brothers, or any fetus, upon arrival in the new world, the newborn is left with no recollection of his fetal past. No one has any remembrance of life in a dark and moist environment and getting fed through a tube attached to the navel (at least not with the conscious mind).

Death, as we perceive it, is an exit on one side and an entrance to another. As dark and tragic it may look to us, we will not know the exact answer until we join the one that has departed and arrive at the new destination.

When we lost Stephen, I created a foundation in his name almost immediately. I thought to myself, *I don't want his name to be a reminder of sadness and tragedy. He is no longer in the physical world, able to do what he had planned to do, but his name can still go on living. A lot of good*

can come out of it. Lives could be changed, hospitals could be built, orphanages could be helped, scholarships could be given. His life does not have to end here. It will have a meaning, a purpose, a continuation of 22 years well lived.

I could have mourned his death for the rest of my life and asked, "Why him?" over and over again. But I chose not to. I chose to make him proud and decided to alter lives with his short existence and bring some good to this world. I knew the unthinkable had happened, and there was absolutely nothing anyone could do. So, I had to ask, "Now what?" I knew I needed to move forward in a positive direction. I knew I had to save myself and my family. I knew I had to help others. It just so happened that by helping others, I helped myself.

Stephen always wanted hundreds of entries to pop up when his name was Googled. I am helping him do that, knowing he is watching me with a smile. What happened to him remains a tragedy, but we have given it new meaning. All of us did. My friends joined in. His friends joined in. Everyone in the community got involved in our events. Besides the annual fundraiser, Justin and his friends arrange basketball games, barbecue parties, spinning events in his honor. They brought people together and created a sense of contribution among the younger generation. They started seeing and experiencing all the various ways in which they could help make a difference. The suffering and the sadness were turned into achievement and accomplishment.

How many successful people do we know who thought they had it all figured out, until that reality check of a day arrived—a medical condition, a sudden tragedy or loss—and rocked their perfect world? It's how they chose to take a stand towards those uninvited and uncalled-for circumstances that defines their liberty and their true power. The attitude one chooses in any situation or difficulty is his or her ultimate freedom. Viktor Frankl says it best, "It does not really matter what we expect from life, but rather what life expects from us."

It is on us to decide how to overcome the suffering caused by guilt or pain or death. It is on us to choose not to drown in the sea of sadness. Suffering is a chronic and accepted part of everyone's life; some are handed more than others. There are no limits to suffering. There is no quota on suffering. Life will test each person individually, and each person will feel the pain independently. In time through his own experience every single living person will answer and respond to the inevitable changes of life.

To be miserable is easy; there is no effort required. It becomes a habit almost immediately, and after awhile people feel that they have invested so much in their misery that it has become their best friend, their life companion. Misery understands them. Like a shadow, it follows them everywhere. After a while it feels just and right to be unhappy.

Feeling like a victim is addictive. You welcome it to the point where little by little it takes over your day-to-day life. It grows stronger every day. Before long it has absolute power over you. And you forget along the way that you are the one that gave misery complete control. You forget that if you invited him to your daily life, you can get rid of him, too. Misery is one of the oldest human habits. But it is your choice to dispose of it. The most difficult part is the realization that you are the master of your mind and not a slave to its desires. That you are the only one that is able to put those thoughts in your mind, and that only you are the one can decide to change them.

You have to make a conscious decision. There is no need to stay in darkness. Bring the smallest candle or a flashlight into a room and you get rid of the absolute darkness right away. Lack of light creates darkness. But the opposite scenario does not apply. You cannot carry darkness in a box or in your hands to a bright room and make it dark. You need to make an effort to do that. The doors and the windows have to be tightly closed, the curtains have to be pulled, and the light switch has to be off. Still, carry one candle into that room and the darkness is gone.

Just bring light into your life, step out, and allow for love and unconditional love to fill up your heart. Let the kindness of your friends penetrate your soul. Welcome and breathe in their compassionate words and their thoughtfulness. Step into the sun and let its brightness cover and touch your body like a warm and soft blanket. Sun never differentiates, never judges; it shines equally on a tall cypress tree and a lowly wild weed. Embrace the light and what it offers. Feel it in your heart. "Love helps those who are being loved and helps those who love, more." Love is light and fear is darkness. The heart that can love is fearless, and it's potential is limitless. That is why Jesus said, "God is love." Reach out and be open to any possibility. So long as you do that, darkness has no way in.

We should not continue on living the rest of our lives asking, "Why did this happen?" It did happen, and it's done. We cannot un-happen or undo it. "How" we react to the circumstances or "what" we can do about them are what we should ask ourselves.

We were discussing exactly that at one of my classes on Rumi with Dr. Nasrin Beraghdar. She told me with her kind voice, "Soheila, the pressure and the hardship of your life had created cracks in your soul. You have two choices, you can either focus on those crooked, ugly, brown lines, or notice the light that is free to shine through them."

By living in your past and worrying about your future you are losing your today, your now. You are sacrificing your everyday for yesterday or the next day. The past is buried and the future is anybody's guess. The only sure thing that you have is NOW. "Don't wait for the perfect moment, take the moment and make it perfect."

I can stand in the here and now today and wonder: was I wrestling with God? Was God wrestling with me? Was the bliss and love I experienced having Stephen in my life for 22 years worth the agony of losing him? Did we lose by Fariborz's death or did we gain by having such a wonderful person in our lives for 47 years? Was the world a better place because he was in it for a short time, or it would have been better off not having him in it at all? Would I trade the heavy, suffocating feelings of sorrow and grief caused by their losses for never having known my sister, my brother or my son?

What kind of a world would it be if all the people who didn't make it to old age were never born, if only to spare their loved ones the profound pain that comes with losing them? Would that be a better world? It is a commonly said that "only the good die young." And while it may be a cliché, it is also true that these young people do a tremendous amount of good before they depart this world. They make a real difference. They touch people's lives. They leave love behind.

In truth, there is no "wrestling with God." There is no "winner" or "loser." It is just a dance: two steps forward, one step back. One step forward, two steps back. Universe plays a tune and we dance to it as best as we can. Each one of us, to the best of our abilities. Ours became a dark and sad tune. But even the darkest and the longest night is always followed by the morning light. That is for sure.

Nothing is more real than nature. The God that I am looking for and seeking is hiding in nature and in my heart. The answer to every question for me lays in nature. Hence, I learned to follow her laws and notice her secret codes. A simple example, the trees and the plants dance to the music of the wind, no matter how strong the storm. The more flexible and adaptable the tree, the better chance of survival. We, too, have to be responsive to the circumstances surrounding us. We, too, have to dance, even if it is alone and in the dark.

We all come into this world from one door and leave from a different one. And in the time between we are all here to fulfill our stories, play our parts, make our marks—good or bad—and then leave. What kind of mark do I intend to leave behind? In honor of the loves of my life that departed before me, I choose to leave a mark of love. I choose to live for the "Whys" in my life. I choose to stop wrestling with God and start resting with him. I choose to dance to his melody, as best as I can. I choose to notice the light that is shining through the cracks. I choose to follow my heart until we meet again—maybe not anytime soon, but ... when it's time.

Until then, keep dancing amongst the stars.

About the Author

Soheila Adelipour moved from New York to Los Angeles after the tragic death of her college-age son in 2007. She founded the Stefan Adelipour For Life Foundation, which puts on an annual event to benefit the less fortunate in remembrance of her son.

Email: sadelipour19@gmail.com
Facebook: facebook.com/soheila.adelipour
Instagram: instagram.com/soheilaadelipour